CHRISTIAN RESPONSES TO THE NEW AGE MOVEMENT

A CRITICAL ASSESSMENT

JOHN A. SALIBA

GEOFFREY CHAPMAN

Geoffrey Chapman
A Cassell imprint
Wellington House, 125 Strand, London WC2R 0BB
370 Lexington Avenue, New York, NY 10017-6550
www.cassell.co.uk

First published 1999

British Library Cataloguing-in-Publication Data
A catalogue record for this book is available from the British Library.

ISBN 0–225–66852–1

Typeset by York House Typographic Ltd, London
Printed and bound in Great Britain by
Biddles Ltd, Guildford and King's Lynn

CHRISTIAN RESPONSES TO THE
NEW AGE MOVEMENT

CONTENTS

PREFACE

It is becoming increasingly difficult to pick up a popular magazine and not to come across the New Age advertised or talked about in some form or other. Three major weekly news publications, *Time*, *Newsweek*, and *U.S. News and World Report*, have carried several articles on the New Age during the last four years. Various other magazines, like *Family Circle*, *New Scientist*, the *Humanist*, *Forbes*, *Omni*, and *Discovery* have all highlighted the movement. The New Age has come to mean also big business, since magazines like *Money*, the *Wall Street Journal*, *Marketing Week*, and *Publishers Weekly* have dealt with the financial incentives that the demand for New Age publications and products has given rise to. Film stars like Shirley MacLaine have added luster to the nation-wide campaign to announce the coming of the New Age. It is not surprising that we read about New Age Spirituality, New Age Health, New Age Politics, a New Age Dictionary, and, on the lighter side, the *New Age Baby Name Book*.[1]

Not that the New Age Movement has not met any critical reactions. The *Christian Century* and *Christianity Today*, which can probably be numbered among the most widely-read Christian publications, have replied with a barrage of negative assessments. Further, Richard Blow, writing in the *New Republic*, has attacked the New Age on the grounds that it is morally and spiritually barren.[2] Yet, in spite of these attempts to relegate the New Age to a menacing fad or to a superstitious craze, the fact remains that the signs of its presence in our midst abound and clamor for an explanation and a response. A decade ago Fergus Bordewich, reporting on the education scene in Colorado, said that 'critics abound, but in Colorado the New Age Movement reaches from the schoolroom to the board room'.[3] His observations still apply today not just to Colorado but to different countries. There are probably few industrialized nations in the world which have not felt the impact of New Age ideology and practices.[4]

Truly enough, there are signs that the New Age might be waning and that the very name 'New Age' is losing its appeal. Some scholars argue that the New Age itself is in crisis because its promises of a golden age have not materialized. In a recent conference[5] it was suggested that the term 'Next Age' (or 'Next Stage', or 'New Edge') might more accurately designate the post-New Age movements that are likely to flourish as some of the key elements in the current New Age ideology cease to be relevant.

There are some indications that, in the United States at least, the label 'New Age' is already being dropped from bookstore shelves and substituted by a more respectable, though certainly misleading, designation, namely 'Metaphysics'.[6] Yet the books which had appeared under the labels 'New Age' and 'Occult' are still available. Publications on New Age topics are still voluminous; in fact, in the United States, the sale of New Age books experienced a sharp increase from 1992 to 1995.[7] The Internet is loaded with hundreds of thousands of references to New Age topics, thus making New Age ideas and products readily available to an even wider audience. The name 'New Age' might be ephemeral but some key components of its ideology and many of its practices are not.

Scholars continue to show interest in the progress and development of New Age thought and practices. Recent publications support the view that, while several aspects of the New Age might be passing fads, its basic religious and spiritual orientation are still popular.[8] The influence of the New Age on mainline religion is substantial and still conceived as a challenge to Christian theology.[9] Even if the New Age were to cease to exist as an independent religious force in modern culture, its presence will survive in the spiritual lives of many people who have found it meaningful and satisfying and in the churches which have adapted some of its beliefs and practices to their theology and ritual.

The reactions of Christians, which is the topic of this book, have become a major component of the New Age. In order to understand the New Age and its effects on culture one must look into, not only the scholarly studies on the movement, but also the vast Christian literature that describes, evaluates, and attacks its ideology and practices. The development of the New Age depends, in part, on the interpretations and responses of the Christian churches.

The scope of this book is thus to survey and evaluate the many

Christian responses to the New Age and to make suggestions as to how Christianity can react meaningfully to a modern spiritual phenomenon that is having an impact on the lives of many people at the end of the second millennium. After attempting to describe the movement's ideology and goals both from a scholarly perspective and from the viewpoint of those involved in it (Chapter 1), several chapters will examine critically three responses to the New Age Movement, namely those offered respectively by the evangelical/fundamental (Chapter 2), Protestant and Eastern Orthodox (Chapter 3), and Roman Catholic (Chapter 4) branches of Christianity. The final chapter will then draw up principles of evaluation and apply them to several specific New Age beliefs and practices.

NOTES

1. This is the title of a book authored by Sue Browder and published by Warner Brothers, New York (rev. ed., 1987).

2. 'Moronic convergence', *New Republic* 198 (January 25, 1988): 24ff.

3. *New York Times Magazine* (May 1, 1988): 38.

4. In Japan, for example, many of the so-called new religions have been influenced by the New Age. One issue of the *Japanese Journal of Religious Studies* (vol. 22, Fall 1995) was dedicated to the presence of the New Age in Japan.

5. 'La crisi del New Age e la nascita di un nuovo fenomeno: il Next Age' is the theme of a conference held in Turin in April, 1998, and sponsored by the Alleanza Cattolica and by CESNUR, the Turin-based center for the study of new religions.

6. The word 'metaphysics' is used to refer to a branch of philosophy that deals with the concepts of 'existence' and 'nature'. Although the New Age certainly has a lot to say about these topics, its mode of proceeding differs from philosophy. Moreover, many of the areas that fall under the New Age, such as parapsychology, do not form part of metaphysics as understood by philosophers. Cf. W. H. Walsh, 'Metaphysics, Nature of' in *The Encyclopedia of Philosophy*, ed. Paul Edwards (New York: Macmillan Publishing Co., 1967), vol. 5, pp. 300–07.

7. See Erica E. Goode, 'The eternal quest for a New Age', *U.S. News and World Report* 122 (April 7, 1997): 22–24.

8. Among the more recent publications one can consult (1) Wouter J. Hanegraaff,

New Age Religion and Western Culture: Esotericism in the Mirror of Secular Thought (Albany: SUNY Press, 1988); (2) Jon P. Block, *New Spirituality, Self, and Belonging: How New Agers and Neo-Pagans Talk about Themselves* (Westport, CT: Praeger, 1998); and (3) Stuart Rose, 'An examination of the New Age Movement: who is involved and what constitutes its spirituality', *Journal of Contemporary Religion* 13 (1998): 5–22.

9. See, for instance, John P. Newport, *The New Age Movement and the Biblical Worldview* (Grand Rapids, MI: Eerdmans, 1998).

1
.

THE MEANING OF THE NEW AGE

The founding of the Findhorn community in Scotland in 1965 was an important milestone in the movement which bears the label of the 'New Age'. In fact, Findhorn 'was seen as embodying its principal ideals of transformation'.[1] The quest for a universal consciousness, the goal of harmony with nature, the vision of a transformed world, and the practice of channeling, all of which have become hallmarks of the New Age Movement, were present at Findhorn from its foundation.[2] The success of this community led to its becoming a model for, and/or an inspiration to, other groups, such as Alternatives in London, Esalen in Big Sur, California, and the Open Center and Omega Institute in New York.[3]

While the modern roots of the movement have been traced to the emergence of the Theosophical Society in the second half of the nineteenth century, and while several foundations and institutions since then have contributed to the ideology and practices of contemporary New Agers, there is little doubt that the New Age as a social and spiritual movement emerged in the late 1960s and became a significant force in Western culture in the 1980s.[4]

It might be relatively easy to pinpoint the birth of a movement whose goals and practices have become international.[5] It is much less easy, however, to define it and to enumerate its main features. It is almost impossible to categorize all the activities and practices that might be ascribed to it. J. Gordon Melton[6] lists Leslie Shepard's *Encyclopedia of Occultism and Parapsychology*[7] with the sources that survey the movement. Shepard's monumental work includes references to different types of religious and spiritual organizations, to an immense variety of magical and divinatory practices, and to a whole range of extrasensory perceptions. And William Frost remarks that all the entries in Rosemary Ellen Guiley's *Harper's Encyclopedia of Mystical and Paranormal Experience* 'pertain to the interest of the New Age movement'.[8] This encyclopedia contains entries on the world's great religions, various Christian sects, occult topics and organizations, psychic phenomena, and mysticism. It is certainly not surprising that a definition of the New Age is somewhat elusive and an exhaustive inventory of its features and practices a herculean task.

The New Age can be misunderstood for a number of reasons. First, the movement borrows and reinterprets ideas from diverse sources, such as Eastern religions, and integrates them with concepts taken from the Judeo-Christian tradition. Second, many of its beliefs and practices are indistinguishable from the occult. Third, it has no over-arching structure that specifies its teachings and regulates, guides, and evaluates its practices. Consequently, New Agers can differ among themselves rather substantially in both religious beliefs and spiritual practices. Even commonly-held beliefs, like that in reincarnation, may not be universally held by those who align themselves with the movement. And many of the practices routinely linked with the movement, like the use of crystals for healing, are definitely not universal.

Besides, the movement is made up of disparate organizations that differ in the kind of commitment they expect or demand from their followers. Rodney Stark and William Bainbridge[9] have conveniently distinguished among three levels of organization that characterize new religious movements. The first consists of 'audience cults' that have no formal organization. Their members do not form a community; they learn the cult doctrines and practices through literature and the news media, rather than through formal instruction and initiation. The second is made up of 'client cults' which are more organized in their teachings. Members of these groups establish a client relationship with those who promulgate their particular teachings. The clients themselves are largely unorganized and relate to the cult leaders just as patients relate to their doctors or therapists. The third refers to 'cult movements' that are organized religious bodies offering membership through initiation into a religious or spiritual community and requiring commitment and regular participation.

The differences between these groups are applicable to the New Age Movement where one finds (1) those who get involved through attendance at New Age fairs and through individual assimilation of New Age thought through various sources of information, including literature and public talks; (2) those who regularly consult individual channelers and/or astrologers for advice and guidance; and (3) those who join highly organized movements like the I AM Movement, the Church Universal and Triumphant, and the Aetherius Society.

In order to understand the New Age it will be useful to consider first, how New Agers themselves envision it and, secondly, how scholars have attempted to describe and analyze its ideology and practices. In anthropological terms these represent, respectively, the emic and the etic approaches to the understanding of societies, cultures, and religions. The former (emic) stands for the insider's point of view and emphasizes the subjective meanings shared by a social, cultural, or religious group; the latter (etic) gives the outsider's perspective and concentrates on the theoretical and formal categories used to understand another society, culture, or religion.[10]

THE NEW AGE: THE INSIDER'S VIEWPOINT

Those who advocate the coming of the New Age start with the assumption that there is something wrong with the world as we know it. The recent advances in technology and the growing ecological awareness have sharpened people's perception of contemporary global crises. Science and materialism, it is believed, have suffocated the human spirit and stifled human attempts to experience the holy. Organized religions appear to have overregulated and possibly distorted the innate human desire for genuine spirituality or religiosity. Those who proclaim the New Age insist, therefore, that changes both on the individual and social levels are called for, changes that stress holistic values rather than individual desires for wealth and power and that focus on one's inner experiences rather than on explicit statements of belief.

From this point of view, the New Age is a symbolic or metaphorical expression of the human quest for a transformative, creative, and free existence. Those involved in the New Age Movement envisage the human race as one family living and sharing the same planet in peace and harmony, since all people have the same origin and destiny. Compassion, love, and ministry to the needs of others are qualities that ideally identify those who want to join the New Age Movement, where all people are invited to participate in its goals of social, material, and spiritual improvement or betterment. The New Age is a time when people delve more deeply into the mysteries of God, of the universe, and of the self and when they become more open to God's love and companionship in their daily lives.

Some leading representatives of the New Age portray it in ideal-istic terms.[11] David Spangler, a major theoretician of New Age ideology, presents a highly personalized view of the meaning and goals that the New Age offers. He writes:

> For me the New Age has always been a combination of things: a myth, a metaphor, a paradigm shift, a call to imagine a positive future and then to build it. New Age activities to me mean push-ing back the frontiers of human knowledge through science, working with alternative energy sources, seeking understanding and harmony between cultures, and building the spirit of com-munity in our society. I found the New Age in understanding and protecting the environment, in recognizing and honoring the sacredness of everyday life and in developing non-adversarial forms of politics. The New Age agenda includes inventing empowering styles of economics and business to deal with structural unem-ployment, poverty and hunger, as well as developing whole systems, points of view and a spirit of planetary wholeness that would lessen the dangers of nuclear war.[12]

And again he asserts that the 'New Age is fundamentally a change of consciousness from one of isolation and separation to one of com-munion, attunement, and wholeness'.[13]

David Spangler argues that the popular image of the New Age as a future event is a form of 'disillusionment' that limits people's creative abilities. For him, it is not an apocalyptic or messianic event; it is rather already in existence here on earth. He declares that the 'New Age idea has little to do with prophecy. It is an invitation to encounter today in a joyous, nurturing, and creative way.'[14] And he insists that:

> The New Age is here now. Earth has entered a new phase of energy expression. It is important to realize that this new pattern of con-sciousness was not imposed from outside. The New Age is a result of education, a drawing out from within. It has always existed in essence, just as future ages yet to come now exist as unrealized potentials.[15]

And again:

> The New Age idea calls us to replace projection with vision. It is prophetic not in the sense of precognitively describing the future but in calling us to live with a transformative vision that opens us to the metaphoric and regenerative qualities of life.

> Thus, the New Age is not something yet to come. It is the character of the time in which we are living! It is the age in which we encounter the new on a yearly or monthly or even weekly basis.[16]

The same idea is reinforced by William Irwin Thompson,[17] who labels any apocalyptic trend a 'messianic delusion' or 'messianic compulsion'. The meaning of the apocalypse, as George Trevelyan[18] maintains, is, therefore, symbolical. Such a view is thus opposed to that proposed by, for example, Benjamin Creme, who expects a messianic figure to introduce the New Age and who has repeatedly announced that Christ, the Maitreya, is already here on earth ready to initiate the New Age of synthesis.[19] Popular figures of the New Age, like Ruth Montgomery, promote the same millennial expectations and believe that the Piscean Age, which began with the coming of Christ, is now reaching its culmination. For her, the human race is now at the threshold of a new age, that of Aquarius, an age of love and fellowship.[20] Montgomery holds that 'walk-ins', who are enlightened human beings who have gone through multiple reincarnations and now inhabit adult bodies, bring messages of the end and other signs of the coming millennium.

The New Age vision adopted by those magazines and journals that are dedicated to give information about and to promote New Age ideals and spirituality is sometimes in harmony with Spangler's position and contains no explicit messianic or millenarian reference. The statement of purpose of one such journal, *Magical Blend*, expresses its conception of the New Age as follows:

> *Magical Blend* accepts the premise that society is presently undergoing a fundamental transformation. A new world is being born, and whether this birth is to be an easy or difficult one will depend largely upon the individual. It is our aim to chart the course this transformation is taking and to assist the individual to cope with and contribute to the birthing process. Since we believe that people's thoughts influence their reality, our goal is to channel people's thoughts into positive, uplifting areas, and in so doing, to act as a catalyst to encourage the individual to achieve his or her highest level of spiritual awareness. We endorse no one pathway to spiritual growth, but attempt to explore many alternative possibilities to help transform the planet.[21]

David Spangler[22] also rejects the position of those who equate the New Age with psychic phenomena and the occult, with the pursuit of pagan religions and Eastern philosophies, or with involvement in channeling, crystals, and reincarnation. And he points out that the claim of one's divinity, portrayed in New Age literature, is not of the essence of the New Age. He rejects this claim because it

> is a prescription for selfishness and a withdrawal from the world. It ignores social justice and closes itself to the real pain of others and to the way in which we are all responsible for creating the conditions that contribute to that pain.[23]

His theology of the New Age does not have the human person as its center. He insists:

> Therefore, for those of us who profess belief in a New Age, it is important to understand that the New Age is essentially a symbol representing the human heart and intellect in partnership with God building a better world that can celebrate values of community, wholeness and sacredness. It is a symbol for the emergence of social behavior based on a worldview that stimulates creativity, discipline, abundance and wholeness; it is a symbol for a more mature and unobstructed expression of the sacredness and love at the heart of life.[24]

The average person involved in the New Age Movement does not, however, stop at picturing the New Age in this appealing, idealistic manner. The more prevalent view takes the 'Harmonic Convergence' that took place in August 1987 as the final 25-year cycle of this planet as outlined in the ancient Mayan calendar. After this period the advent of the Golden or New Age, the Millennium, or the Promised Land is expected. New Agers usually consider the New Age a near future event that will transform history as we know it. Those who proclaim it are prophets on a planet destined for a fundamental metamorphosis the like of which can hardly be conceived. In this New Age human beings will develop enormous psychic powers and become more content, spiritual, and creative. They will, in a sense, become like God.[25]

Many of those involved in the New Age have already begun preparing themselves for the millennium. In their endeavor to be ready for this great event, their New Age activities are centered on three major practical concerns. First, there is a felt need to develop the psychic powers that are believed to be inherent in human nature and that will be characteristic of human interactions in the future. Secondly, there is a great desire to get in touch with the supernatural and paranormal dimensions of life, a desire that expresses itself in efforts to contact spirits or the God that dwells within every human being. And finally, New Age people are dissatisfied with what the Judeo-Christian tradition has to offer and are seeking knowledge and guidance from alternative philosophies and theologies.

New Age practices

The optimistic, utopian, and romantic depictions of the New Age must be translated into practical programs for those who wish to embark on the journey towards self-transformation and the creation of a better world. One of the most articulate formulations of the practical agenda of the New Age Movement has been proposed by Marilyn Ferguson, whose seminal work[26] 'has been accepted more than any other single book as a consensus statement of the New Age perspective'.[27] Stressing that the world is going through a radical evolution or a paradigm shift, Ferguson believes that a powerful and vast network of people from all levels of society are working to bring about a new consciousness that will lead to a renewal of society.

Marilyn Ferguson does not stop with the discussion of the transformation of one's consciousness and world view that are essential to the New Age. She outlines eight broad means by which such a change of awareness can be achieved, namely:[28] (1) autogenic training; (2) self-help and mutual-help networks; (3) hypnosis; (4) various kinds of meditation (such as Zen and Transcendental Meditation); (5) shamanic and magical techniques; (6) seminars like 'est' (The Forum), and Silva Mind Control; (7) mystical systems proposed by such groups as Arica and Theosophy; and (8) body disciplines and therapies, such as hatha yoga, Rolfing, and T'ai Chi.

The variety of alternative spiritual and psychotherapeutic practices summed up by Ferguson offer a fairly comprehensive catalogue of activities from which New Agers can take their pick. They form the bulk of materials discussed and recommended in New Age journals.

In order to understand what the New Age means to the majority of people who subscribe to its philosophy and theology, one can profitably look at the main areas of interests and concerns that appear with constant regularity in New Age journals and catalogues. The New Age endorses diverse methods that are believed to be necessary if planetary transformation is to occur. A comprehensive survey of the features of the New Age can be found, for example, in *The New Age Catalogue: Access to Information and Sources*,[29] which classifies the materials under the following eight headings: (1) Intuitive development/channeling; (2) Create your own reality/transformational journeys; (3) Transitions/birth; (4) Spirituality; (5) Holistic healing and health; (6) Bodywork/movement; (7) New lifestyles/communities; and (8) The Planet/planetary visions.

These categories require clarification since many of them fall outside medical, psychological, and religious traditions. It should be noted that the above classification should not be interpreted rigidly for there is a lot of overlapping between the themes and practices. Further, New Agers do not, and obviously cannot, become involved in all the activities indicated by the endless resources that they find in New Age books, magazines, and journals. These areas of New Age involvement can be described as follows:

(1) Intuitive Development/channeling. This includes channeling, psychic functioning, chakras/auras, crystals, divination, astrology, numerology, tarot, palmistry, graphology, dowsing, oracles, and the I Ching.

To many New Agers channeling is at the heart of their involvement in the New Age Movement. Basic to channeling is the assumption that knowledge of self and others can be achieved through self-reflection or through some inner, higher aspect of their personality. More specifically, channeling can be described as the communication of information to or through a human being from paranormal sources. These sources can be of two kinds: (1) other entities, such as spirits of the dead, angels, or ascended masters (i.e., highly evolved individuals who no longer need to live on earth to continue their spiritual growth),[30] or (2) the individual's innermost being, which has a divine, supernatural dimension that cannot be reached through ordinary human consciousness.[31] In either case, channeling is seen both as a beneficial, sometimes healing, experience in that it enhances one's spiritual growth, as well as a useful means of helping others through the information or knowledge one acquires in the process.

The first kind of channeling (also called spirit channeling) has a long history and resembles traditional mediumship. It requires a spiritual or non-material entity and a human being through which this entity speaks. Probably the classic example is Edgar Cayce,[32] known as the sleeping prophet, who taught that by delving into, and becoming attuned with, the subconscious and deeper levels of their minds people will be able to communicate with the spirits of the dead, spirit guides, and archangels.

A more recent example of this kind of channeling are the so-called 'Lazaris Videotapes'. Jack Pursel, one of the more noted channelers, believes that Lazaris, a being who has reached the spiritual plane, communicates through him and that the instructions and information he receives cannot come through normal agencies. Thus, to give a few specific examples, Lazaris teaches what the Higher Self is, how one can get in touch and develop a relationship with it, and in what way one can use such experiences for spiritual growth. There are also directives about practical matters, such as achieving intimacy and loving relationships, forgiveness, and unconditional love, and details about the healing powers of crystals and their uses in past civilizations like Atlantis, Mesopotamia, and Ancient Egypt.[33]

Other well-known channelers, such as Jane Roberts, who channels Seth, J. Z. Knight, who channels Ramtha, and Elwood Babbitt, who channels Mark Twain, Einstein, Wordsworth, Jesus and Vishnu, have contributed to the popularity of the phenomenon.[34] Their publications (books and video and audio tapes) are readily available in bookstores and/or by mail. Even more popular is the lengthy channeled document, *A Course in Miracles*,[35] which purports to divulge revealed knowledge from a spirit source. Its author, Helen Schucman, claims that the words came to her mentally through the process of inner dictation. The book was first published anonymously and implied that the source of knowledge it imparts is Jesus Christ. Not all channels are as well known as the above. There are many other people who are channeling various kinds of entities whose purported messages are recorded in New Age magazines.[36]

A typical example of the second kind of channeling is provided by Kathleen Vande Kieft, who describes channeling as 'a form of intuitive knowledge issuing from the place of divine access *within yourself*'.[37] She further explains that this store of knowledge can be called 'the High Self', the 'God-self', or the 'inner teacher'. Channeling does not come from a discarnate entity, but rather from one's own being, or more precisely, from a force within the person that is deeply compassionate, infinitely knowledgeable, and instantly accessible. Consequently everyone can channel since everyone can tap into this individual form of superconscious revelation. Vande Kieft actually dedicates a large section of her book to teaching people how to channel their inner selves.

Because channeling is believed to be within the reach of everybody, channelers readily offer instructions on the methods that can be used to develop one's inherent powers to become a channeler. Developing one's psychic skills seems to be a prerequisite. There are numerous organizations and publications that are dedicated to this task.[38] Meditation is universally admitted to be necessary for anybody desiring to embark on the spiritual journey of channeling. Sharpening one's intuition through such means as the tarot, numerology, astrology, and the I Ching, makes one receptive to spirit entities seeking to make contact with human beings to guide them on their spiritual path.

(2) Create your own reality/transformational journeys. Under this category are listed self-help, subliminal programming, meditation, dreamwork, astral projection/out-of-the-body experiences, search for consciousness, relationships, rebirthing, brain/mind technology, inspiration, creativity, and various schools, institutes, and retreats.

The search for a new age is exemplified in one's life experiences, particularly those journeys that open up one's perceptions and transform one's view of self and reality. Of the myriad accounts that claim such transformations, that of actress Shirley MacLaine has received great publicity. One of her books[39] has been hailed as 'a classic in transformational literature'.[40] MacLaine's personal encounters led her to explore the mysteries of karma, reincarnation, and the 'higher self'. She talks of seeing a blinding, loving light that leads people to acquire a greater receptivity and openness to a higher consciousness or self. According to her and others who report such experiences, the light or the energy is something within the individual.[41] Physical, mental, and spiritual growth flow from tapping into this inner source of light and energy.

This journey into one's deeper self must be vigorously pursued by the individual who has embarked on the path of self-discovery and transformation. Since this personal metamorphosis is reached through one's own efforts, self-help becomes the operative term. The phrase 'create your own reality' has become a catch word among New Agers. This means, according to MacLaine, that people are the creators of the very situations in which they live and they, therefore, have the choice to bring about those conditions.[42] To do so, one must first of all become aware of the need for change. Then one must take the initiative to improve oneself and to search for those methods conducive to happiness and wholeness. Advice as to how to embark and proceed on one's transformational journey is given regularly in New Age literature.[43] Visualization, self-hypnosis, subliminal programming, meditation, dreamwork, astral projection, and out-of-the-body experiences are examples of New Age techniques for achieving transformation.

One of the most important techniques is creative visualization.

Insisting on the need to acquire a positive attitude, one which imagines and expects satisfaction and pleasure, the promoters of this path towards personal change contend that learning to listen to one's own intuition is a primary requirement for self development. The power of positive thinking must be practiced and nurtured in order that one may reach the goals set. Shakti Gawain describes creative visualization as 'the technique of using your imagination to create what you want in your life'.[44] She maintains that

> When we create something, we always create it first in a thought form. . . . The idea is like a blueprint; it creates an image of the form, which then magnetizes and guides the physical energy to flow into that form and eventually manifest it on the physical plane. . . .
> If we are basically positive in attitude, expecting and envisioning pleasure, satisfaction and happiness, we will attract and create people, situations, and events which will conform to our positive expectations. So the more positive energy we put into imaging what we want, the more it begins to manifest in our lives.[45]

Gawain then proceeds to give four basic steps for effective creative visualization: (1) Set your goal; (2) create a clear idea or picture; (3) focus on it often; and (4) give it positive energy.

The same principles are emphasized in what some writers call 'attitudinal healing'. Our thoughts and attitudes about people and events causes conflict and distress. People are responsible for their own thoughts and attitudes which they can control and change. 'Attitudinal healing involves correcting our misperceptions and removing the inner obstacles to experiencing peace.'[46]

Underlying the New Age tenet that an individual can create his or her own reality are two principles that derive from the new psychology and the new physics. The first deals with human relationships and insists that one must discover and develop one's own friends, lovers, and/or soul mates.[47] The second postulates a new model of the physics of the mind, a model that claims that (1) positive subliminal affirmations can bring changes to one's life without effort, conscious thought patterning, or strain[48] and (2) sensation, feeling, thought, and intuition are deeply linked with the physical process of the universe.[49]

Many procedures are available for the person who wishes to embark on the journey of self-transformation. Subliminal and neuro-linguistic programming are practical means which are backed, according to some New Agers, by hard scientific data. These two forms of self-programming are based on the assumption that an individual can only be conscious of a small amount of the information that one's body, mind, and brain can assimilate. One can, however, subject oneself to receive information without being conscious that one is learning new data, that is, one exposes oneself to subliminal messages that may enhance development without effort or strain. Listening to tapes that have subliminal messages could reaffirm positive thoughts on both conscious and subconscious levels of the mind and thus enable the individual to create the reality one desires. Neuro-linguistic programming (NLP) makes people more cognizant of the essential elements of excellence in any field and helps them organize the data, making it more teachable to others. Further, NLP 'provides very effective techniques for achieving rapport with anyone more easily and for making the use of language and sensory acuity more effective in gathering information and establishing clear goals'.[50]

Meditation, dream interpretation, and astral projection are additional methods people can adopt to expand self discipline, awareness, and knowledge. By so doing, individuals would be choosing not only the methods through which they change but also the goals of their endeavors. They will be, in fact, creating their own realities; in other words, assuming responsibility for their own personal growth and betterment.

(3) Transitions/birth. This area covers birth, near-death experiences, death and dying, reincarnation, and walk-ins.

Another interest of the New Age is the processes of human birth and dying. Besides the stress on natural childbirth, there is an insistence that birth itself is a spiritual experience and that mothers can have greater influence on the children they give birth to.[51] Current research about fetal development is integrated within the framework of holistic and humanistic ideals about parenting in an effort to create a workable model of the best environment for the birth and training of children. Sandra Sol, for example, writes:

> The supreme ideal birth to me would be where both parents had released their own Birth Traumas *before conception* of the child. This is my idea of perfection because there would be little or no psychic contamination to the fetus and little fear of the birth itself.
>
> This could be done easily and pleasurably if both parents were willing to get rebirthed for at least a year prior to conceiving a child. The guidance of a Spiritual Master who is powerful enough to wash out Birth Trauma is also extremely helpful.[52]

Just as birth is a transition into life, so also is death. The description of near-death experiences has become a subject of research. The studies of Elisabeth Kübler-Ross,[53] Raymond Moody,[54] and Kenneth Ring[55] on subjects who had been pronounced clinically dead and then revived have been adduced to support the importance of cultivating positive attitudes towards death and dying. People who have had a near-death experience often go through a radical change in which their spiritual values change. Near-death experiences have strengthened belief in the afterlife; so much so that these experiences are cited as proofs of the existence of a spiritual soul or entity and of life after death. Since death is seen as a stage or change in one's existence, two major preoccupations become topics for discussion.

The first is the preparation for death. If death is, like birth, a rite of passage, then it is appropriate to talk not only about how the individual should prepare for such a great event, but also about how those who survive deal with this transition that intimately affects their own lives. If one anticipates death and gets ready for it, then it is appropriate to discuss one's right to die (active and passive euthanasia).[56]

The second revolves around the spirits of the dead. It seems to be a common folk belief that the spirits of the dead can become earth-bound or else return to haunt or possess the living. The 1982 film *Poltergeist* (directed by Steven Spielberg) highlighted this preoccupation in a most graphic fashion. Edith Fiore, a psychologist, has tried to give substance to the popular belief that evil spirits and wayward souls can possess human beings almost at random. In one of her books[57] she explains that the spirits of many dead people are in a state of confusion, fear, and disorientation; and they consequently tend to attach themselves to and possess living persons. In her psychological practice Fiore helps both the spirit entities and the possessed individuals to bring about a successful release.

The transition to the next life leads naturally into a discussion on reincarnation, one of the most widely-held beliefs of those committed to the New Age. Though reincarnation is not a topic of debate within the traditional Christian churches, it has emerged, under the influence of Theosophy, as one of the most popular doctrines in contemporary Western culture. Many New Agers hold that remembering one's past lives can have important therapeutic benefits. If one's feelings, anxieties, hangups, and fears come from past events, including those that occurred in one's previous lives, then past-life therapy can become a valuable tool for eliminating both mental and psychological problems.[58]

(4) Spirituality. The areas covered by this heading are: Mystics and Masters, Spiritualism, Native American religious beliefs and practices (such as Shamanism), Women's Spirituality, and Earth Religions.

Another area of interest in the New Age is spirituality which, in current usage, describes 'those attitudes, beliefs, practices which animate people's lives and help them to reach out towards super-sensible realities'.[59] Influenced by Eastern religions,[60] participants in the New Age strive for developing their spirit or soul, for reaching higher levels of awareness, and for experiencing union with God. Hence, mystics and masters are considered necessary guides of the spiritual life.

It is an accepted principle in New Age circles that there are diverse paths to spiritual improvement and enlightenment and that all religions have ultimately the same goal and somewhat similar methods to reach it. Therefore, uniting practices from diverse religious traditions is common. The presence of Eastern religious groups in the West has provided an opportunity for the mingling of spiritual exercises that had been customarily judged to be unreconcilable.

One example of an Eastern path that has spread to the West is Sufism, that is, Islamic mysticism. The Sufi Order in the West, founded by Pir Inayat Khan, is probably the most organized and widespread form of Sufism in the Western world.[61] The symbolic representation of this movement encapsulates some central New Age themes. It consists of a heart with wings attached to it, denoting its ideal. The heart is the receptacle on earth of the divine. When the divine resides in the heart, the heart soars heavenward. Inside the heart is a drawing of a crescent and a star. The crescent (a quarter moon) symbolizes responsiveness to the holy. The heart, like the moon, grows fuller as it approaches the divine. The star in the heart of the crescent represents the divine spark that is reflected in the human heart as love.[62]

Although Sufism is Islamic in origin, Sufism in the West has taken a much broader approach to spirituality. Instead of defining themselves as Muslims, Western Sufis prefer to describe their organization as a more encompassing spiritual order, one that focuses on a way of life and a world view that sees the divine in all life and respects the sacredness of all religious traditions. Consequently, in Sufi worship, elements of different religions are incorporated to signify that all paths ultimately lead to the one supreme being.

Another form of spirituality which has been planted in the Western world is Zen, a form of Japanese Buddhist meditation aimed at helping the individual acquire a new viewpoint for looking into the essence of things.[63] The end result of Zen is satori, an experience that cannot be communicated to others by words or arguments. A person who experiences satori discovers that all life vibrates with divine meaning and creative vitality. Zen, which cannot be taught, is a state of absolute peace of mind comparable to that achieved by mystics throughout the ages.

Two other forms that manifest this spiritual quest are Spiritualism[64] and earth religions.[65] Spiritualism stresses the survival of one's personal identity at death and the existence of a spiritual dimension with which human beings can be in constant contact. Communications with the spirits of the dead through mediums figure prominently in spiritualist organizations. Spiritualism also teaches that there is a spark of divinity that dwells in all human beings – a religious theme that pervades New Age thought.

The revival of earth religions (also referred to as Paganism or Witchcraft) is related to a spirituality that looks on earth as a manifestation of the divine. Finding God in nature is central to these religions where the mother goddess receives priority. Some members of the feminist movement have tapped into this form of spirituality, which they believe has broken away from the male-oriented religions and is more in tune with woman's nature and psychology.

(5) Holistic healing and health, with special attention being given to oriental medicine, homeopathy, herbology, and nutrition.

The influence of New Thought is most explicitly seen in the attitudes towards disease and in the methods of healing that the New Age Movement constantly promotes. Two predominant themes can be detected in this respect: (1) a world view that recommends a return to nature and (2) a position that strongly believes that mind (and spirit) can influence matter.

Holistic health (or alternative or natural healing) covers a vast variety of nontraditional treatments approved by the New Age Movement. Directories of holistic health include such practices as acupuncture, acupressure, biofeedback, body cleansing, bodywork, chiropractic, flower essence therapy, herbology, homeopathy, macrobiotics, polarity therapy, reflexology, visualization, and yoga.[66] The guiding principle behind the above-mentioned techniques is that a person can cure oneself with the right mental attitude and with natural processes that have not been contaminated by modern farming methods and artificial medications.

The quest for holistic health has become a persistent preoccupation for those who are committed to the New Age. The *New Age Journal* publishes a yearly directory on holistic health,[67] a directory that provides names of healers who practice alternative medicines, descriptions of therapies, lists of health spas and retreats, and tips for choosing and evaluating a practitioner.

A recent directory divides holistic healers into eight broad categories according to the techniques they practice: (1) Bodywork and massage therapy (such as acupressure, chiropractic, Rolfing, shiatsu and reflexology); (2) Counseling (examples: astrology, intuitive arts, holistic psychiatry, hypnotherapy, neuro-linguistic programming, and past-life/regression therapies); (3) Energy techniques (examples: polarity therapy, therapeutic touch, and several Asian techniques); (4) Holistic health (examples: Anthroposophic medicine, Ayurvedic (Hindu) medicine, holistic dentistry, medicine, and nursing, and health spas and retreat centers); (5) Movement therapies (examples: Alexander technique, Feldenkrais method, Kripalu yoga, yoga therapy, and T'ai Chi); (6) Natural health therapies (examples: acupuncture, aromatherapy, biofeedback, homeopathy, macrobiotic counseling, and meditation); (7) Health Specialists (examples: those who practice cancer therapies, holistic vision therapies, and pain and stress management); (8) Bodywork/movement, consisting of polarity therapy, massage, acupressure, yoga, T'ai Chi, chiropractic therapy, and sports.[68]

(6) Bodywork/movement. Related to the above emphasis on holistic medicine is the contemporary craze for exercise and bodily activities in general as ways to better health and longer life. 'Bodywork', as it is called, is designed to 'restore the body to its maximum state of well-being by reversing the negative effects that physical and emotional traumas have had on the body in the course of a lifetime'.[69] Among the many forms of 'bodywork' are included 'mentastics', a form of mental gymnastics, massage, yoga, sports, and various communal lifestyles.

Communes in the Western world have a long history and have experienced a minor revival in recent times.[70] Many of the so-called New Age communities, which may or may not be organized as communes, offer the opportunity of novel lifestyles that incorporate the principles of the New Age, especially the need to return to nature. Adopting a new lifestyle may entail the use of natural products (such as natural furniture polish, bedding, and clothing), New

Age literature, music, and art, and responsible investing that is socially conscious and opposed to big business.

The New Age is often advertised through the work of small communities that publish magazines that disseminate information on the topics mentioned above, that is, topics ranging from spiritual exercises to healing practices. References to these communities are found in New Age journals and local magazines and newsletters distributed in major cities.[71]

The principles and goals of the New Age seem to permeate the whole of culture. There is also New Age fiction, New Age travel, and New Age music. For New Agers travel ceases to be an activity pursued just for business or for relaxation. Like pilgrimages in traditional religions, it has the goals of enlightenment, spiritual nourishment, and transformation. Similarly, music is not just a form of artistic entertainment, but a path to higher consciousness. 'New Age music', in the words of Steven Halpern, 'is really a return to roots, an existential exegesis to the primordial power of sound.'[72] It is 'a carrier wave for consciousness'. It is based on 'harmony and consonance' and can be used as a form of 'psychospiritual technology'.

(8) The Planet/planetary visions. This area comprises planetary visionaries, global concerns, earth changes, earth spirit, ancient mysteries, and UFOs.

Finally, New Agers are troubled by the current state of the Earth as a whole and worried about its future. The optimistic possibilities of renewal of self, society, and the world are foremost in the minds of those who envisage a better planet to live in. Marilyn Ferguson's book, *The Aquarian Conspiracy*, is one of the basic manuals that express the hope of planetary transformation that will benefit all people. A key element in this change is the harmonious relationship between human beings and nature.

Visions of the future are, therefore, central in the minds and hearts of New Age people. John Naisbitt's popular book on the 'restructuring of America'[73] is seen as forecasting the future in ways that are in harmony with the projections of New Age thinkers, even though the author had no intention of writing a New Age manual. Prophetic utterances about the future are sought for and taken seriously. The prophecies of Nostradamus,[74] a sixteenth-century prophet, have achieved a certain amount of popularity. Recent events, such as the elections of the last two popes and the rather mysterious death of Pope John Paul I, have been traced to his insights. Apocalyptic and millennial longings are back in vogue, which explains why the 'Harmonic Convergence' is believed to have been a significant event in the history of the human race. The New Age has brought with it a new eschatology.

Apprehensions about the future and speculations about the past history of the human race are also hallmarks of the New Age. Interest in ecological changes taking place on the planet, as well as in projects and initiatives directed to secure world peace, rank high. A new curiosity about human origins was sparked by Erich von Däniken's book, *Chariots of the Gods: Unsolved Mysteries of the Past*.[75] The quest for ancient mysteries and for UFOs are major interests among many people involved in the New Age Movement. Such quests, however, easily take on a mythological flavor as in the stories about Atlantis, Stonehenge, the Pyramids of Ancient Egypt, and the Inca ruins of South America. These narratives are told to corroborate a spiritual history of a human race that, because of human pride and the misuse of science, lost its mystic and psychic powers and began its long decline. UFO experiences are given religious and spiritual significance and become the bases for alternative religions.[76]

THE NEW AGE: SCHOLARLY PERSPECTIVES

One of the most authoritative compilations on the New Age Movement has been made by J. Gordon Melton, Jerome Clark, and Aidan A. Kelly, who define the New Age as follows:

> The New Age Movement can be defined by its primal experience of transformation. **New Agers** have either experienced or are diligently seeking a profound personal transformation from an old, unacceptable life to a new, exciting future. One prominent model for transformation is healing, which has given rise to what is possibly the largest identifiable segment of the movement, the holistic health movement.[77]

They then proceed to describe the contents of the movement under seven broad headings: (1) 'Altered States: Channeling and Walk-ins, Dreams, Meditation, Music, Past Lives, and Reincarnation'; (2) 'Mystery Theatre: Lost Continents, Power Spots, Tarot Cards, and UFOs'; (3) 'On the Road to Samadhi: Yoga'; (4) 'Positive States: Health and Healing'; (5) 'Star Karma: Astrology, Celebrities, and Related Matters'; (6) 'Temple of Cosmic Wisdom: Metaphysics, Occultism, and Spirituality'; (7) 'Worldview: Community Life, Education, Environment, Love, Peace, Planetary Consciousness, and Politics'.

This eclectic classification provides an overview not only of New Age activities but also of the religious ideology characteristic of New Agers. Although it does not coincide with that given in the *New Age Catalogue*, it refers practically to all the materials typically found in New Age literature.

Massimo Introvigne prefers to describe, rather than define, the movement in the following words:

> The New Age is an extremely fluid and fleeting reality. It is certainly not a movement, a 'sect', an association to which one subscribes or to which one adheres. It is rather a climate, an ambience, an atmosphere, an assortment of realities that share certain familiar surroundings, but that also presents differences and contradictions.[78] [my translation]

He explains that New Age beliefs and practices flow from three chief sources: (1) Alternative spiritualities (promoted by, for example, Eastern religions, metaphysics and esoteric Christianity, spiritism, occultism, neo-Paganism, UFOs and extraterrestrials, and astrology); (2) Alternative therapies (comprising holistic medicine, vegetarianism, alternative psychologies, especially those of Carl Jung and Robert Assagioli, and the recovery movement or healing); and (3) Alternative social organizations (which include the commune movement, ecology and the new science, and the new politics).

The variety and complexity of the movement is summed up by William Frost, who asserts that the movement 'is about holistic medicine, transcendental meditation, Yoga and Zen, the liberation of consciousness, the Buddhist enlightenment, the Christian mystical tradition, relaxation to embrace the divine energy, communication with the dead, near-death experiences, acupuncture, reflexology, Hinduism, Taoism, Jainism, Animism, Sufism, the noosphere of Teilhard de Chardin, utopian communities, the celebration of world Peace and love'.[79]

Guiley finds the term New Age Movement controversial for three main reasons: (1) it includes such a wide range of interests and outlooks that it eludes definition; (2) it connotes that there is something 'new', which is misleading; and (3) it has no national or international organization or leaders. But she detects certain features in the movement that characterize it as an entity distinct from other religions or spiritualities. She states that among New Agers:

> There is a general interest in pursuing *sadhana*, a spiritual path,

toward self-realization; in transforming the world through spiritual consciousness that unifies all religions; and in looking after planetary concerns.[80]

And she specifies a few general illustrative ideas that permeate the movement, namely the beliefs that one creates one's own reality, that divinity exists within, and that human beings need a renewed recognition of the feminine principle and the use of 'feminine' traits such as intuition.

In an attempt to deal with the contradictory world views found in the New Age, Paul Greer[81] argues that the movement embraces two practical antithetical types of theology regarding divinity, humanity, and nature. These he labels 'patriarchal' and 'ecological'; the former being characterized by a separatist, anti-ecological view of the self, the latter by the importance placed on earth as the natural abode of the human race, by the belief in the interdependence of all living organisms, and by an acceptance of diversity.

Several scholars seem to maintain that the New Age Movement has already made a great impact on the religious ideology and spiritual practices of many people. Peter Occhiogrosso, for example, in a recent book on world religions, treats the New Age as a major religion and dedicates, as he does with each of the great religious traditions, a whole chapter to exposing its tenets.[82]

Occhiogrosso starts by observing that no single definition can encompass all the sects, movements, teachings, techniques, and personalities that comprise the New Age Movement and that the name 'New Age' is entirely inadequate. He recommends that the New Age should be approached with the same openness and respect accorded other religious traditions. The New Age is a genuine religious movement that embraces diversity and encompasses not only various forms of spirituality but also all kinds of minority groups. Besides Eastern meditation and yoga, the New Age incorporates 'an increased awareness of nutrition and the value of preventive medicine, alternative approaches to healing, ecological concerns, an integration of business procedures with the common good, a reconsideration of the value of intuition as opposed to strictly logical thought, and, above all, an acknowledgment of the invisible realm of spirit'.[83] Its preeminent goal is the evolution of a universal religion. It upholds certain principles, such as individualism, practicality, and a commitment to social justice, that are already part of Western culture.

Further, Occhiogrosso thinks that apocalyptism, the expectation that the world is coming to an end and the anticipation that it will be replaced by a better one, is the most common New Age belief. And he specifies one particular feature that distinguishes this apocalyptic world view from that found in other religious traditions:

> Many New Agers believe that the apocalypse will take the form of a vast transformation in human consciousness, a move up to the next level of awareness, for which we all need to prepare. Although some New Agers envision this change as potentially explosive and destructive, most view it as an inevitable but benevolent event; preparing for it through meditation and other spiritual practices, they say, will help reduce the confusion and fear that some people may experience during the transition.[84]

This apocalyptic dimension of the New Age Movement is echoed by Michael York, who writes:

> Its vision of an imminent and comprehensive change in collective human consciousness often rests on belief in supernatural and/or extra-terrestrial mediation. The diversity within the movement might best be pictured as conforming to three 'camps': the occult which seeks personal change through channeling, crystals and magic; the spiritual which centers on individual growth and trance state attainment through meditation and related techniques; and the social which stresses human potential development mainly as a means for collective social change.[85]

Other writers prefer to talk of the millenarian ideals that they believe are prevalent in the New Age Movement. Reender Kranenborg,[86] for example, argues that the dawning of the Age of Aquarius is central to the movement which has adopted and adapted Theosophy's evolutionary-eschatological view of history. He discusses two different schools of thought regarding the millennium. The first revolves around the belief that the Age of Aquarius will arrive with the coming of the Maitreya, a view popularized by Benjamin Creme. The second is based on the view of history as evolving through different ages, the present being the Age of Pisces (or the Christian age). In general the New Age Movement's predictions for the future are optimistic.

In spite of the diversity, the apocalyptic vision is, according to some scholars, a principal theme within the New Age Movement. Charles B. Strozier[87] points out that there are three forms of apocalyptic in the movement, namely catastrophic, magical, and efficacious. The catastrophic sees the coming millennium as being born in violence and destruction; the magical conceives of the New Age as one that will be ushered in by aliens or spirits; and the efficacious insists that human actions will be responsible for the transformation of our world in the coming New Age.

It is not surprising that scholars studying the New Age Movement have described it as 'a highly amorphous and confusing area'.[88] James Lewis, for instance, has remarked that 'one almost always has difficulties deciding where the phenomenon begins and ends'.[89] He has further questioned whether the label 'New Age' is a meaningful category. Certainly, its hope for a new world and its use of occult practices to achieve its ends are hardly novel.

Most scholars admit that the New Age Movement is genuinely religious in nature, even though it lacks the organization and specification of beliefs and rituals found in the main traditions. Consequently, they tend to include it as part of the twentieth-century religious scene. Julia Mitchell Corbett,[90] for example, in her survey of religion in America, inserts the New Age under the category 'Alternative Religion in the Popular Mode'. The focus of the New Age is on the individual and on small group involvement without any links to traditional ecclesiastical settings. Admitting that it is just as hard to define the New Age as it is to estimate the number of people involved in it, she leans to Melton's view that the primal experience of transformation is the keynote of New Age involvement.

For Corbett, the following major themes recur frequently in New Age literature: (1) the stress on holism as a reaction to the dualism that has characterized Western thought; (2) the immanence of the divine; (3) the interrelatedness of all things; (4) concern for ecology; (5) the need for change both in the individual and in culture at large; (6) compassionate service to people and to community; (7) the underlying unity of all religions; (8) the development of a planetary culture; (9) the development of communal lifestyles; (10) the stress on cooperation rather than competition; and (11) the acceptance of the Eastern teachings on karma and reincarnation. Central to the lifestyle of New Agers is the selection of a spiritual path and participation in rituals and meditation that are held to be essential for self transformation. Holistic health and alternative healing methods are preferred to standard medical practices in the West. The New Age, according to Corbett, is not alien to American culture but has been part and parcel of it almost since its inception.

In like manner, Steve Bruce,[91] a sociologist, treats the New Age as one facet of contemporary religion. He lists eclecticism and diffusiveness as central features of the movement which creates 'a milieu in which people acquire, absorb, and learn a variety of beliefs and practices that they combine into their own pockets of culture'. Besides improving the self, the New Age advances a new science and a new ecology. It tends to be inclusive in its attitude towards diverse beliefs. A key element in New Age thought is the power or divinity of the self. Among the sociological features of the New Age movement, Bruce observes that (1) there is an inverse relationship with the strength of traditional churches; (2) New Agers tend to come from the affluent and educated section of society; and (3) women tend to be more attracted to it than men.

Scholars, further, seem to agree that the New Age Movement promulgates attractive spiritualities. However, they are also aware that the movement is inherently problematic and that it will probably not survive in the form in which it became so popular in the 1980s.

Scholarly evaluations of the New Age

Peter Occhiogrosso sums up one of the criticisms which have been leveled at the New Age Movement by stating that it lacks a 'logical, sharply structured theory'. For him, the 'greatest potential weakness of the New Age may be its confusing conglomeration of beliefs, the often vague nature of their definitions, and an overall lack of focus'.[92] He reiterates Ken Wilber's critique of its underlying philosophy of higher consciousness. Wilber, in his book *Transformations of Consciousness*,[93] voiced the danger of treating prerational states, such as myth and magic, as rational structures and of confusing genuinely mystical experiences with regression and schizophrenia. The New Age, with its stress on the nonrational and its encouragement of trance states, could be a form of escape from reality rather than a genuine transformation.

Some of the more popular practices of the New Age Movement, like channeling and the use of crystals for healing, are easily open to both criticism and ridicule. Peter Occhiogrosso[94] speculates that channelers may be in touch with delusional states of consciousness rather than with spiritual entities. And Gordon Melton observes that channeling and the use of crystals have contributed to the 'downfall' of the New Age Movement. He writes:

> Crystals presented a more substantive problem [than channeling]. Many outrageous claims were made concerning the supposed 'scientific' properties of the crystals to store and transmit energy.

> In the end those who promoted the use of crystals were forced to
> back away from any scientific claims and had to defend the use of
> crystals entirely on less attractive spiritual grounds.[95]

Rosemary Ellen Guiley voices serious reservations about the movement. While admiring the ecumenical stance of many New Agers,
she warns that 'there is a danger in New Age ecumenism, in that the
individual may remain religiously rootless, skipping about and col-
lecting a superficial grab bag of only the most convenient doctrines
and practices'.[96] She accepts Jacob Needleman's[97] concern that the
goal of unlocking higher energies within the psyche can become a
selfish (maybe narcissistic) pursuit without inner discipline and
without the guidance of reliable knowledge and the support of an
established community. She also suggests that involvement in the
New Age may consist of flirtation without serious commitment. And
though she dismisses as extreme the attacks against the movement
that have come largely from Christian fundamentalists, she observes
that 'the criticisms of narcissism, superficiality, exploitation, and
fraud have some legitimacy – but there is not a single field which
does not have its abusers'.[98]

More radical criticisms have come from scholars who find that
most New Age tenets are based on pseudoscientific beliefs like astrology and channeling. Paul Kurtz[99] expresses the standard scientific
view when he declares quite categorically that New Agers make
'highly questionable claims that do not stand up to critical evaluation'. Other writers[100] have argued against reincarnation and past-life
regression and have questioned the foundations of New Age music,
politics, and economics. One journal in particular, *The Skeptical
Inquirer,* has dedicated much time and space to attacking and often
ridiculing New Age beliefs and practices. The contributors to this
journal, which is published by the Committee for the Investigation
of Scientific Claims for the Paranormal (CISCOP), reject all New Age
beliefs as irrational and unsubstantiated by scientific evidence and
most New Age practices as magical.

Attacks against the New Age are common in psychological quarters. M. D. Faber, in a recent book, delivers what is probably the most
damaging assessment of the movement. He writes:

> I regard New Age thinking as essentially *regressive or infantile* in
> nature. It is absorbed, I contend, in matters of symbiotic merger,
> omnipotence, narcissistic inflation, and in magical thinking and
> wishing generally. New Age thinking makes war on reality; it deni-

grates reason; it denies and distorts what I consider to be the existential facts of our human experience; it seeks to restore the past, specifically, the before-separation world, in an idealized, wish-fulfilling form that has little if any connection with the adult estate ... it bears *no relevance whatsoever* to any and all questions of veracity, authenticity, actuality, or validity, as it is a purely *practical or pragmatical criterion*; it exacts too high a price, namely loss of reason, autonomy, and maturity, for whatever adaptive reward it offers the practitioner.[101]

Joseph Chuman,[102] writing from a humanistic perspective, accuses New Agers of refusing, or being powerless, to correct their assumptions, thus committing the 'error of solipsism, or the belief that the outside world is exclusively an object of our own consciousness'. New Agers are berated for turning off their critical faculties and for proclaiming 'a metaphysical dualism with an exuberance and gusto that would have caused St. Augustine to blush', while the New Age is further charged with being 'founded upon an utterly unsubstantiated metaphysics and a disreputable epistemology', and for 'irresponsibly confusing imagination with fact'.[103] Henry Gordon, epitomizing the attitudes of the Committee for the Scientific Investigation of Claims of the Paranormal (CSICOP), declares unequivocally that the field encompassed by the New Age is 'nonsensical drivel'.[104]

While few scholars would doubt the New Age's impact on modern society, many would question its depth and significance. Bruce, for one, points out that it is hard to assess the influence New Age ideas and practices are having on society as a whole. He sums up his survey by stating that the

New Age religion cannot aspire to promote radical and specific change because it does not have the cohesion and discipline of the sect. The New Age will not have the impact that Methodism had. But, as has already happened with aspects of its environmentalism and its holistic approach to health, some of its ideas may find themselves stripped of their more esoteric parts and accepted into the cultural mainstream. More important than its immediate impact on the lives of individuals is the part that it plays as symptom and as cause in the erosion of faith in orthodoxies and the authority of professional knowledge.[105]

Criticisms of the New Age have also come from the anti-cult movement. While these reactions to New Age beliefs and practices are colored by a negative stance against new religions in general, it must be admitted that the critique proffered by anti-cultists is similar to that found in more balanced scholarly works. Many of the goals of the New Age are said to be unrealistic. Its psychology 'recalls the emotional irrationalism of the romantic period'.[106] Further, the New Age has been criticized for endorsing a view of personal responsibility that is a kind of 'rationalized and often uncaring narcissism'.[107]

The debate in anti-cult literature has centered on whether the New Age is harmful to those who become involved in it. On the one hand, members of the American Family Foundation (AFF)[108] and of the Committee for the Scientific Investigation of Claims of the Paranormal (CSICOP) agree that, while brainwashing doesn't seem to be integral to New Age groups, membership tends to develop destructive cultic behavior. On the other hand, experts who are sympathetic to the New Age Movement rate New Age beliefs and practices as either neutral or even mildly beneficial. And even those who maintain that membership in most new religious groups is harmful seem ready to make an exception in the case of those who are involved in the New Age. Researchers at the American Family Foundation who conducted a comprehensive survey admitted that their questionnaire 'was not the product of evenhanded, objective scientists'.[109] Arthur Dole analyzed the responses to these surveys and concluded that:

> if some aspects of the New Age are fraudulent, dollar-driven, magical, superstitious, anti-scientific, and cultic, other aspects are sincere and benign attempts to find alternative paths to religious fulfillment, to encourage tolerance, responsibility, and love of others, and to develop personal potential. Skeptics, anti-cult specialists, and other outsiders may need to revise some of their conceptions about the New Age.[110]

Probably one of the more favorable scholarly evaluations of the New Age Movement is that of Mary Farrell Bednarowski. In her review of fourteen representative books,[111] she underscores five themes that permeate the movement: (1) the need for a new world view that avoids dualist concepts (such as body/spirit, matter/consciousness, and male/female); (2) the belief that the divine is immanent and that, consequently, all things are interrelated; (3) an optimism about the possibility of both individual and social transformation; (4) a concern for ecology and, hence, an insistence on the need to develop a planetary consciousness; and (5) the assumption that underlies the above themes, namely, the pervasive presence of the evolutionary process.

Bednarowski contends that, though the movement is indeed eclectic and though disagreements within its ranks are numerous, the common themes make it less amorphous than it appears at first sight. She holds, however, that the movement leaves unanswered many of the questions it raises. Thus, for example, whether the paradigmatic change is inevitable and positive is not always clear. In like manner, the process of salvation promised by the movement is open to conflicting interpretations.[112] Moreover, Bednarowski is not sure 'what role does the New Age Movement play in American culture'. She speculates that the movement may function, not just as a resurgence of the metaphysical tradition, but as a forum where religious questions are discussed outside the boundaries of traditional theological discourse and where the relationship between religion and the social and physical disciplines can be reassessed. It can also act as a catalyst for looking at social issues (like ecology) from unconventional and innovative perspectives and as a testimony of the vitality of popular religion in an age when organized religion appears to be on the decline.

UNDERSTANDING AND EVALUATING THE NEW AGE MOVEMENT

Given the complex picture and all-encompassing nature of the New Age, it is not surprising that it has elicited many reactions from Christian commentators. The New Age needs to be evaluated because it deals with both theoretical and practical matters that affect people's lives. Its influence is widespread. It offers a critique of traditional religions, particularly Christianity. And it borrows ideas from a variety of religious sources and reinterprets them. Moreover, it advances alternative theologies and spiritualities.

It is unfortunate, however, that the Christian reaction to the New Age Movement has been marred by misunderstandings and apprehensions. Hence one must proceed with caution and inculcate, from the very start, what the New Age is not. Based both on the writings by New Agers and on scholarly studies of the movement, the following major conclusions can be drawn:

(1) The New Age Movement is not an organization in the ordinary meaning of the term. It has no centralized headquarters, no legislative or even counseling body of experts in the field. Hence, no general policy statements or directives are ever issued. There is too

much diversity within the movement to allow for the emergence of an organized religion. Hence, it would probably be better to talk of New Age movements that share a basic ideology and religious orientation (with lots of differences in theory and practice).

(2) The New Age Movement is not a secret organization, planning to take over any specific country or the world or to eradicate any particular religion. There is no covert plot. While certain proponents of the New Age who are recognized as its leaders do sometimes meet, they operate more as individual leaders who manage to attract a clientele. And while there is a lot of 'networking' between New Agers,[113] their methods can be more accurately described as evangelical rather than revolutionary.

(3) Nobody is forcing people to conform to New Age ideas or to join New Age groups. Most New Agers are adult (and not very young ones at that). Evangelization and recruitment are done largely through personal contacts, meetings open to the public, and attractive publications.

(4) There is no direct link between the New Age Movement and Satanism, unless one assumes that anything non-Christian must have a connection with evil forces or demons. A few New Age beliefs, for example, those regarding magic and psychic powers, are also espoused by contemporary Satanists, as are some New Age practices, such as the consultation of one's horoscopes. Satanic groups have claimed that the New Age of Satan has started. It would be illogical and incorrect to conclude, however, that all New Agers are Satanists.

Hence, the New Age Movement should be approached as any other social and/or religious movement, that is, without any fear or panic. This doesn't mean that one can or should extend to it an uncritical welcome and accept its beliefs and approve of its many practices. Rather, one should employ discretion, distinction, and discrimination.

There are three dimensions or aspects of the New Age Movement that call for an evaluation and critical assessment:

(1) The first is philosophical. The New Age offers a distinct world view.[114] New Agers are worried about the scientific and environmental changes that are taking place in our times and postulate that these changes require new attitudes and priorities. Those committed to the New Age point out that political, economic, and religious developments are turning the world into a global village and that, consequently, people must strive to acquire a fundamental change in their awareness and priorities.

(2) The second is religious or theological. Central to the New Age is the belief that there is a spiritual dimension to human existence and that it should not be separated from other major aspects of human life. The New Age tries to achieve a synthesis of Eastern and Western theologies. It endeavors to develop a positive spirituality that lies within everybody's reach. Moreover, its spirituality fits into Western individualism and encourages people to construct their own religion by picking and choosing from a large assortment of beliefs and practices, none of which are rejected as unorthodox or unethical. The New Age also strives to find a synthesis between religion and science.[115]

(3) The third level is a practical one. The New Age is not only an ideology but a program of action that includes methods for acquiring self-knowledge and rituals for self-transformation. Astrology and channeling, for instance, are commonly-used tools for self-development and knowledge. Healing is one of the practical applications of the New Age and would encompass holistic health practices (such as the adoption of microbiotic diet) and magical rituals (such as the use of crystals and mantras to ward off disease and evil influences).

One of the difficulties inherent in any evaluation of the New Age Movement is the large diversity of beliefs and practices that it embraces. Thus, for instance, the practice of channeling and the concern for the environment, both of which are popular features of the New Age Movement, require different kinds of appraisals. Because of this, a Christian response to and evaluation of the New Age Movement as a whole may not be feasible. Understanding the New Age is a prerequisite not only for evaluating it but also for assessing the numerous Christian responses that have been made over the last quarter of a century.

NOTES

1. Gordon Melton, Jerome Clark, and Aidan A. Kelly, *New Age Encyclopedia* (Detroit: Gale Research Inc., 1990), p. 171.

2. See The Findhorn Community, *Faces of Findhorn: Images of a Planetary Family* (New York: Harper and Row, 1980); and David Spangler, *Visions of Findhorn: Anthology* (Forres, UK: Findhorn Foundation, 1976).

3. For a list of New Age organizations in different parts of the English-speaking world, see Eileen Campbell and J. H. Brennan, *The Aquarian Guide to the New*

Age (Wellingborough, UK: Aquarian Press, 1990), pp. 339–48.

4. The historical roots of the New Age are discussed in several essays in *Perspectives on the New Age*, ed. James R. Lewis and J. Gordon Melton (Albany: SUNY Press, 1992), pp. 13–67. For a brief history see J. Gordon Melton, 'A history of the New Age Movement' in *Not Necessarily the New Age: Critical Essays*, ed. Robert Basil (Buffalo, NY: Prometheus Press, 1988), pp. 35–53. J. Gordon Melton, Jerome Clark, and Aidan A. Kelly, in their *New Age Almanac* (Detroit: Gale Research, 1991), pp. xi–xvi, provide a chronology of the New Age from 1975 to 1990.

5. See, for example, Michael York, 'New Age in Britain: an overview', *Religion Today: Journal of Contemporary Religion* 9.3 (1994): 14–21; and *Perspectives on the New Age*, ed. James R. Lewis and J. Gordon Melton, section iv, 'International Dimensions', pp. 213ff.

6. 'Introductory essay: an overview of the New Age Movement' in *New Age Encyclopedia*, p. xxxii.

7. Detroit: Gale Research, 2nd ed., 1984. Since the publication of the *New Age Encyclopedia*, a two-volume 3rd ed. of Shepard's work was published by Gale Research in 1991.

8. *What Is the New Age? Defining the Third Millennium Consciousness* (Lewiston, NY: Edwin Mellen Press, 1992), p. 33.

9. 'Concepts for a theory of religious movements' in *Alternatives to American Mainline Churches*, ed. Joseph H. Fichter (Barrytown, NY: Rose of Sharon Press, 1983), pp. 12–19. Stark and Bainbridge's analysis has been further amplified by Bainbridge, who adds a fourth group or level which he calls 'private' and which consists of individuals and very small groups 'without a leader or professional practitioner, and without any large-scale communication or organization'. See his recent book, *The Sociology of Religious Movements* (London and New York: Routledge, 1997), p. 374.

10. Charlotte Seymour-Smith, *Macmillan Dictionary of Anthropology* (London: Macmillan Press, Ltd, 1986), p. 92.

11. For some basic materials on the New Age, see *The New Age: An Anthology of Essential Writings*, ed. William Bloom (London: Rider, 1991). Besides descriptions of the New Age, this collection of essays contains sections on the inner voice, healing, the human potential, and Gaia.

12. *The New Age* (Issaquah, WA: Morningtown Press, 1988), p. 3. See also his *New Age and Beyond* (Issaquah, WA: Morningtown Press, 1989).

13. *Visions of Findhorn: Anthology*, p. 17.

14. 'Defining the New Age' in *The New Age Catalogue: Access to Information and Sources*,

by the editors of *Body, Mind and Spirit* (New York: Doubleday, 1988), Introduction.

15. *Visions of Findhorn: Anthology*, pp. 16–17.

16. 'Images of the New Age' in *Reimagination of the World: A Critique of the New Age, Science, and Popular Culture*, ed. David Spangler and William Irwin Thompson (Santa Fe, NM: Bear and Co., 1991), pp. 23 and 25.

17. 'The big picture and the messianic delusion' in *Reimagination of the World*, ed. David Spangler and William Irwin Thompson, pp. 73–81.

18. *A Vision of the Aquarian Age: The Emerging Spiritual World View* (Walpole, UK: Stillpoint Publishing, 1984), pp. 11ff.

19. *The Reappearance of Christ and the Masters of Wisdom* (Los Angeles: Tara Center, 1980), pp. 24ff. Creme claims that Maitreya the Christ delivered 140 messages to him between September 6, 1977 and May 27, 1982. Cf. Benjamin Creme, *Messages from Maitreya the Christ* (Los Angeles: Tara Center, 2 vols, 1980 and 1982).

20. *Strangers Among Us* (New York: Fawcett Crest, 1979), pp. 29ff.

21. *Magical Blend*, issue 28 (October 1990), inside of front cover. Some minor additions and clarifications have been recently made to this statement of purpose; see *Magical Blend*, issue 44 (April 1995): 1.

22. *The New Age*, pp. 17–19.

23 'The New Age: the movement toward the divine' in *New Age Spirituality: An Assessment*, ed. Duncan S. Ferguson (Louisville, KY: Westminster/John Knox Press, 1993), p. 95.

24. *The New Age*, pp. 20–21.

25. See, for example, Bill Barol, 'The end of the world (again)', *Newsweek* 110 (August 17, 1987): 70–71; and Otto Friedrich, 'New Age harmonies', *Time* 130 (December 7, 1987): 62–66. The interest in the Harmonic Convergence seems to have declined sharply since 1987. Cf. J. Gordon Melton, et al., 'Harmonic convergence' in *New Age Encyclopedia*, pp. 204–05.

26. *The Aquarian Conspiracy* (Los Angeles: Jeremy B. Tarcher, 1980).

27. J. Gordon Melton et al., *New Age Encyclopedia*, p. 121.

28. *The Aquarian Conspiracy*, pp. 86–87.

29. This volume is published by the editors of *Body, Mind and Spirit* (New York: Island Publishing Company, 1988).

30. Cf. Jon Klimo, *Channeling: Investigations on Receiving Information from Paranormal Sources* (Los Angeles: Jeremy P. Tarcher, 1987); and Sanaya Roman and Duane Packer, *Opening to Channel: How to Connect with Your Guide* (Los Angeles: Lumin Essence Publications, 1987).

31. See, for examples, Kathleen Vande Kieft, *Innersource: Channeling Your Unlimited Self* (New York: Ballantine, 1988).

32. Herbert B. Puryear, *The Edgar Cayce Primer: Discovering the Path to Self-Transformation* (Virginia Beach, VA: A.R.E. Press, 1982).

33. Many of the messages channeled by Lazaris are available only on audio and/video tapes published by Concept: Synergy in Los Angeles. See, for instances, 'Crystals: their power and use' (audio tape) and 'Achieving intimacy and loving relationships' (video tape).

34. Robin Westen's book, *Channelers: A New Age Directory* (New York: Putnam, 1988), provides an account of 18 channelers (pp. 85–179) and a New Age channeling directory for the United States and Canada (pp. 185–219). For records of individual channelers see Jane Roberts, *The Seth Materials* (New York: Bantam Books, 1970); *Ramtha Channeled through J. Z. Knight*, ed. Lee Steven Weinberg (Eastwood, WA: Sovereignty, 1986); and Charles H. Hapgood, *Voices of the Spirits through the Psychic Experiences of Elwood Babbitt* (Turners Falls, MA: Fine Line Books, 1975).

35. Tiburion, CA: Foundation for Inner Peace, 1974.

36. Consult, for instance, *Sedona: Journal of Emergence!* (October 1995), where a whole section (pp. 44–79) is dedicated to recording information from spirit sources delivered through various channelers.

37. *Innersource: Channeling Your Unlimited Self*, p. xiii.

38. See, for example, Enid Hoffman, *Develop Your Psychic Skill* (West Chester, PA: Para Research, 1981); Dick Sutphen, *How to Rapidly Develop Your Psychic Ability* (Agoura Hills, CA: Valley of the Sun, 1985); R. M. Miller, *A Psychic Energy Workbook: An Illustrated Course in Practical Psychic Skills* (New York: Aquarius Press, 1986); and John Friedlander, *The Practical Psychic* (York Beach, ME: Samuel Weiser, 1991).

39. *Out on a Limb* (New York: Bantam Books, 1983).

40. *The New Age Catalogue*, p. 40.

41. See, for example, W. Brugh Joy, *Joy's Way: A Map for the Transformational Journey* (Los Angeles: Jeremy P. Tarcher, 1978).

42. This theme runs throughout her book *It's All in Playing* (New York: Bantam, 1987); see, for instance, pp. 15–16, 19, 33, 38, 114, 173–74.

43. Cf. Tom Rusk and Randy Read, *I Want to Change But I Don't Know How* (Los Angeles: Price/Stern/Sloan Publishing, 1986); and Shakti Gawain, *Living in the Light: A Guide to Personal and Planetary Transformation* (New York: Bantam, 1993).

44. Shakti Gawain, *Creative Visualization: Use the Power of Your Imagination to Create Whatever You Want in Your Life* (San Rafael, CA: New World Library, 1991), p. 13.

45. Ibid., pp. 19–20.

46. Gerald G. Jampolsky and Diane V. Cirincione, *Change Your Mind, Change Your Life: Concepts in Attitudinal Healing* (New York: Bantam, 1993), p. 7.

47. A lot of New Age literature deals with this topic. See, for instance, Tina B. Tessina, *Love Styles: How to Celebrate Your Differences* (Van Nuys, CA: Newcastle Publishing, 1987); Jess Stern, *Soul Mates* (Des Plaines, IL: Bantam Books, 1984); and Ken Keyes, *A Conscious Person's Guide to Relationships* (Coos Bay, OR: Cornucopia Books, 1979).

48. For a list of sources, including audio tapes, on subliminal programming, cf. *The New Age Catalogue*, p. 60.

49. See, for example, Fred Alan Wolf, *Star Wave: Mind, Consciousness, and Quantum Physics* (New York: Macmillan, 1984), and *The Body Quantum: Mind, Consciousness and Quantum Physics* (New York: Macmillan, 1986). Wolf maintains that quantum physics provides a basis for a new religion and for an understanding of the human spirit.

50. *The New Age Catalogue*, p. 85.

51. See, for example, Jeannine Parvati Baker, Frederick Baker, and Tamara Slayton, *Conscious Conception* (Berkeley, CA: North Atlantic Books, 1986); and Michel Odent, *Birth Reborn* (Westminster, MD: Pantheon Books, 1984).

52. Sandra Sol, *Ideal Birth* (Beverly Hills, CA: Celestial Arts, 1985), p. 97. The process of regressing to birth and prenatal states of consciousness is called 'rebirthing', a process during which people are made to 'relive physiologically, psychologically, and spiritually the moment of their first breath, and release all of the trauma connected with it'. Cf. Mark Kastner and Hugh Burroughs, *Alternative Healing: The Complete A–Z Guide to Over 160 Different Alternative Therapies* (La Mesa, CA: Halcyon Publishing, 1993), p. 208.

53. *On Death and Dying* (Riverside, NJ: Macmillan Publishing, 1969).

54. *Life After Life* (Des Plaines, IL: Bantam Books, 1975).

55. *Life at Death: A Scientific Investigation of Near-Death Experience* (Fairfield, NJ: William Morrow and Co., 1980).

56. See Dereck Humphry and Ann Wickett, *The Right to Die: Understanding Euthanasia* (Hagerstown, MD: Harper and Row, 1986).

57. *The Unquiet Dead: A Psychologist Treats Spirit Possession – Detecting and Removing Earthbound Spirits* (Garden City, NY: Doubleday, 1987).

58. Dick Sutphen, *Past Life Therapy: Regression Album* (Agoura Hills, CA: Valley of the Sun, 1981).

59. Gordon S. Wakefield, 'Spirituality' in *Dictionary of Christian Spirituality*, ed. Gordon S. Wakefield (Philadelphia: Westminster Press, 1983), p. 262.

60. One should note that misinterpretations of Eastern religions abound in New Age writings. See, for example, Andrea Grace Diem and James R. Lewis's critique of Fritjof Capra's misrepresentation of Hinduism and over-idealization of Eastern religions in general in their essay 'Imagining India: the influence of Hinduism on the New Age Movement' in *Perspectives on the New Age*, ed. James R. Lewis and J. Gordon Melton, pp. 49–51.

61. For basic outlines of Sufism, see Cyril Glassé, *The Concise Encyclopedia of Islam* (San Francisco: HarperSanFrancisco, 1991), pp. 375–80; and Andrew Rippin, *Muslims: Their Religious Beliefs and Practices*, vol. 1: *The Formative Period* (London: Routledge, 1990), pp. 117–28.

62. This description is a summary of the Sufi Order in the West's own explanation of its symbol. Cf. *The New Age Catalogue*, p. 124.

63. See, for example, D. I. Suzuki, *An Introduction to Zen Buddhism* (Westminster, MD: Grove Press, 1964).

64. Cf. Ruth Brandon, *The Spiritualists: The Passion for the Occult in the Nineteenth and Twentieth Centuries* (New York: Alfred A. Knopf, 1993). For a short account of Spiritualism in the West see Leslie Shepard, *Encyclopedia of Occultism and Parapsychology*, vol. 2, pp. 1582–1600.

65. Consult, for instance, Monica Sjoo and Barbara Mor, *The Great Cosmic Mother: Rediscovering the Religion of the Earth* (Hagerstown, PA: Harper and Row, 1987).

66. *The New Age Catalogue*, p. 149. For a description of over 160 different types of alternative therapies see Mark Kastner and Hugh Burroughs, *Alternative Healing* (La Mesa, CA: Halcycon Publishing, 1993).

67. The editors of the *New Age Journal* publish yearly source books on the New Age and on holistic health. Cf., for instance, *Holistic Health: Directory and Resource Guide 1994–1995, New Age Journal* 11.6 (1994) and *The Annual Sourcebook for 1996, New Age Journal* 12.9 (1996). Many other magazines that deal with holistic health, such as *Natural Health: The Guide to Well-Being* and *Health Consciousness*,

are excellent sources for alternative healing techniques. In the United Kingdom, the journal *Kindred Spirit: The Guide to Personal and Planetary Healing* provides a regular resource directory that emphasizes alternative healing techniques. See, for example, *Kindred Spirit,* issue 39 (Summer 1997), pp. 65–84.

68. *Holistic Health: Directory and Resource Guide 1994–1995,* p. 61.

69. *The New Age Catalogue,* p. 178. For descriptions of various kinds of 'bodywork' see Milton Trigger and Kathy Guadagno, *Traeger Mentastics: Movement as a Way to Agelessness* (Barrytown, NY: Station Hill Press, 1987); Randolph Stone, *Polarity Therapy* (Sebastopol, CA; CRCS Publications, 1986); Lucinda Hall, *The Book of Massage: The Complete Step-by-Step Guide to Eastern and Western Techniques* (Old Tappan, NJ: Simon and Schuster, 1984); Dan Millman, *The Warrior Athlete: Self-Transformation through Total Training* (Walpole, NH: Stillpoint International, 1979); Duane Juhan, *Job's Body: Handbook for Bodywork* (Barrytown, NY: Station Hill Press, 1987); and Joseph Heller and William A. Henkin, *Bodywise: Regaining Your Natural Flexibility and Vitality for Maximum Well-Being* (Los Angeles: Jeremy P. Tarcher, 1991).

70. See John Mercer, *Communes: A Social History and Guide* (Dorchester, UK: Prism Press, 1984); Benjamin David Zablocki, *Alienation and Charisma: A Study of Contemporary American Communes* (New York: Free Press, 1980); and Andrew Rigby, *Communes in Britain* (London: Routledge and Kegan Paul, 1974).

71. This is especially the case in the United States where quarterly or monthly magazines listing New Age resources and opportunities are distributed freely in many cities. Examples of these are *Common Ground: Resources for Personal Transformation* (in San Francisco, California) and *PhenomeNews* (in Detroit, Michigan).

72. 'What is New Age music?' in *The New Age Catalogue,* p. 204.

73. *Megatrends: Ten New Directions Transforming Our Lives* (New York: Warner Books, 1982). Among the areas of change Naisbitt includes (p. 2) the 'giving up our dependence on hierarchical structures in favor of informal networks'.

74. See, for instance, *The Prophecies of Nostradamus* (New York: Putnam Publishing Group, 1975) and *The Final Prophecies of Nostradamus* (New York: Perigee, 1989), both ed. Erika Cheetham. For a popular account, cf. Dava Sobel, 'The resurrection of Nostradamus: tripping through time with the man who saw tomorrow', *Omni* (December 1993): 42–51.

75. New York: Berkley Publishing, 1969.

76. Cf. John A. Saliba, 'Religious dimensions of UFO phenomena' in *The Gods Have Landed: New Religions from Other Worlds,* ed. James R. Lewis (Albany, NY: State University of New York Press, 1995), pp. 15–64.

77. *New Age Almanac*, p. 3.

78. *Storia del New Age, 1962–1992* (Piacenza, Italy: Cristianità, 1994), pp. 16–17.

79. *What Is the New Age: Defining the Third Millennium Consciousness* (Lewiston, NY: Edwin Mellen Press, 1992), p. 31.

80. *Harper's Encyclopedia of Mystical and Paranormal Experience* (San Francisco: HarperSanFrancisco, 1991), p. 403.

81. 'The Aquarian confusion: conflicting theologies of the New Age', *Religion Today: Journal of Contemporary Religion* 10.2 (1995): 152ff.

82. *The Joys of Sects: A Spirited Guide to the World's Religious Traditions* (New York: Doubleday, 1994), chapter 7, 'The New Age and beyond', pp. 467–584.

83. Ibid., p. 469.

84. Ibid., p. 473.

85. 'The New Age and neo-Pagan movements', *Religion Today* 6.2 (1991): 1–2.

86. 'Contemporary millenianism and the New Age Movement', *Exchange: Journal of Missiological and Ecumenical Research* 23.1 (1994): 44–57.

87. *Apocalypse: On the Psychology of Fundamentalism in America* (Boston: Beacon Press, 1994), pp. 228ff.

88. Eileen Barker, *New Religious Movements: A Practical Introduction* (London: Her Majesty's Stationery Office, 1989), p. 189.

89. 'Approaches to the study of the New Age Movement' in *Perspectives on the New Age*, ed. James R. Lewis and J. Gordon Melton, p. 1.

90. *Religion in America* (Upper Saddle River, NJ: Prentice Hall, 3rd ed., 1997), pp. 292–98.

91. *Religion in the Modern World: From Cathedrals to Cults* (London: Oxford University Press, 1996), pp. 197–229.

92. *The Joys of Sects*, p. 471.

93. Boston: New Science Library, 1986.

94. *The Joys of Sects*, p. 511.

95. 'Whither the New Age?', *The Way* 33 (1993): 207.

96. *Harper's Encyclopedia of Mystical and Paranormal Experience*, p. 405.

97. See his book *The New Religions* (Garden City, NY: Doubleday, 1980).

98. *Harper's Encyclopedia of Mystical and Paranormal Experience*, p. 406.

99. 'The New Age perspective', *The Skeptical Inquirer* 13 (Summer 1989): 366.

100. See *Not Necessarily the New Age: Critical Essays*, ed. Robert Basil.

101. *New Age Thinking: A Psychoanalytic Critique* (Ottawa: University of Ottawa Press, 1996), pp. 14–15.

102. 'A critique of New Age thought', *Religious Humanism* (Spring 1992): 56.

103. Ibid., p. 58.

104. *Channeling into the New Age: The 'Teachings' of Shirley MacLaine and Other Such Gurus* (Buffalo, NY: Prometheus Books, 1988), p. 28.

105. *Religion in the Modern World*, p. 225.

106. Steve K. Dubrow-Eichel and Linda Dubrow-Eichel, 'Trouble in paradise: some observations on psychotherapy with New Agers', *Cultic Studies Journal* 5 (1988): 178.

107. Ibid., p. 180.

108. See Arthur Dole, Michael Langone, and Steve Dubrow-Eichel, 'The New Age: fad or menace?', *Cultic Studies Journal* 7 (1990): 69–91 and 'Is the New Age Movement harmless?: critics versus experts', *Cultic Studies Journal* 10 (1993): 53–77.

109. Arthur Dole, Michael Langone, and Steve Dubrow-Eichel, 'Is the New Age Movement harmless?', p. 70.

110. 'Some conceptions of the New Age', *Journal of Religion and Health* 32 (1993): 275.

111. 'Literature of the New Age: a review of representative sources', *Religious Studies Review* 17 (1991): 209–16.

112. Ibid., pp. 215–16.

113. Consult Jessica Lipnack and Jeffrey Stamps, *Networking: The First Report and Directory* (Garden City, NY: Doubleday, 1982).

114. See, for example, Louise B. Young, *The Unfinished Universe* (New York: Simon

and Schuster, 1986); and Brian Swimme, *The Universe Is a Green Dragon: A Cosmic Creation Story* (Santa Fe, NM: Bear & Co., 1984).

115. Cf., for instance, Fritjof Capra, *The Tao of Physics: An Exploration of the Parallels Between Modern Physics and Eastern Mysticism* (Boulder, CO: Shambhala, 1991; first published 1965).

2.

EVANGELICAL AND FUNDAMENTALIST RESPONSES TO THE NEW AGE MOVEMENT

By far the majority of Christian writings on the New Age Movement stem from evangelical or fundamentalist sources that analyze and evaluate it from Christian biblical and theological perspectives.[1] These writings are not primarily intended to offer descriptive accounts of the movement, though in point of fact many such accounts are commonly included. They are concerned with the teachings and activities of the New Age on two levels, namely, the doctrinal and the pastoral.

The perception of the New Age as a serious competitor to traditional Christian values and commitment has determined the goals which most evangelical and fundamentalist Christians share in their responses to the New Age. These goals have been directed towards: (1) specifying and explaining clearly orthodox Christian doctrine; (2) refuting the teachings of the New Age and showing that they cannot be reconciled with Christianity; (3) exposing the weaknesses of the New Age tenets; (4) denouncing many of its leaders; and (5) alerting Christians to the subtle dangers posed by New Age beliefs and practices. Some writers have endeavored to present a less defensive and confrontational attitude. John Ankerberg and John Weldon, for example, state that their reasons for writing about the New Age are

> 1) to provide reliable information in brief and popular language on the New Age Movement; 2) to challenge readers to critically reexamine their own worldview; and 3) to express love for those who would like to be our friends by sharing our concerns as to the nature and implications of this topic.[2]

Not all these reasons, however, are borne out by their treatment of New Age beliefs and practices. Although plenty of information is provided, nowhere do the authors even remotely challenge their readers to any serious reflection on their Christian beliefs and practices. And the sharing of the authors' concerns is done in such a way that it rarely elicits much love towards those who are involved in the New Age.

THE DANGERS OF THE NEW AGE MOVEMENT

There is unanimity among Christian evangelicals and fundamentalists that the New Age Movement is an important religious development in the second half of the twentieth century and that its presence should be a source of concern to all Christians.[3] The New Age is certainly not a passing fad.[4] Elliot Miller, for example, thinks that the movement 'has become a *third major force* vying with traditional Judeo-Christian religion and secular humanism for cultural dominance'.[5] Others maintain that so many people are involved in New Age thought and activities that one cannot dismiss the movement as a harmless pastime.[6] Besides, it has already affected all levels of society and has made noteworthy inroads in education, health, psychology, the arts, business, industry, politics, religion, science, and entertainment.[7] Moreover, it is leading people to abandon their Judeo-Christian values in favor of those of the occult[8] and has thus become a threat to the very foundation of the Judeo-Christian faith as well as to the very existence of objective truth.[9]

The New Age, besides being a significant spiritual movement, is also a dangerous one. The majority of evangelicals and fundamentalists who have written on the New Age go to great lengths to convince their readers that dabbling in its beliefs and practices leads to disastrous consequences, psychologically, sociologically, and spiritually. The New Age is metaphorically compared to an uncaged lion that will devour all unless the necessary precautions are taken.[10]

Like other religious movements, the New Age has been accused of using mind control methods to regulate and manipulate people,[11] of indoctrinating its leaders,[12] and of hypnotizing audiences during talks and other presentations.[13] Randall N. Baer, who was formerly involved in the New Age, claims that Christ delivered him 'from the New Age brainwashing that bonds a person to the horrors that lurk beneath the surface of the New Age'.[14]

The New Age Movement is sometimes linked with a host of social abnormalities. Walter Martin thinks that the members of Jim Jones's Peoples Temple were 'victims of a fanatic influenced by New Age teachings'. He traces the tragedy to New Age teachings, especially those regarding the divine nature of human beings and the relativistic world view.[15]

Others accuse New Agers of all kinds of behavior that cannot be justified from the standpoint of Christian morality and/or that are plainly against established social and legal norms. Such behavior would include homosexuality, free-thinking sexual ethics, social nudity, divorce, abortion, and the use of illicit drugs.[16] In addition, some writers have detected a connection between the New Age and human sacrifice. Kenneth R. Wade formulates a general thesis about the consequences of monism, karma, and reincarnation. In his view these do not lead to peace, harmony, and love. On the contrary, since, for the New Age, life is small, insignificant, and temporary, it follows that wars, murder, and human sacrifice are its natural results.[17] Some, like Paul DeParrie and Mary Pride,[18] charge the New Age with advocating suicide and euthanasia, hastening the death of patients for their organs, practicing 'cannibalism' for research, as well as sacrificing children by using them, among other things, as organ farms.

Constance Cumbey is deeply concerned that many people 'are unaware of the political aims of the Movement to eliminate several billions from the earth's population and millions from that of the United States prior to the year 2000 – a goal only accomplishable by mass genocide'.[19] The New Age Movement could, therefore, be a religious or spiritual trend that might eventually eclipse Christianity. It certainly is a social, cultural, and political force that aims to achieve radical changes in all areas of human life. No moral restraints will hinder its march to achieve world domination. Cumbey's warnings about the disastrous repercussions that follow involvement in the New Age are frequently articulated in Christian literature. Spiritual, social, and psychological reasons are lumped together to persuade people that anything connected with the New Age should be avoided at all costs and that measures must be taken to openly confront and thwart its agenda.

John Eidsmore, for example, thinks that the New Age Movement is more dangerous than secular humanism[20] and enumerates seven reasons to prove that, particularly because of its principle 'we create our own reality', it is spiritually dangerous. He warns people to avoid any involvement in it because

> (1) It leads people to believe God has promised things which He
> has not promised; (2) It leads to disillusionment when the

promised things do not materialize as expected; people think that either God has not lived up to His promises or we have failed Him by not exercising the necessary faith, using the right techniques, etc.; (3) It leads to obsession with material blessing; (4) It causes people to lose sight of the fact that God often gives His greatest blessings through tragedy and adversity; indeed, it is through these that we often have our greatest growth; (5) It gives Satan and his demons the opportunity to confuse believers and lead them astray by giving us that which we have requested from God; (6) It can cause people to lose their industry and initiative and depend upon visualization to get what God wants them to work for; and (7) It can lead people to believe the results were obtained by their own power of visualization, rather than by the sovereign act of God.[21]

Douglas Groothuis[22] points out that all occult practices, condoned or encouraged by the New Age, are explicitly forbidden by the Bible. Yoga, for instance, because of its roots in Hinduism, can lead a person astray from Christian belief. His list of 'spiritual' maladies caused by involvement in the occult consists of the following eight elements, four of which are psychological or physical: (1) medium-istic affinity; (2) resistance to the things of God; (3) character and emotional disorders; (4) breeding grounds for mental illness; (5) oppression for descendants (who inherit a predilection for the occult); (6) suicide; (7) ghosts and poltergeists; and (8) frequent diseases.

Other writers combine dire religious, psychological, and social consequences that flow from the New Age and include deep self-deception, rejection of Christ, false happiness and contentment, and family disruptions among the dangers of the movement. Randall Baer,[23] for example, maintains that personal identity prob-lems accompany belief in reincarnation and in the acquisition of great spiritual or supernatural (or shamanic) powers.[24] He develops a lengthy catalogue of problems, mostly psychological, that flow from involvement in the New Age:

> A short-term rush of energy and peace into one's life followed by a fall-off into anxiety, disorientation, depression, and a driving desire for another occult experience to alleviate the inner empti-ness.
>
> A severe fall-off in job performance, family relations, and other responsibilities as the person becomes more self-absorbed, dis-tracted, and moody.
>
> A change in personality marked by a hyper-happy, starry-eyed,

blissful enthusiastic attitude. This floating on a New Age cloud nine mentally can sometimes last for months, but usually ends with disappointment, frustration, and sometimes disillusionment, or seeking out yet another New Age high.

A progressively absorbing addiction to seeking the advice of psychic readers and channels to gain egostrokes, security about the future, self-glorification, answers to problems, etc. This can be as addictive as any drug, and sometimes more expensive.

An absorption into some grand vision quest – like preparing for a UFO beam-up or discovering an ancient artifact of world-importance in Peru or some other planet-shaking event – to the extent of totally ignoring the rest of one's life (job, family, mortgage, etc.) as it disintegrates.

An awakening of the *kundalini* ('serpent-power' said in the occult to lay dormant at the base of the spine) through occult practices can lead to many severe problems including: mental/emotional upheavals and breakdown, intense involuntary body spasms, severe brain and perceptual distortions, and sometimes even psychosis and insanity.

An abrupt intrusion of a demon-spirit into one's life leading to various kinds of possession and control.

An erosion of Biblical morals into a more lax and liberal viewpoint that opens the way to committing sins such as adultery, fornication, and spiritism.

An overload of occult energy into one's system, resulting in a type of 'circuit overload' – severe hyper-tension and anxiety, mental and emotional disorders, deep depression, rapid breakdown of psychical health, and others.

An increasing hardening of the heart and dulling of the ear to the Good News of Jesus – this becomes particularly ingrained the more one delves into the New Age.[25]

The theory that these dangers follow involvement in the New Age Movement is corroborated by its connection with occult practices that are deemed to be both physically and psychologically harmful.[26]

Finally, the New Age is conceived as an anti-Christian movement whose goals are to supplant the Judeo-Christian tradition. Constance Cumbey feels sure that New Agers have 'deep and abiding hatred' for Jews, Christians, and orthodox Muslims, all of whom have been threatened with extermination.[27] She declares that 'New Agers generally do not openly repudiate Christianity. More subtly than that, at least for the moment, they often clothe New Age concepts in Christian language and – like Hitler – undermine Christianity while pretending to be its friends.'[28]

Texe Marrs concedes that the New Age embraces people from different religious traditions into its fold. But he complains that the movement has no room for Christians. Instead it has plans to wipe them all out because they are unfit for the new religious and sociopolitical order. He states:

> The plan of the New Age is to take over every Christian church and every Jewish temple in the world and to turn these great and small architectural structures into centers for the New Age World Religion. This is an absolute fact.[29]

He admits, however, that it is impossible to prove this, since one cannot 'gain access to the actual documents that reveal outright a hideous, hidden intent to persecute, purge, or kill all the Bible-believing Christians at some point in the future after the Antichrist ascends to dictatorial power'.[30] Yet he manages to outline in some detail a thirteen-point master plan, concocted by Satan, to take over the world, establish one New Age religion and sociopolitical order ruled by the Antichrist, indoctrinate all in the New Age ideology, and weed out, by extermination, if necessary, those Christians who resist.[31] This anti-Christian element in the New Age is noted also by other Christians[32] who adhere to more moderate views than those propounded by Constance Cumbey and Texe Marrs.

Not all evangelicals would concur with Cumbey's and Marrs's extreme views. John Ankerberg and John Weldon present a more modest view that, while recognizing that many New Agers have negative feelings towards Christianity, concedes that malicious intentions cannot be ascribed to all of them. They write:

> Given the teachings of the NAM, the rejection of Christianity is quite logical, although not all in the New Age are openly hostile to the Christian faith. Indeed, many members come from nominal Christian backgrounds or are liberal Christians and for this reason are seeking to combine Christianity and the New Age. Nevertheless, there are those who have openly asserted that it was their dislike for orthodox Christian faith which led them into the NAM . . . In addition, some who are fanatically committed to the NAM and are also familiar with Christian teachings are openly antagonistic to Christianity because they realize that the Christian faith is a formidable barrier to New age views . . . and to New Age goals.[33]

DESCRIPTIONS OF THE NEW AGE MOVEMENT

In reviewing evangelical and fundamentalist treatments of the New Age Movement it is important to bear in mind that they are motivated largely by the fear and/or concern that its beliefs and practices are a serious threat to Christianity. Descriptions of the New Age are, consequently, so colored by theological evaluations and denunciations that it is often difficult to distinguish between the descriptions themselves and the opinions of the authors. Further, many Christian commentators have adopted a theory to explain the presence and influence of the New Age Movement and they dwell especially on those elements which buttress their particular theoretical slant.

Definitions of the New Age

Attempts at defining the New Age abound. Many evangelicals and fundamentalists are convinced that the New Age Movement is a religion, even though it is a false and counterfeit one. John Eidsmore, for example, states:

> Since the New Age Movement recognizes a spiritual reality, offers explanations for man's origins, man's place in the present universe, and man's ultimate destiny, and offers diagnoses and solutions for man's basic spiritual problems, the New Age Movement must be considered a religion.[34]

His view is echoed by John Ankerberg and John Weldon, who write:

> The New Age Movement (NAM) is a title that refers to a worldview or philosophy of life that many people hold. The NAM can be properly called a religion because it is based on religious views; for example, New Agers hold to pantheism, a belief that everything is part of God.[35]

Constance Cumbey is even more explicit in her view that the New Age Movement has all the trappings of an organized religion. She insists without hesitation:

> Make no mistake about it! The New Age Movement *is* a religion complete with its own Bibles, prayers and mantras, Vatican City/Jerusalem equivalents, priests and gurus, born-again experiences (they call it 'rebirthing'), spiritual laws and commandments, psychics and 'prophets', and nearly every other indicia of religion.[36]

Some writers seem less certain of the institutional elements of the New Age, though they still hold that a religious ideology is the common feature that binds New Agers in a cohesive group distinguishable from members of other faiths. For Elliot Miller, for instance, the New Age Movement is

> an extremely large, *loosely* structured network of organizations and individuals bound together by common values (based in mysticism and monism – the world view that 'all is One'), and a common vision (a coming 'new age' of peace and enlightenment, the 'Age of Aquarius').[37]

In a similar way, Ron Rhodes defines the New Age as a movement (not a cult or religion) that is made up of:

> a loosely structured network of individuals who share a vision of a new age of enlightenment and harmony (the 'Age of Aquarius') and who subscribe to a common 'worldview' [of monism, pantheism, and mysticism].[38]

Gordon R. Lewis concurs and avoids the term 'religion' in his broad definition that stresses the movement's overriding goal of transformation. He asserts that:

> The new-age movement generally may be defined as a spiritual, social and political attempt to transform individuals and society through mystical experiences of alleged oneness with the energy of the cosmos and occult techniques for ending the threat of nuclear destruction and inaugurating a new era of global peace.[39]

All seem to think that the New Age Movement is one of the strongest social and spiritual forces in the West and that something must be done to stem its spread. Consequently, its main features must be clearly identified and contrasted to those of Christianity.

Main characteristics of the New Age

Many evangelical and fundamentalist books provide extensive and comprehensive outlines of New Age beliefs and practices, stressing their incompatibility with Christian doctrines. These outlines differ slightly in content, but they are all structured to emphasize doctrinal matters, especially those that relate to the concept of God and the unique place of Jesus Christ in the history of religions. Probably the three most often mentioned characteristics of the New Age are pantheism, monism, and the deification of humanity. Reincarnation and evolution are, at times, included as important components of the movement.

It is useful to reproduce a number of efforts by evangelicals and fundamentalists to categorize the content of New Age ideology and practice. Several begin by listing what they consider to be essential Christian beliefs and then show, directly or by implication, that none of the New Age tenets can be, even remotely, harmonized with them. Bob Larson, for example, lists five major religious themes found both in Christianity and the New Age. He briefly denies what the New Age teaches about each topic and then adds the correct Christian doctrine:

> 1. **God**: God is not a man's Higher Self, an inner manifestation of divinity. There is only one God, eternally existent in three persons: Father, Son, and Holy Spirit.
> 2. **Jesus Christ**: Christ is not an office, a status of enlightenment. Jesus is the God-man, born of a virgin, sinless. Having died on the cross and been raised from the dead, he ascended to the right hand of the Father and will return personally in power and glory.
> 3. **Man**: Man is not a god in embryo, a divine being whose realization of his divinity must be awakened. Man has fallen from a right standing before God through disobedience. So now man is conceived in sin, and he is destined for damnation unless he is spiritually reborn by the Holy Spirit.
> 4. **Creation**: All that exists is not part of God. Creation is different in substance and nature from God and was created by him to declare his glory.
> 5. **Redemption**: Man's spiritual awakening or transformation cannot be achieved by affirming his supposed divine essence or cultivating mystical phenomena. Regeneration by the Holy Spirit through faith in Jesus Christ is absolutely essential for the salvation of lost and sinful man.[40]

John Ankerberg and John Weldon have the same theological principles in mind when they summarize the religious views of the New Age under nine topics that form the backbone of Christian theological speculation. These authors are convinced that the New Age views are antithetical to Christianity and must be outrightly rejected. In their opinion, the New Age can be recognized by the answers it gives to key religious questions about God, the Holy Spirit, salvation, etc. They characterize New Age beliefs as follows:

God – an impersonal, all-pervading energy.

The Holy Spirit – an energy that can be used creatively or physically.

Jesus Christ – a New Age teacher and illustration of an enlightened individual who realized that He was God.

Man – inwardly good and divine; thus he carries within himself all that he needs for time and eternity.

Salvation – development of psychic powers and higher consciousness. This is achieved by looking inside one's self and practicing New Age techniques to develop psychically and finally attain awareness of personal divinity.

Sin – ignorance of personal divinity manifested in errors of consciousness.

Death – the moment one hopes to experience a merging with God, the all-pervading energy of the universe. This only comes if personal transformation or enlightenment has been obtained.

Satan – normal consciousness – man existing in his state of unrealized potential.

Heaven–Hell – good or bad states of consciousness in this life.[41]

They then summarize the movement's ideology in four basic beliefs: (1) all true reality is divine; (2) personal enlightenment is important; (3) altered states of consciousness, psychic powers and spirit contacts are the means to achieve enlightenment; and (4) political activism is necessary to help people bring about a united world. These imply a broad consensus on some key elements, namely, that God is an impersonal force of which human beings are a part; that humans are ignorant of their divine nature; and that New Age beliefs and practices lead to the solution of all human problems.

Amano Yutaka and Norman Geisler add several elements to the above features of the New Age. Instead of starting with the concept of God, they begin by listing both an epistemological underpinning of the movement and a theological assumption regarding revelation. Their inventory of nine major traits, which they buttress by copious quotations from New Age sources, consists of: (1) Knowledge of the truth. Logical thinking is subordinated to experience; (2) Revelation. The Bible is both incomplete and inadequate and must be amended by continuous revelations to New Age prophets; (3) God. Ultimate reality is conceived as impersonal and as pervading all reality; (4) Christ. The New Age stresses the 'Christ spirit' rather than the historical Jesus, who was not the only Son of God, a unique person who brought salvation to the world; (5)

Human nature. The emphasis in New Age ideology is that human beings are spiritual beings who are essentially divine; (6) Sin and morality. These are relative and depend on human choice, not on God-given laws; (7) Salvation. Human redemption is the realization of one's divinity and is achieved by self-reflection and effort. Reincarnation is part of the process that leads to salvation or realization; (8) Universalism. All religious paths are believed to lead to God; (9) Future events. The reappearance of Christ. For the New Age, a reincarnation of the Christ spirit will return to bring peace and unity and to set up a new world religion and a new economic and political system.[42]

A similar pattern is followed by Walter Martin,[43] who selects the following ten basic subjects around which the beliefs of both Christianity and the New Age are grouped: (1) God; (2) the Trinity; (3) Jesus Christ; (4) Atonement; (5) Salvation; (6) Heaven, Hell, and the Last Judgment; (7) demonic powers; (8) the Second Coming of Christ; (9) reincarnation; and (10) the New Age. He specifies what Christians believe and then adduces scriptural quotes to show how none of the New Age beliefs are compatible with Christianity. One of the more interesting (and somewhat original) elements of his list is that he includes the concept of a 'New Age' as an essential element of both Christianity and the New Age Movement, even though he maintains that there is a radical difference between the conceptions of a new age proposed by these two religions.

Douglas Groothuis lists six distinctive teachings (which he calls counterfeits) of the New Age: (1) all is one; (2) all is God; (3) humanity is God; (4) a change in consciousness; (5) all religions are one; and (6) cosmic evolutionary optimism.[44] These he later amplifies into nine 'counterfeit' parallels to Christianity, which imply that, unlike Christianity, the New Age offers fake and mistaken answers to the ultimate questions of life: (1) Evolutionary optimism: a counterfeit kingdom; (2) Monism: a counterfeit cosmos; (3) Pantheism: a counterfeit humanity; (4) Transformation of consciousness: a counterfeit conversion; (5) Create your own reality: a counterfeit morality; (6) Unlimited human potential: counterfeit miracles; (7) Spirit contact: counterfeit revelation; (8) Masters from above: counterfeit myth; (9) Religious syncretism: a counterfeit religion.[45]

One of the more recent undertakings to outline New Age thought in schematic form and to submit a Christian response is that of Ron Rhodes, who is an editor with the Christian Research Institute in Santa Ana, California. He lists nine characteristics that most New Agers would subscribe to: (1) eclecticism; (2) religious syncretism; (3) monism; (4) pantheism; (5) deification of humanity; (6) a quest for personal and planetary transformation; (7) networking; (8) ecological orientation; (9) belief in a coming utopia.[46]

He then dedicates a whole section to the theology of the New Age and examines seven areas: (1) biblical interpretation; (2) the doctrine of revelation; (3) the doctrine of God; (4) the person of Jesus Christ; (5) the doctrine of human nature; (6) the doctrines of sin and salvation; and (7) the doctrine of the second coming of Christ. In each instance he schematically analyzes the New Age position, expounds the arguments used by New Agers to support their beliefs, and meticulously refutes each one of them.

Other writers try to simplify the contents of the New Age by reducing them to a handful of basic beliefs. For Elliot Miller, for example, the New Age can be characterized by two principles, namely: (1) all is One (monism) and (2) ultimate reality is an impersonal force, or simply awareness or bliss.[47] He then, more specifically, identifies a New Ager by the following: (1) acceptance of pantheism; (2) involvement in, and/or experience of, mystical states or occult practices; (3) belief in a coming New Age of peace and enlightenment; and (4) participation in the New Age network to hasten the coming of the New Age. If not all these characteristics are present, then the individual has an affinity to the New Age Movement, but is not technically a New Ager.[48]

In some cases, the description of the New Age is more a reflection of the author's negative evaluation of the movement. Constance Cumbey, for instance, provides a simplified, if not simplistic, summary of the major tenets accepted by New Agers:

> While their theology is obfuscated in deliberate gobbledy-gook, it is not complicated. A Christian may read the main tenets in the third chapter of the book of Genesis. Basically they involve (1) an attack on the authority of God's word; (2) a denial that one will die (reincarnation); (3) a claim that man can be as a god himself; and (4) a deification of Lucifer and other demonic entities (the Masters of Wisdom theory).[49]

In her overview she lists the following main premises of the New Age: (1) the law of rebirth (reincarnation); (2) the theory of the

Solar Logos (or Trinity), a hierarchy of beings in which Jesus comes last; (3) belief in evolution; and (4) the doctrine of wholeness, implying that all things are interconnected or interdependent.[50]

Although the number and importance of the main characteristics ascribed to the New Age by evangelicals and fundamentalists differ, there is agreement on what many of the philosophical and theological tenets of the movement are. And in spite of the generalizations and negative evaluations that are made on the New Age, the features described present a fairly accurate (though at times misleading) picture of the general religious trends and beliefs within the movement.

THEORIES EXPLAINING THE RISE OF THE NEW AGE MOVEMENT

The rise and success of the New Age Movement have elicited various theories to explain its emergence and persistent presence in the second half of the twentieth century. Five major theories dominate evangelical and fundamentalist literature: (1) the revival of religion theory; (2) the conspiracy theory; (3) the satanic theory; (4) the infiltration theory; and (5) the apocalyptic theory. These theories, though distinct, are not mutually exclusive. In fact, most evangelical and fundamentalist writings combine and endorse more than one of them. And, frequently, the view that Satan is ultimately responsible for the New Age is reflected in all the above-mentioned theories.

The revival of religion theory

Although the New Age Movement appears to be a novel phenomenon in the latter part of the twentieth century, most Christian evangelicals and fundamentalists do not perceive anything particularly new in its beliefs and practices. On the contrary many see it as a revival of ancient Paganism going as far back as Babylon.[51] Texe Marrs[52] thinks that it is a revival of the satanic religion of Babylon which included the beliefs in evolution, human divinity, and reincarnation, was centered on the worship of spirits, and encouraged sexual license. Kenneth R. Wade[53] maintains that it is a return to ancient religion when human sacrifice was prevalent, while others[54] state simply that it incorporates many pagan themes.

The link between the New Age and the occult is mentioned in practically all Christian commentaries. The New Age is so permeated with esoteric thought and rituals that it could easily be seen as a modern revival of the occult. New Agers, according to John Ankerberg and John Weldon,[55] have embraced diverse occult beliefs, like magic and ESP, and practices, like channeling and the consultation of one's horoscopes. This return to involvement in occult matters is said to be an 'escape from reason' leading to a kind of 'irrational spirituality'.[56]

The New Age is also interpreted by some as a revival of Gnosticism. Peter Jones, for example, develops the view that the New Age Movement is a modern form of the old gnostic heresy. The denial that God created the universe, the insistence that salvation is achieved by human effort, the belief that the kingdom of God is within the individual, the acceptance of Jesus as a revealer of gnosis, and the tolerance shown to different approaches to truth are said to be among the main pillars of both Gnosticism and the New Age.[57] This connection is occasionally made by scholars whose main goals are not to evaluate the movement from a Christian perspective.[58]

Another view is to consider the New Age as a revival of a tradition that has always existed in Western culture. Philip C. Almond suggests that 'the New Age may fruitfully be seen as the resurgence of what may be called the Western esoteric tradition of neo-Platonism, particularly of its theurgic elements of Gnosticism, of Hermeticism, of medieval magic and alchemy'.[59]

More recent roots of the New Age Movement are sometimes mentioned. Constance Cumbey, for example, traces its origins to the Theosophical Society. But then she links both Theosophy and the New Age with Nazism.[60] In each of her two books she dedicates a whole chapter[61] to the question of whether the New Age is a revival of Nazism. She argues that the early writings of the Lucis Trust and the Theosophical Society indicate that there is more than mere ideological similarities between the modern New Age Movement and Nazism.[62] She seems convinced that the movement 'is identical in basic cosmology and beliefs to *both* Nazism and the Ku Klux Klan'.[63] She even thinks that the movement 'has characteristics of a well-thought out military operation patterned after Hitler's organization of the "Third Reich"'.[64] Such links between the New Age and Nazism have been noted by other Christians. Texe Marrs, for example, believes that the same tactics used by Nero, Caligula, and Hitler, may be employed by New Age masters.[65]

Not all Christian commentators, however, conclude that the New Age is merely a revival of some ancient religion or philosophy, a revival instigated largely by Satan. Some stress that historical and sociological factors must, to some degree, account for its emergence. Rhodes[66] lists five precursors and/or influences antecedent to the movement: (1) nineteenth-century Transcendentalism; (2) revival of the occult, especially through the Theosophical Society, Anthroposophy, the Arcane School, the I AM Movement, spiritism, and astrology; (3) the inadequacy of secular humanism; (4) the counterculture of the 1960s; and (5) the influx of Eastern ideas. By so doing, he draws attention to more natural causes that are responsible for its emergence and indirectly, and, maybe unintentionally, de-emphasizes the theory that the New Age is a well-conceived satanic plot to overthrow Christianity.

The theory that the New Age Movement is a revival of one or several forms of ancient religion or occult philosophy easily lends itself to speculation about who is behind it. Who is responsible for initiating and leading the return to a religion that contradicts the main teachings of Christianity and entices Christians to abandon their faith?

The conspiracy theory

One of the earlier theories of the New Age Movement was formulated by Constance Cumbey, whose position stimulated plenty of discussions and disagreements both outside and within evangelical circles and has left a lasting impact on Christian literature on the New Age. Cumbey draws up an elaborate scheme in which New Agers are the executors of a master plan to take over the earth. The plan includes the installation of a new Messiah, the establishment of a new world government, and the promulgation of a new religion under Maitreya, the fifth incarnation of the Buddha. The great plan consists not only of a religious goal, but also of political, social, and economic designs. In the new world order there will be no room for Christianity.[67]

Thus, Cumbey contends that the political goals of the movement include a mandatory religion as well as the creation of various authorities that control all aspects of human life. She thinks that its organizers would like to establish a universal socialism similar to that introduced in Germany by Hitler and that everybody will be interconnected 'by incredibly sophisticated computers that are Orwellian in scope'.[68] She develops an intricate chart showing how New Age origins, beliefs, and goals can be correlated with those of

Nazism.[69] Cumbey is not alone in linking the ideology and goals of the New Age with those of Nazi Germany. Elissa Lindsey McClain,[70] for example, believes that the New Age has a world plan that is 'practically identical to Adolph Hitler's SS Occult Bureau on which Nazism was founded'. Such conspiratorial views are easily linked with apocalyptic themes in which the Antichrist and the number 666 occupy a major role.[71] These alarmist views are echoed by others, like Salem Kirban, who believe that there is a New Age plan to conquer the whole world which will be ruled by one government, thus preparing the way for the Antichrist by the year 2000.[72]

The majority of evangelicals and fundamentalists do not accept the view that human beings could be responsible for such an elaborate and well drawn-up plan to promote and enforce the New Age agenda. They also reject the view that natural forces, by themselves, could account for its influence and success. They prefer to interpret the pervasive presence of New Age ideology as a result of supernatural agencies and, more specifically, to the machinations of Satan who is the master-mind and the architect or conspirator of the plot.

The satanic theory

Christians who believe that Satan is behind the revival of New Age ideas and values are quickly led to conclude that involvement in the movement is a form of Satanism. Some go as far as to identify the New Age with Satan,[73] others accuse New Agers of being devil worshipers[74] or the devil's messengers,[75] and still others affirm that the movement 'is simply opening the doors to his [Satan's] destructive influence in our culture even wider than before'.[76]

Texe Marrs, for instance, declares that there is certainly 'a conspiratorial network' but this has been devised by Satan himself.[77] He adds[78] that 'while the New Age may not be a secretive *human* conspiracy in the classic sense of the word, it *is* nevertheless a conspiracy, one of global proportions'. And though its leaders may work independently, they '*all* are seized by the very same *satanic impulse*' and 'every New Age believer is a victim of a *demonic conspiracy* to promote Satan's plan to rule humanity and overcome God'. He maintains, moreover, that the leaders of the New Age have devised a colossal plan aimed particularly at children and to be executed by a well-planned network of satanic workers. Basing his conclusions on Alice Bailey's views, rather than on hard data, he constructs a New Age blueprint for educating children to reject the religion of their parents and to accept the principles of the New Age. Included in this plan are the abolition of patriotism and the traditional family unit and the teaching of New Age religious beliefs, such as karma and reincarnation, to all children.[79]

Douglas Groothuis asserts that the New Age is not new at all. 'It is the most recent repeat of the second oldest religion, the spirituality of the serpent.' Referring to the Biblical story of the temptation and fall of Adam and Eve (Genesis, ch. 3), he maintains that Satan initiated a new religion that opposed the one true faith given by God to the first human beings. Satan's 'offer was to forsake God's way of life and to believe in the serpent's promise that in rebelling against God they could "be as Gods" and "would not die"'.[80] The New Age beliefs that people share in God's divinity and can create their own reality are modern replicas of the ancient temptations. Besides, for Groothuis, Satan ultimately inspires all false religion. He finds this connection between the New Age and Satan confirmed by two main facts: (1) the contradictions between the New Age and the Bible; (2) the presence of occult activities in New Age practices.

First of all, the New Age is a religion that contradicts the Bible and, as such, represents evil and has to be the work of Satan. John Ankerberg and John Weldon do not doubt that 'orthodox Christianity views the New Age Movement as a false religious world view, motivated and taught by Satan's demons masquerading as benevolent spirit guides concerned with the welfare of humanity'.[81] They see similarities between the doctrines of the New Age and those of both Witchcraft and Satanism. They explain:

> Although they are by no means identical, there is general agreement among them that 'all is one,' 'all is God,' and that we are our own gods. There is also agreement on the personal use of both occult power and the spirit world. And there is agreement on the rejection of absolute morality, including Christian values.[82]

In addition, they believe that there is some connection between the New Age Movement and a satanic network, even though, they regret to say, this connection is not recognized by most people.

Second, the close link between the New Age Movement and the occult is another indication that the former is satanic in origin.[83] Randall Baer defines the New Age as essentially 'a Satan-controlled, modern-day mass revival of occult-based philosophies and practices in both obvious and cleverly-disguised forms'.[84] Thus, for instance, channeling is invariably interpreted as a manifestation of evil spirits.[85] And Atlantean warriors, ascended masters, spirit guides, etc., are all demonic entities with evil intentions.

The tendency to see paranormal and occult activities as initiated by Satan is a standard feature of Christian evangelical and fundamentalist literature. The supernatural powers displayed by psychics, for example, are judged to be 'manifestations of evil spirits, of demons or Satan himself'.[86] Any contact with all forms of divination, including astrology, 'leads to deception and can result in demonization of various kinds'.[87] And telepathic communications and channeled information from extraterrestrials are probably demonic in nature.[88] Douglas Groothuis states:

> But demons – and their director – are also being welcomed by increasing numbers of 'civilized westerners' through numerous occult practices, including divination (Tarot cards, I Ching, runes, psychic readings), trance-channeling (mediumship), non-Christian meditation or other potentially demon-inducing or demon-inspired activities, all of which are forbidden and called 'detestable' by Scripture.[89]

Texe Marrs lists fortune-telling, levitation, fire-walking, body tattoos, numerology, mental imagery, ESP, palmistry, astral travel, astrology, hypnotism, yoga, necromancy, color therapy, heavy metal music as ancient satanic teachings and practices.[90]

The assumption that diabolical activity is responsible for the spread of New Age ideas and practices fits well with the theory that there is a satanic plot to undermine Christian beliefs and morals. It also corroborates the view that New Age ideals are inexorably penetrating Western culture. Peter Jones writes:

> In spite of its apparent tolerant, pluralistic, and diffuse nature, the New Age has a coherent agenda, orchestrated from a diabolical center, moving and reproducing ineluctably, like algae in a lake.[91]

Since there is no concrete evidence of a secret national or international organization promoting this nefarious plot, and since the activities of Satan to promulgate the New Age are beyond human scrutiny, proponents of the conspiracy theory argue that the goals of the New Age are being realized through subtle and covert infiltration into Western culture.

The infiltration theory

The theory of cultural infiltration is a common explanation of how the leaders or promoters of the New Age are gradually reaching their goal of world domination both in religion and politics. According to this theory the principles espoused by New Agers are affecting all social and economic classes, government, business, education, and entertainment. This is done by unobtrusive and shrewd means that are not discernable by the majority of people.[92]

Walter Martin, for instance, postulates that many New Agers have joined popular clubs, like the Sierra Club and Amnesty International, and are inundating all their members with New Age ideology.[93] Television programs, toys, and music have incorporated New Age symbols and ideas and are having a great impact on the younger generations. Texe Marrs[94] dedicates several chapters to illustrate how sorcery and witchcraft are rampant in TV programs for children, how games like 'Dungeons and Dragons' are aimed at advancing New Age themes, and how New Age instrumental music 'is even more deadly to the spirit than heavy metal rock'. Eastern thought, adopted by the New Age Movement, has invaded Western culture and manifests itself even in apparently innocuous and popular movies such as *Star Wars*.[95] New Age ideology is so prevalent that people adopt it unconsciously by the process of socialization.

Several evangelical writers are more worried that the New Age is creeping into the churches and corrupting Christianity in cunning ways. They think that New Age ideas and practices, presented in Christian garb, are being too readily accepted by many Christian and social organizations. They are further convinced that part of the New Age plan is to take over the Christian Church by a stealthy infiltration or that occult initiates are trying to penetrate and subvert the Christian churches.[96]

The theme that the New Age is creeping into Christian circles and corrupting the Christian faith is reiterated throughout evangelical and fundamentalist writings. Erwin W. Lutzer and John F. DeVries, for example, maintain that Satan is infiltrating the Church by building bridges to gain access to people's minds and hearts.[97] They mention five such bridges: those of psychology, the science of the mind, inner healing, spiritual healing, and ecumenism. And Samantha Smith and Brenda Scott critically examine the work of one particular writer and popular speaker, namely, Madeleine L'Engle, whose writings have, in their opinion, deeply penetrated mainstream Christianity.[98] These authors believe that under the guise of 'Christian literature' her books introduce the occult into the Church. The Episcopal Cathedral of St. John the Divine in New York[99] and St. James Church, Piccadilly, in London[100] are identified as centers through which New Age ideas are disseminated under the auspices of established Christian churches. Like a Trojan horse, the New Age has found its way into the Christian Church and is undermining it from within.[101]

There seems to be agreement that this influence is especially evident in liberal Catholic and Protestant circles. Hunt and McMahon's view, articulated in their book, *The Seduction of Christianity*, namely, that the New Age has filtered through even evangelical churches, is, however, hotly debated.[102]

The apocalyptic theory

The theory that the New Age Movement is a grandiose satanic plot to take over the world easily lends itself to the belief that the world has reached the apocalyptic climax which many think is forecasted in the Bible.

One of the most elaborate and influential theories that interprets the New Age in apocalyptic terms is that of Constance Cumbey. In her book, *The Hidden Dangers of the Rainbow*, she bases her imminent apocalyptic vision on biblical sources (Daniel 11:31 and Revelation, ch. 13) and schematically shows how various biblical prophecies are fulfilled in the New Age.[103] Cumbey, writing in the early 1980s, maintains that the New Age Movement's leadership is proposing to implement all the systems set forth in Revelation and that the New Age plan will be in action by June 21, 1983.

Cumbey's views are echoed, although sometimes in subdued form, in evangelical and fundamentalist literature on the New Age. Among the more extreme views are those of Dave Hunt and T. A. McMahon who argue that the New Age is 'the "great delusion" that the Bible warns will sweep the world in the "last days" and cause humanity to worship the Antichrist'.[104] They find evidence of this in the false prophets, the false Christs, and the fake miracles that proliferate in New Age circles.[105]

Another writer who wholeheartedly subscribes to this theory is Texe Marrs, who dedicates a whole chapter to interpret the signs that will mark the coming Antichrist.[106] He holds that Lord Maitreya is the Antichrist, the Beast with the number 666, the Antichrist foretold in the books of Daniel and Revelation. Like Cumbey, Marrs thinks that the Antichrist will appear soon and even goes as far as to suggest that the last year of the twentieth century might witness the final stages of the battle between God and the powers of evil. Other writers have propounded similar interpretations of the New Age.[107] In fact, so common is the association of the New Age with the coming of the Antichrist that the reader is bound to conclude that evangelicals and fundamentalists make use of the presence of the movement to support their millennial and apocalyptic ideology and to promote their missionary plans.

Moderate views

Although the above-mentioned views dominate both evangelical and fundamentalist literature on the New Age, it must be emphasized that unanimity does not exist. While practically everyone would agree that the New Age is largely a revival of previous beliefs and practices and that it is making inroads in Western culture and Christianity,[108] some question or explicitly reject the conspiracy, satanic, and apocalyptic theories.

Criticism of the conspiracy theory

Constance Cumbey's version of the conspiracy theory and modified versions of it are still widely discussed and sometimes accepted in Christian literature on the New Age Movement, even though Cumbey herself is no longer actively involved in denouncing the New Age. Many commentators, however, have rejected her view as a form of sensationalism. Russell Chandler, for example, is fully aware of the weaknesses of conspiracy theories where facts 'are mishandled, claims are undocumented, conclusions are biased, and logic is flawed at vital connection points'.[109] He also criticizes Dave Hunt for overreacting to the dangers of the New Age Movement and for interpreting anything faintly resembling it as part of the plot. Elliot Miller concurs and dedicates an appendix to his book to a criticism of Cumbey's theory which he thinks is 'riddled with mishandled facts and logical fallacies'.[110]

That more careful commentators on the New Age have doubted the facts adduced in support of the conspiracy theory does not come as a surprise. Some of the purported plans of New Agers are nothing but wild, unrealistic speculations. Texe Marrs, for instance, asserts that the New Age religion will eventually have its own 'unholy Bible'; and that its leaders are '*already making plans for this Bible and have mapped out the major elements it is to contain*'.[111] But he fails to provide even a clue as to where he acquired this startling information. Besides, one might add that the variety of beliefs found among New Agers would make the creation of such a Bible practically impossible.

Other evangelicals, while inclined to support some form of conspiracy to account for the rise and success of the New Age Movement, are still reluctant to give it their whole-hearted endorsement. Groothuis,[112] for example, insists that 'conspiratorial speculations should be tempered by several cautions'. He acknowledges that not every New Age group is working with all others in a plot to overrun Christianity and take over the world. He prudently advises that concrete evidence must be adduced to support the conspiracy theory. The fact that New Agers network among themselves does not necessarily mean that they are involved in a worldwide plot. He fears that conspiratorial theories are prone to blame the New Age for all human problems. To those who insist that powerful demonic forces are using the New Age to dominate the earth, he affirms that the Bible 'never consigns the universe or history totally to demonic powers'.

Similar, more balanced views are held by Kerry D. McRoberts, for example, who, while concurring with the opinion that the spirituality embraced by the New Age is antagonistic to Christianity, rejects the conspiracy theory. In her opinion the 'New Age Movement is better understood as the result of a dynamic historical, cultural process ... rather than a conscious, monolithic conspiracy of international proportions and decades of planning'.[113]

Even those who still find the conspiracy theory attractive have tried to temper their views. Kevin Logan,[114] for instance, sees no 'human-based conspiracy' at all and comments that the Christian claims of a world-wide plot 'damages our credibility and integrity'. He supports the view, however, that there is a conspiracy of evil in the spiritual realms. And Walter Martin[115] holds that some conspiracy actually exists, but not all New Agers are involved. He maintains that the conspiracy is not highly developed and that no individual has been chosen as a world ruler. Consequently, he counsels Christians not to respond with hysteria.

Criticism of the satanic theory

One of the difficulties of the satanic theory is that it leads to the conclusion that there is nothing worthwhile in the New Age Movement and that many, if not all, New Agers are, consciously or not, part of a diabolical plot. There are several evangelical and fundamentalist voices of moderation that have been less inclined to denounce the New Age *in toto* and have observed that (1) there is something valid in New Age ideology which cannot be dismissed as totally incompatible with Christianity and that (2) not all New Agers are to be condemned or judged to be in league with the devil.

The inclination of evangelical and fundamentalist Christians to dismiss all New Age beliefs and concerns as unchristian or anti-Christian has been questioned. Bob Larson, though highly critical of the New Age Movement, begins by stating:

> Not all tenets of the New Age Movement are objectional to orthodox adherents of the Christian faith. Evangelicals share several of the Movement's concerns, including:
>
> 1. **Environmentalism:** Respecting all living things and eradicating pollution from Earth.
> 2. **Peace:** Desiring world peace and working to avoid nuclear conflagration.
> 3. **Ethics:** Encouraging a moral climate in commerce and placing human needs above monetary incentives.
> 4. **Spirituality:** Evoking a renewed interest in the transcendent and encouraging a nonmaterial approach to existence.
> 5. **Human Rights:** Minimizing hunger and conquering disease, poverty, and inequities in underdeveloped countries.[116]

Similarly, Don Rhodes, in his directions for witnessing to New Agers, advises evangelists to look for common ground. He writes: 'Possible common ground discussions to focus on could include ecology, rejection of humanism, patriotism, human rights, or social justice.'[117] It is a pity that neither Larson or Rhodes saw it opportune to dedicate some time to explore these common and unifying features.

Elliot Miller[118] is quite insistent that the condemnation of all New Agers is both unfair and unrealistic. New Agers, he admits, are sincere and intelligent and their beliefs are not irrational or inconsistent. They are world-affirming. They have a social consciousness and desire personal and spiritual fulfillment. They embrace a vision of the future that includes world peace, unification, and ecological balance. And they can be genuinely humanitarian.

He, further, disagrees with the general fundamentalist tendency to locate evil in everything the New Age stands for. He insists that some New Age emphases are good. The orientation toward health and human growth, for example, is a positive feature in the movement, as is the stress that human beings must take responsibility for the planet and work to avoid an ecological disaster. And while many evangelicals and fundamentalists assume that New Agers support the use of (illegal) drugs, Miller acknowledges that mysticism in the New Age is largely drug-free. He favors dialogue with New Agers.

According to Douglas Groothuis there are several pitfalls that Christians can succumb to when considering the New Age Movement. Besides those of ignoring the movement or absorbing its ideology, he mentions the dangers of labeling everything approved by the New Age as evil ('The Quarantine Mentality') and of condemning it *in toto* ('The Paranoid Mentality').[119]

Criticism of the apocalyptic theory

Objections have also been raised against the opinion that interprets the advent of the New Age Movement in apocalyptic terms. Among the more vociferous opponents of the apocalyptic theory is Gary North, who writes:[120]

> The revival of occultism in this century, and especially since 1965, is not the sign of the end of the world, the triumph of Satan, the second coming of Christ, or any other apocalyptic event.

North sees the occult revival and cultural disintegration as concomitant events taking place in the latter part of the twentieth century. He speculates that these developments are actually a sign of a 'humanist civilization's *dying gasp*'. Consequently, he does not preach an impending doom, nor does he react to the New Age with fear. On the contrary, he states explicitly that the 'Christian answer is not terror, retreat, and hopelessness', but rather 'Christian reconstruction'.[121]

Elliot Miller examines the apocalyptic theory in some depth and provides reasons for and against the view that the end of the world and the second coming of Christ are imminent. He then suggests that Christians should indeed be prepared for the end to come at any time, but they should still commit themselves to productive earthly endeavors. The presence of the New Age Movement is for him not an indicator of the impending doom. It is rather a strong reminder of the task Christians have to transform the world. He states:

> I am convinced we need to recognize that in some respects the rise of the New Age Movement is a reproof to the church for our undiscerning identification with society's status quo, and our considerable neglect of social matters.[122]

TYPES OF RESPONSES TO THE NEW AGE MOVEMENT

The proliferation of New Age beliefs and practices has led evangelicals and fundamentalists not only to take a clear stand on doctrinal issues, but also to devise ways to respond to and counteract what they perceive to be a threat to Christian orthodoxy. Mary Ann Lind identifies three kinds of general responses to the New Age: (1) the 'ostrich' approach, which minimizes or ignores the effects it is having on Western culture and religion; (2) the 'alarmist' approach, which tends to see the New Age everywhere and which the author believes is an overreaction; and (3) the more moderate approach which considers the New Age as a significant trend in the West (cf. 2 Thessalonians 2:9–11) and which encourages Christians to respond accordingly.[123]

Evangelicals and fundamentalists cannot be accused of ignoring the presence of New Age beliefs and practices. Some of them have certainly portrayed alarmist tendencies in their criticisms of anything even vaguely connected with the New Age. The relatively moderate approaches tend to be openly confrontational and are concerned with propounding apologetic arguments to refute New Age tenets and with employing standard techniques to evangelize those committed to New Age ideology.

More specifically Christian replies to the New Age can conveniently be grouped under three headings which express the relationships Christians have established with New Agers: (1) confrontational, in which the New Age is resisted; (2) apologetical, where Christian doctrine is clearly expressed and New Age teachings evaluated from a biblical standpoint; and (3) pastoral, where advice is given to Christians to prepare themselves to counteract the movement's influence or to New Agers to draw them back into the Christian fold.

Confronting the New Age

Those writers who dwell on the various dangers brought by the presence and activities of the New Age and who subscribe to one or more of the theories described above usually encourage open resistance to the New Age. Christians are called to do battle with the New Age on a spiritual and/or a social level. They are roused to resist a religious and cultural movement which is seen as a threat to Judeo-Christian values and cultural mores. In the words of Texe Marrs, they are urged to '[c]onfront and fight New Age apostasy wherever you find it'.[124]

Several evangelicals and fundamentalists see the New Age movement as a kind of battle ground in which Christians muster their forces to overcome the enemy. John Ankerberg and John Weldon advise Christians to become informed about this new religious movement and to criticize its tenets from a Biblical standpoint. They then add that the Christian could 'effectively prepare for spiritual warfare (Ephesians 6:10–18) and to use the Bible intelligently' for God's word 'is living and active and sharper than a two-edged sword, and piercing as far as the division of soul and spirit . . . (Hebrews 4:12)'.[125] They temper this belligerent approach with the observation that human arguments cannot overcome the New Age which is a form of demonic deception and can, therefore, only be met with prayer. They exhort Christians to react to the New Age with earnest prayer, patience, courage, love, and respect.

Lengthy catalogues of ways Christians can battle the New Age are frequently given. John Eidsmore, for instance, besides drawing attention to the need to beware of the deceitful ploys of Satan and to be strong and confident in one's faith, advises Christians to take action by defending their rights in the courtrooms, legislating against satanic practices, and resisting New Age pressures.[126]

Those who are disturbed with the inroads the New Age is making in the educational system insist that practical measures must be taken to neutralize the negative impact on children. John Ankerberg, Craig Branch, and John Weldon advise parents and educators to: (1) understand their rights; (2) be firm; (3) be gracious (avoid emotional reactions); (4) be informed; (5) be active politically; (6) raise the issues directly with the teacher; and (7) go through channels.[127]

Apologetics and theological debates

By far the more common form of confrontation consists of the use of apologetics and theological arguments to counteract New Age teachings. Walter Martin dedicates a chapter outlining the ways Christians could use the Bible to counteract the New Age by defending orthodox doctrine and by evangelization.[128] He gives several guidelines that Christians might employ in their contacts with New Agers. Besides the need for prayer and knowledge of the Bible, Martin counsels Christians to seek the common ground they share with New Agers and to dwell more on questioning them than imparting correct doctrine. He recommends that Christians, rather than criticize New Agers, should compliment them 'for their efforts in the area of conservation and concern for the well-being of the planet as well as the creatures that live on it'.[129] Yet he strongly believes that Christians must study the New Age to reveal the weakness of its moral relativism and the inconsistency of its world view. And he encourages Christians to distribute books and tapes as a means of evangelizing New Agers.

A typical apologetical response to the New Age Movement is that of David K. Clark and Norman L. Geisler, who focus on pantheism which they maintain is central to the New Age.[130] After exposing the pantheistic views of several Western and Eastern philosophers, they describe the New Age world view as fundamentally pantheistic. They then proceed to refute it.

A popular approach is to engage New Agers in debates on those beliefs which are perceived as incompatible with Christianity. One of the best examples of this method is presented by Ron Rhodes, who encourages Christians to draw attention to the difficulties inherent in New Age beliefs.[131] Rhodes, in fact, begins his section on witnessing tips by briefly observing that the discussion should start with some common ground, like ecology, rejection of humanism, etc. But he does not dwell on and expound these issues, the resolution of which could improve the relationship between New Agers and Christians. On the contrary, such a discussion is merely an indirect way intended to lead the conversation to those areas of serious disagreement and to engage in acrimonious debates.

Rhodes lists seven problematic areas or weak tenets of the New Age: (1) mysticism; (2) pantheism and the problem of evil; (3) relativity; (4) God; (5) reincarnation; (6) the uniqueness of Christ; and (7) sin. In each case he locates the main flaws with the New Age beliefs. Thus, to cite a few examples, he observes that a good evangelist should point out to the New Ager that mystical revelations are too uncertain and can lead to spiritual deception and that belief in reincarnation is inconsistent with a monistic world view and with the teachings of Jesus.

Counseling Christians

In their instructions of how to witness to New Agers, most evangelicals and fundamentalists stress the need for self-preparation. To resist the New Age and its cunning infiltration tactics into Western culture and religion, Christians must first of all be solid in their own belief system. Christians must be aware, be prepared, and be Christians in action.[132]

In spite of his overall pessimistic outlook towards the New Age, Texe Marrs forecasts victory for Jesus and advises parents to (1) call on God; (2) arm themselves with knowledge; (3) read and trust in God's word; (4) witness to others; (5) present a simple message; and (6) give thanks (to God). He advises parents to be vigilant and watch out for twenty warning signs of New Age Satanism. Among these signs he includes dabbling in ESP, the practices of channeling, acupuncture, and reflexology, and interest in occult and magical books.[133] Besides, he thinks that the following psychological signs indicate that a youngster is getting too involved in the New Age: 'Severe mood swings, a drop in grades, intense introspection, depression, loss of sleep, frequent nightmares, paranoia or excessive fear, and restlessness'.[134] He finally gives the following seven steps that a person might take to overcome satanic and occult involvement:

> (1) Confess your involvement.
> (2) Break the contact – and contract – with evil.
> (3) Get rid of *all* Satanic articles and items.
> (4) Ask our Lord Jesus Christ to forgive you and wash you clean of *all* the sins of your life.
> (5) Acknowledge to God verbally that *he* is your deliverer. Praise him for your deliverance.
> (6) Pledge to obey God, to read your Bible, to pray frequently, and to witness to others.
> (7) Stand daily against Satan, always with the full assurance that God *is* almighty and that His strength is always sufficient.[135]

EVALUATION OF THE
EVANGELICAL/FUNDAMENTALIST APPROACH TO
THE NEW AGE

Several scholars have attempted to survey and evaluate the evangelical and fundamentalist literature on the New Age Movement. One of the more comprehensive, though limited, of such endeavors is that of James E. Rosscup, who teaches at a Christian seminary.[136] Rosscup selects 32 books which he divides into seven categories: (1) general surveys (scholarly and popular); (2) special areas of thought (such as astrology and channeling); (3) novels against the New Age; (4) evangelism: Satan's forces and God's; (5) books by former New Agers; (6) New Age appeal to women; and (7) New Age infiltration into the lives of children. Over half the books reviewed are listed in the first category.

On the whole Rosscup gives a favorable reading of the majority of Christian responses to the New Age. In his catalogue of scholarly works he includes Elliot Miller's *A Crash Course on the New Age*, Douglas Groothuis's two volumes *Unmasking the New Age* and *Confronting the New Age*, Karen Hoyt's *The New Age Rage*, Randall Baer's *Inside the New Age Nightmare*, and Gary North's *Occultism and the New Humanism*. Rosscup doubts the conspiracy and apocalyptic theories of the New Age found in several popular books on the New Age.

More critical assessments on the Christian responses to the New Age have been made by James Lewis and Irving Hexham. Lewis,[137] in a survey that includes over 40 books, distinguishes between 'fair' and 'unfair' criticisms that conservative Christian literature has leveled at the New Age Movement. He defines as 'fair' the analyses of the New Age that distinguish its beliefs from those of Christianity and that detect some satanic inspiration in its rise and popularity. On the other hand he thinks that the attacks against New Age leaders as being consciously in league with Satan, the lumping of the movement with everything from Nazism to secular humanism, and the accusation that brainwashing and hypnotism explain involvement as 'unfair'. He then identifies and evaluates five key works, namely, Constance Cumbey's *Hidden Dangers of the Rainbow*, Douglas R. Groothuis's *Unmasking the New Age*, Karen Hoyt's *The New Age Rage*, Russell Chandler's *Understanding the New Age*, and Ruth Tucker's *Another Gospel*.

While Lewis finds Cumbey's accusations 'the least responsible', he concedes that she had made some accurate empirical observations. Cumbey developed her conspiracy theory from a standard manual of New Age ideology, namely, Marilyn Ferguson's book *The Aquarian Conspiracy*, even though she ends up giving the word 'conspiracy' a negative connotation never intended by Ferguson. Her observation that occultism, from which many New Agers derive their views and practices, had an important place in Hitler's Nazi Germany can be substantiated by historical data. And she correctly sees the works of Alice Bailey as the source of the idea of the New Age.

Lewis thinks that Groothuis is correct in choosing monism as the central theme in the New Age. This evangelical author, however, misunderstands monism and attributes to it features (like the absence of ethical distinctions and its inability to provide meaning) that are inapplicable to most New Agers. Hoyt's collection of essays provide, in Lewis's opinion, 'a generally fair evaluation', though the treatment of Hinduism is rather weak. Lewis finds many factual errors in Chandler's book. Of these major works, he maintains, Ruth Tucker's contains the best description of the movement, though it contains little analysis and adopts the alarmist stance found repeatedly in Christian responses to the New Age.[138]

After dealing with these key works, Lewis surveys the literature from 1980 up to 1989. He points out that by the mid-1980s an anti-New Age genre had emerged and that many books are, in fact, of 'poor quality'.

Another examination of evangelical responses to the New Age is that of Irving Hexham,[139] who credits Francis A. Schaeffer with the best apologetic and analytical critique of the ideology that later became known as the New Age. Hexham believes that serious evangelical reactions to the New Age began in the mid-1980s after the publications of the works of Constance Cumbey and Dave Hunt. Many of the evangelical responses to the New Age have been written by individuals who had been previously involved in it and can, therefore, be better described as testimonies. These books, according to Hexham,

> follow a similar pattern: ensnarement by the New Age, gradual dis-illusionment, and conversion, followed by a desire to expose the evils of the movement. Few pretend to scholarship, although most throw in a few academic-sounding examples to add authority to their case. Needless to say, most of these books are sensational tracts with little real value.[140]

Hexham judges several evangelical works, particularly those of Karen Hoyt, Russell Chandler, Elliot Miller, and Douglas Groothuis, to be better approaches. But he finds that there are still many popular evangelical books on the New Age that belong more to fiction than to serious scholarship.

The best feature of these evangelical responses to the New Age is, according to Hexham, their success in alerting people to the influence the New Age is having in education. He agrees that the infiltration of New Age ideas is dangerous. He argues, however, that this danger lies, not in any New Age plan to take over the world, but in the fact that the New Age 'represents an unscientific ethos which has a detrimental effect on scholarship'.[141]

Hexham dwells on eight major weaknesses in the evangelical reactions to the New Age Movement. He remarks that evangelicals tend (1) to misuse footnotes (by quoting evangelical sources to add authority); (2) to adopt poor scholarly methods (such as quoting writers out of context); (3) to accept fantastic claims (such as Kirlian photography) of New Agers much too readily; (4) to create guilt by association (such as judging reincarnation to be amoral because it is a basic belief in Witchcraft); (5) to be reductionistic; (6) to fail to define adequately some key terms (e.g., monism); (7) to adopt alternative words (e.g., dualism) without realizing that they are equally problematic; and (8) to force their opponents into a preconceived theoretical framework (as, for example, in the indiscriminate way they describe pantheism).[142]

Chrissie Steyn[143] reviews the literature from a South African perspective and divides the materials into the following kinds of works, namely: (1) those written by New Agers; (2) those which predate the movement; (3) those consisting of books that deal with issues of concern to New Agers; and (4) those describing and evaluating the movement from scholarly (academic disciplines, such as religious studies and sociology), scientific (humanistic), or Christian perspectives. Her observations on the first three categories are minimal, but she does make some incisive comments both on the Christian responses to the New Age and on those academic books which aim at describing and/or evaluating the New Age. She is suspicious of the Christian responses which, in her opinion, vary from 'well researched but negative evaluations' to 'fanatically rabid books in which the movement is usually equated with the demonic'. Like so many other scholars she finds many of these Christian depictions of the New Age inaccurate and misleading.

In her criticism of academic studies on the New Age, she remarks that, while their scholarship is flawless, the scholars' 'subjective allegiance' to the movement might account for the positive evaluations they make of it. She criticizes Martin Gardner's book, *The New Age: Notes of a Fringe Watcher*,[144] written from a humanistic perspective, as much too negative. She complains that his 'zeal in exposing all paranormal claims borders on the vitriolic so that ultimately his work can hardly be distinguished from the hostile attacks of Christian authors'.[145]

The evangelical/fundamentalist reactions to the New Age Movement may be justly criticized for their inferior academic quality. They have, however, raised the following significant questions: (1) How important is the New Age?; (2) Is it a dangerous movement?; (3) How accurate are Christian depictions or caricatures of it?; and (4) How convincing are the theories that have been advanced to explain its rise?

How important is the New Age?

Given the widespread and persistent coverage of the New Age Movement by Christian evangelicals and fundamentalists, one wonders whether its importance has been overrated. And given the possibility that the New Age as a movement is already waning, one questions whether the attacks and denunciations against it have been, at best, wasted energies that might have been better directed elsewhere.

The importance of the New Age, however, might not lie in its viability as an enduring movement. In fact, if one considers its lack of organization, its tendency to embrace divergent and incompatible viewpoints, and its stress on the individual's decision to make one's own choices regarding what to believe and what to practice, the New Age cannot compete with the major religious traditions, especially Christianity. But it is probable that, precisely because of these qualities, its significance should not be downplayed, much less ignored. In an age when all aspects of human life have fallen under the influence of bureaucracies, when variety has become the spice of life, and when individual human freedom is a primary value, the New Age is bound to influence many people, even if most do not become fully committed to its world view.

Several arguments can be brought forward to support the theory that the New Age is important enough to be taken seriously. First of all the beliefs and practices central to the New Age have already permeated Western culture and religion. For example, the New Age view of Jesus, belief in reincarnation, and interest in channeling, topics discussed in Chapter 5, have entered mainstream religion and/or culture and can hardly be dismissed as marginal.

Secondly, the New Age Movement has raised serious issues that are relevant to the changing sociocultural conditions of the late twentieth century. Two of the more prominent examples of this are healing and ecology. The progress of medicine over the last fifty years has led both to the lengthening of the average life-span and to the ability to manipulate human life itself. But in spite of these advances, sickness is still rampant and modern medicine has brought to the fore a host of political and ethical issues that clamor for our attention. The rise of holistic medicine and healing, both of which are central to New Age thinking, should be understood in the context of some of the failures and shortcomings of modern medicine. Traditional churches have been slow to respond to the questions raised by modern science. In like manner, New Age interest in ecology is a response to the current environmental crisis. To many, the West appears to lack the ideology and the attitude needed to face the current ecological problems and start applying some remedies before it is too late. The New Age provides a different way of looking at nature, one which appears to be more compatible with its preservation.

Thirdly, the New Age has highlighted the problem of religious pluralism. More than ever before people are now faced with the choice of a large variety of religious options. Conflicts between religious groups are likely to increase with the presence of a variety of religions, each claiming some monopoly on the truth and each seeking to enlist members to its ranks. The syncretistic nature of the New Age seems to encourage the principle of unity in diversity.

Some scholars are already considering the New Age as a major religious option. David Noebel thinks that there are three world views that dominate the Western world, namely, Marxism/Leninism, Secular Humanism, and Christianity. He suggests that the New Age ideology, which he prefers to call 'Cosmic Humanism', is becoming extensive enough to be included as a fourth option. He states that 'people adhering to the Cosmic Humanist worldview are gaining power in our society' and can be considered a 'fourth force' in the Western hemisphere.[146]

Is the New Age a dangerous religious movement?

A recurrent theme in evangelical and fundamentalist responses to the New Age is that acceptance of New Age beliefs and involvement in its practices are dangerous on two counts: (1) spiritually, since they cannot be reconciled with Christianity and, hence, will lead Christians to abandon their faith; and (2) psychologically, since they have drastic effects on one's personality. The first reason for concern seems justified because many New Agers have indeed abandoned their Judeo-Christian background and some have become critical of, and antagonistic to, their previous religious allegiances. One must stress, however, that not all people who accept New Age beliefs and get involved in some of its practices actually end up repudiating their Christian faith.

The charge that the New Age, especially because of some of its occult beliefs and practices, is detrimental to one's psychological health requires some scrutiny, if for no other reason than because it needs to be corroborated by careful study and hard data. Christian evangelicals and fundamentalists make no effort to distinguish between various levels of involvement in the occult and paranormal and between the various types of occult practices. Further, they provide no evidence that they have consulted psychological studies on the occult.

Psychological studies on the occult are, in fact, rather mixed. One such study concluded that there is indeed some connection between belief in the paranormal, mystical experiences, and psychopathology (such as proneness to hallucination).[147] Another found a link between members of occult sects and 'schizotypal thinking', but could not determine whether such thinking preceded, or was a result of, membership.[148] Yet another study contradicts a common assumption, since it found that believers in psychic phenomena are not mentally unstable.[149] While there is little doubt that some people involved in the occult indulge in criminal activity, not all types of occult involvement necessarily lead to crime.[150] One study found that involvement in some areas of the occult indicated a higher incidence of identity disorder and alcohol and drug abuse, but showed no greater correlation with criminal behavior.[151] Some researchers have concluded that there might be a relation between substance abuse and occult participation,[152] but evidence for generalizing their conclusion is far from obvious.

Christian commentators have contended that specific New Age

practices, like astrology, are harmful. One of the most articulate and comprehensive repudiations of astrology is that proposed by John Ankerberg and John Weldon,[153] who hold that those who believe in and practice it are exposed to six different dangers, namely, (1) physical damage; (2) inducements to crime; (3) economic loss; (4) spiritual damage; (5) psychological damage; and (6) moral damage.

It can be convincingly argued that those who become deeply involved in astrology may not be able to harmonize their commitment with the Christian faith and that a fatalistic dependency on the position of the stars is incompatible with the Christian concept of a loving and caring God. But there is little evidence to support the view that astrology is psychologically harmful and much less that it promotes or induces criminal behavior.

There is general agreement in the scientific community that astrology has no basis in fact.[154] However, studies have shown that undergraduate students of astrology are not more neurotic than their peers who have no interest in the field.[155] There is some evidence that astrology may be useful, especially when it functions as a counseling or therapeutic device.[156]

Other charges against the New Age have little, if any, foundation in reality. The accusations, for instance, that New Agers maltreat children is summarily dismissed by Kevin Logan, who confesses that 'the vast majority within paganism and the occult are equally as horrified as Christians at child abuse'.[157]

How accurate are Christian depictions or caricatures of the New Age?

One of the nagging questions that faces any scholar who aspires to evaluate the evangelical and fundamentalist responses to the New Age Movement is whether the overall image these responses give is a reliable and just representation of the movement. The descriptions of the New Age mentioned earlier in this chapter provide lists of beliefs and practices that are commonly found among New Agers. Yet the evangelical/fundamentalist responses to the New Age Movement suffer from at least four major deficiencies.

First of all, the approach these Christian writers take is basically faulty. They start with a list of Christian beliefs and then determine whether New Age ideology is compatible with them. The result is that one does not get a clear picture of what New Agers hold, but rather what Christians think New Age beliefs are. Their process of understanding the New Age begins with a list of doctrinal propositions, a process which contradicts the New Age ethos. Since the New Age is not an organized religious movement with a universally accepted religious text and a well-formulated creed expressed in dogmatic statements, one must approach it with a set of different premises and assumptions. New Agers do not collate a list of tenets that characterize the movement to which they belong. Their beliefs and practices are based on religious and/or spiritual experiences which are, at best, suspect in the eyes of most evangelicals and fundamentalists.

Second, the view of the New Age provided in evangelical and fundamentalist literature is much too generalized. Catalogues of New Age beliefs and practices leave the impression that New Agers share a monolithic world view. But New Agers differ radically among themselves. One example of such generalizations, repeated over and over again in evangelical and fundamentalist writings, is the statement that the New Age is monistic. The variety within the movement makes such a designation almost meaningless. Probably not many New Agers would define themselves as 'monists' and fewer still find such a label attractive and meaningful.

Another example of this over-generalization occurs when the dangers of the New Age are listed. Few efforts are made to distinguish between various levels of involvement in, for example, astrology. People might browse through their daily horoscopes, but few would follow the astrological recommendations seriously, and even fewer would approach their charts in a fatalistic manner. Gordon Melton, Jerome Clark, and Aidan Kelly[158] state that, among New Agers, the trend has been to move away from a literal and/or fatalistic interpretation of astrological beliefs and to psychologize them, hoping to make them more believable.

Third, evangelical and fundamentalist descriptions of the New Age are one-sided and too negative. Even though some Christians concede that the New Age has good qualities, they seem to do so reluctantly. Thus, for example, Miller states that the 'New Age religion is thoroughly occultic, and totally unchristian'.[159] This makes the New Age unredeemable. It fails to acknowledge any good elements in it. And it ignores any similarities it might have with Christianity.

Fourth, the evaluations of the New Age contain a number of factual errors, making them unreliable. A good instance of this is the way Hinduism is treated. While Hinduism is correctly taken as one source of New Age ideas, evangelical and fundamentalist understanding of this long religious tradition of India leaves much to be desired. One of the worst examples of Christian misunderstanding is Bob Larson's depiction of Hindu beliefs and practices as idolatrous and satanic.[160] Another is the portrayal of Hinduism as a non-theistic, monistic system of religious thought. Even a cursory look at an introductory text to world religions would show that there are six main and equally orthodox philosophical systems in Hinduism and that theism plays a key role in the devotional lives of most Hindus.[161] James Lewis[162] has correctly remarked that most Hindus are not monists and the movie *Indiana Jones and the Temple of Doom* (1984) does not accurately represent the Tantric tradition.

Another common error is to lump together Witchcraft, Satanism, Paganism, and Eastern religions as characteristic marks of the New Age.[163] While the New Age borrows many beliefs from various Asian religions, not all New Agers are involved in Witchcraft, and relatively few can be labeled Satanists.

The critique that New Age morality cannot be harmonized with that of Christianity is warranted,[164] though one must remember that New Agers differ in their moral standards. But some writers incorrectly hold that New Agers are 'immoral' because of their belief in reincarnation which is wrongly linked with Witchcraft.[165] At times the reader is left with the definitely false impression that non-Christian religions are basically unethical. While it is true that New Agers tend to subscribe to a kind of 'situation ethics', this does not mean that they are immoral and would indulge in, or approve of, all kinds of criminal and illegal behavior. Popular New Age beliefs, such as karma and reincarnation, do not connote, much less condone, immorality,[166] even if some New Agers have tried to justify their behavior by referring to these Eastern beliefs.[167]

The majority of evangelicals and fundamentalists writing on the New Age Movement reject mysticism as a valid expression of Christianity.[168] They exhibit a deep-rooted suspicion of any mystical experience, which is routinely denounced as non-Christian, a recent importation from the East, and an example of syncretism that is bound to corrupt Christianity. They refuse to take into consideration the rich mystical traditions of both Eastern and Western branches of Christianity.[169]

In like manner, there is little understanding of the role of meditation and contemplation in the Christian's life of prayer. And asceticism and the monastic life are considered to be foreign intrusions in Christianity. History is, in fact, distorted to buttress the denunciations of meditation, contemplation, and asceticism that one finds periodically in literature criticizing New Age ideology. One of the most blatant errors of historical reconstruction is provided by Peter Jones, who confidently assures his readers that

> Buddhist methods of meditation and contemplation entered the Roman Church hundreds of years ago through its trade with Asian nations and pagan conquests, incorporating some of the strange religious traditions. Monasteries were established, where whole orders of monks could study and practice the newly-discovered esoteric traditions of these nations. Disciplinary methods of *self-denial* were adopted from Eastern religions and developed into the vows of poverty, chastity, and obedience.[170]

How convincing are these theories about the New Age Movement?

Of the five theories that evangelicals and fundamentalists adduce to explain the rise of the New Age Movement, those of the revival of religion and of infiltration have a strong empirical base. Historical records show that New Age beliefs and practices have appeared again and again in the history of Western civilization. Similarly, one cannot deny that New Age ideology has become widespread in Western culture, even though it is too early to determine whether its impact will be deep and lasting.

The other theories are dependent on evangelical and fundamentalist ideology where Satan is given a prominent role in the running of human affairs and where apocalyptic views flourish. One can add that the theories are somewhat artificial and contrived. There is not enough emphasis on social and historical causes. The result is that the response to the New Age is hampered. Interpreting the New Age Movement as a satanic uprising against God and/or an apocalyptic sign of the end of the world places the matter completely outside the influence of human intervention. There isn't much one can do against diabolical activity except appeal for God's help.

Finally, one should observe that the evangelical and fundamentalist view of Christianity that emerges in the responses to the New Age Movement is much too static. One detects an implicit assumption that there is a pure form of Christianity that is either welded to the culture in which it was born or unattached to any cultural and historical moorings. The result is that there is little room for development and for the articulation of doctrine in different cultural and historical settings. Anything not explicitly mentioned in the

New Testament is likely to be rejected as a foreign and heterodox intrusion. Attempts to adapt the Gospel message to different cultures are frowned upon as dangerous, since they are more likely to end up distorting Christianity and creating a syncretistic faith.

THE FAILURE OF THE
EVANGELICAL/FUNDAMENTALIST RESPONSE

The appeal of the evangelical/fundamentalist reactions to the New Age Movement is understandable in the light of the current social and religious turmoil. These reactions offer simple, clear answers to the questions raised by the proponents of the New Age. By carefully differentiating Christian doctrines from New Age beliefs, they maintain the boundaries 'that allow a community to strengthen its own sense of identity by contrasting itself with "others" who are portrayed as being the exact opposites as themselves'.[171] Such boundaries are necessary whenever conflicting religious claims challenge, or are perceived as a threat to, one's faith. They perform the function of offering intellectual and emotional security to those who are confused and troubled by the spread of different belief systems and spiritual practices. By responding to the New Age in an emotional manner and by dwelling on its apparently unstoppable onslaught, evangelicals and fundamentalists have further elicited the support of many Christians who are willing to renew their dedication and commitment when their faith seems confronted and endangered by emerging religions.

It must be granted that the evangelical and fundamentalist assault on the New Age contains some valuable critique.[172] There is hardly any doubt that many New Age beliefs differ radically from those proposed by Christianity. One wonders, however, whether the kind of criticism offered has any lasting pastoral value. For in the final analysis the evangelical and fundamentalist response to the New Age Movement is nothing but a monologue or a soliloquy. At best, it is a process of self-affirmation and self-assurance, providing comfort and solace to confused Christians; it contrasts the teachings of the New Age with those of the Bible; and it discovers, to nobody's surprise, that the movement's religious ideology deviates from biblical texts and from orthodox Christian teachings. At its worst, it degenerates into a senseless diatribe or an emotional harangue.

Moreover, this kind of response is likely to have very limited results because it consists largely of repetitive and boring catalogues of Christian doctrines and New Age heresies. Since it appeals largely to those who are already committed Christians, it cannot engage New Agers in a fruitful exchange of ideas or in a constructive discussion on ideological standpoints, spiritual goals, and practical agendas. It does not lead Christians and New Agers alike to reflect on and evaluate their own beliefs and practices. It discourages co-operation with New Agers even on mutually-shared interests and concerns. It leaves the impression that all New Agers are evil persons to be condemned, notwithstanding the half-hearted efforts by a few writers to include all within the embrace of Christian charity.

Further, the evangelical/fundamentalist reply to the New Age fails to give real witness to the Christian message of the Good News, because its methods and message are more attuned to elicit fear and anxiety and to dwell on foreboding and pessimistic outlooks for the future. Moreover, it unintentionally confirms negative impressions of, and elicits antagonistic feelings towards, Christianity, and hence encourages uncooperative reactions from those who have abandoned their traditional faith. Consequently, it cannot be, and in fact has not been, very successful in its goals of stemming the spread of New Age ideology in society at large and in the Christian Church itself or reconverting many New Agers to the Christian faith.

NOTES

1. Evangelical and fundamentalist theologies, in spite of their differences, share a similar approach to the rise of new religious movements and their responses to the New Age can be grouped together as one type of response to this contemporary movement.

2. *Cult Watch: What You Need to Know About Spiritual Deception* (Eugene, OR: Harvest House Publishers, 1991), p. 131.

3. *The New Age Cult* (Minneapolis: Bethany House, 1989), p. 21.

4. Douglas R. Groothuis, *Confronting the New Age: How to Resist a Growing Religious Movement* (Downers Grove, IL: InterVarsity Press, 1988), p. 201; Elliot Miller, *A Crash Course on the New Age Movement* (Grand Rapids, MI: Baker Book House, 1989), p. 19; Mary Ann Lind, *From Nirvana to the New Age* (Tarrytown, NY: Fleming H. Revell, 1991), p. 131; and Constance Cumbey, *The Hidden Dangers of the Rainbow: The New Age Movement and Our Coming Age of Barbarism* (Shreveport, LA: Huntington House, 1983), p. 41.

5. *A Crash Course on the New Age Movement*, p. 183. Cf. Robert J. L. Burrows, 'Americans get religion in the New Age', *Christianity Today* (May 16, 1986): 17.

6. Walter Martin, *The New Age Cult*, p. 7.

7. This is a theme common in evangelical and fundamentalist literature. See, for example, John Ankerberg and John Weldon, *Cult Watch*, pp. 134–35; and Randall N. Baer, *Inside the New Age Nightmare* (Shreveport, LA: Huntington House, 1989), pp. 149ff.

8. Randall N. Baer, *Inside the New Age Nightmare*, pp. 135ff.

9. Walter Martin, *The New Age Cult*, p. 22.

10. John Ankerberg and John Weldon, *Cult Watch*, pp. 131–32.

11. Constance Cumbey, *The Hidden Dangers of the Rainbow*, pp. 85–86; see also Bob Larson, *Larson's New Book on Cults* (Wheaton, IL: Tyndale House, 1989), p. 326.

12. Constance Cumbey, *The Hidden Dangers of the Rainbow*, p. 123.

13. Ibid., p. 184. See also p. 261, where she states that the symbol of a rainbow 'is used as a hypnotic device'. Eric Buehrer, in his book *The New Age Masquerade: The Hidden Agenda in Your Child's Classroom* (Brentwood, TN: Wolgemuth and Hyatt, 1990, pp. 95ff.), maintains that children are being hypnotized into the occult.

14. *Inside the New Age Nightmare* (Lafayette, IN: Huntington House, 1989), p. 2.

15. *The New Age Cult*, p. 47.

16. Randall Baer, *Inside the New Age Nightmare*, pp. 126–28.

17. *Savage Future: The Sinister Side of the New Age* (Hagerstown, MD: Autumn House, 1991), pp. 53–54.

18. *Unholy Sacrifices of the New Age* (Westchester, IL: Crossway Books, 1988), pp. 119–24, 132, and 143–44.

19. *The Hidden Dangers of the Rainbow*, p. 190.

20. *Basic Principles of New Age Thought* (Green Forest, AR: New Leaf Press, 1990), p. 41.

21. Ibid., p. 96.

22. *Confronting the New Age*, pp. 76–83.

23. Randall Baer, *Inside the New Age Nightmare*, pp. 93–98 and 133–34.

24. Ibid., pp. 133–34.

25. Ibid., pp. 97–98.

26. John Ankerberg and John Weldon, *Cult Watch*, pp. 283ff.

27. Constance Cumbey, *Hidden Dangers of the Rainbow*, p. 69.

28. Ibid., p. 146.

29. *Dark Secrets of the New Age* (Westchester, IL: Crossway Books, 1987), p. 204.

30. Ibid., p. 137.

31. Ibid., pp. 16–17.

32. See, for example, Walter Martin, *The New Age Cult*, pp. 70–71.

33. *Cult Watch*, pp. 148–49.

34. *Basic Principles of New Age Thought*, p. 26.

35. *Cult Watch*, p. 133.

36. *The Hidden Dangers of the Rainbow*, p. 40. See also pp. 252–54, where Cumbey lists sixteen New Age beliefs.

37. *A Crash Course on the New Age Movement*, p. 15.

38. *New Age Movement* (Grand Rapids, MI: Zondervan Publishing House, 1995), p. 7.

39. 'The church and the new spirituality', *Journal of the Evangelical Theological Society* 36 (1993): 434.

40. *Straight Answers on the New Age* (Nashville, TN: Thomas Nelson Publishers, 1989), p. xii.

41. *Cult Watch*, pp. 145–46.

42. *The Infiltration of the New Age* (Wheaton, IL: Tyndale House, 1989), pp. 107ff.

43. *The New Age Cult*, pp. 25ff.

44. *Unmasking the New Age* (Downers, Grove, IL: InterVarsity Press, 1986), pp. 19ff.

45. *Confronting the New Age*, pp. 20ff.

46. *New Age Movement*, pp. 8–11.

47. *A Crash Course on the New Age Movement*, p. 17.

48. Ibid., pp. 185–86.

49. *The Hidden Dangers of the Rainbow*, p. 40.

50. Ibid., p. 65.

51. See, for example, Mary Ann Lind, *From Nirvana to the New Age*, p. 16, and Erwin W. Lutzer and John F. DeVries, *Satan's Evangelistic Strategy for This New Age* (Wheaton, IL: Victor Books, 1989), pp. 22ff.

52. *Ravaged by the New Age: Satan's Plan to Destroy Our Kids* (Austin, TX: Living Truth Publishers, 1989), pp. 24–25 and 33; and *Dark Secrets of the New Age*, pp. 25ff.

53. *Savage Future: The Sinister Side of the New Age*, pp. 106ff.

54. See, for instance, John Eidsmore, *Basic Principles of New Age Thought*, p. 37.

55. *Cult Watch*, p. 135. Cf. Amano J. Yutaka and Norman Geisler, *The Infiltration of the New Age*, pp. 31ff.; and Mary Ann Lind, *From Nirvana to the New Age*, pp. 84ff.

56. Kerry D. McRoberts, *New Age or Old Lie?*, pp. 22ff.

57. *The Gnostic Empire Strikes Back: An Old Heresy for the New Age* (Phillipsburg, NJ: P & R Publishing, 1992), pp. 20–24. The same theme is developed by Mary Ann Lind, *From Nirvana to the New Age*, ch. 3, pp. 33ff.; and by David Rankin, 'The New Age and the old Gnosticism', *Lutheran Theological Quarterly* 26 (August 1992): 98–105.

58. See, for instance, Carl A. Raschke, *The Interruption of Eternity: Modern Gnosticism and the Origins of the New Religious Consciousness* (Chicago: Nelson-Hall, 1980). The author interprets the rise of new religious movements (and by implication the New Age) as a revival of a broader form of Gnosticism.

59. 'Understanding the New Age', *Evangelical Review of Theology* 16 (1992): 205. See Robert S. Ellwood and Harry B. Partin, *Religious and Spiritual Groups in Contemporary America* (Englewood Cliffs, NJ: Prentice-Hall, 2nd ed, 1988, pp. 30–72), where an outline of the history of alternative traditions in the West is provided.

60. *The Hidden Dangers of the Rainbow*, pp. 44ff. Other writers also notice the link with the Theosophical Society, but make no reference to Nazism. Cf., for instance, Philip C. Almond, 'Understanding the New Age', pp. 208–09.

61. *The Hidden Dangers of the Rainbow*, pp. 99ff. and *A Planned Deception: The Staging of a New Age 'Messiah'* (East Detroit, MI: Pointe Publishers, Inc., 1985), pp. 83ff.

62. *The Hidden Dangers of the Rainbow*, p. 85.

63. Ibid., p. 254.

64. Ibid., p. 257.

65. *Dark Secrets of the New Age*, p. 32.

66. *New Age Movement*, pp. 24ff. See also Douglas Groothuis, *Unmasking the New Age*, pp. 37ff., who postulates that the movement has sociological roots in the counterculture of the 1960s and 1970s.

67. *The Hidden Dangers of the Rainbow*, p. 20.

68. Ibid., pp. 42 and 99ff.

69. Ibid., pp. 114–20.

70. *Rest from the Quest* (Shreveport, LA: Huntington House, 1983), preface.

71. Constance Cumbey, *The Hidden Dangers of the Rainbow*, p. 22.

72. *The New Age Secret Plan for World Conquest* (Chattanooga, TN: AMG Publishers, 1992).

73. Judy Hamlin, *Shedding Light on the New Age: Six Studies for Women on the Lies and Snares of the New Age Movement* (Wheaton, IL: Victor Books, 1993), p. 15. See also Randall Baer, *Inside the New Age Nightmare*, p. 2. Erwin W. Lutzer and John F. DeVries, in their book *Satan's Evangelistic Strategy for This New Age*, pp. 27ff., develop the theme that Satan is the master strategist who by his deceptive salesmanship lures people away from Christianity into the New Age pagan religion.

74. Constance Cumbey, *The Hidden Dangers of the Rainbow*, p. 136; Dave Hunt and T. A. McMahon, *The Seduction of Christianity* (Eugene, OR: Harvest House, 1985), p. 59; and Kevin Logan, *Close Encounters with the New Age* (Eastbourne, UK: Kingsway Publications, 1991), p. 21.

75. Ronald Enroth, 'The New Age Movement: emissaries of spiritual deception, disguised as angels of light', *Fundamentalist Journal* 7 (Fall 1988): 32–34, 43.

76. Steve Russo, *The Devil's Playground* (Eugene, OR: Harvest House Publishers, 1994), p. 102.

77. *Dark Secrets of the New Age*, p. 53.

78. Ibid., p. 99.

79. *Ravaged by the New Age*, pp. 14ff.

80. *Confronting the New Age*, p. 17. See also Caryl Matrisciana, *Gods of the New Age* (Eugene, OR: Harvest House Publishers, 1985), pp. 22–23, where the New Age is said to be Satan's religion given to Eve.

81. *Cult Watch*, p. 134.

82. Ibid., p. 155. Cf. Kenneth R. Wade, *Savage Future: The Sinister Side of the New Age*, p. 75.

83. Amano J. Yutaka and Norman L. Geisler, *The Infiltration of the New Age*, p. 33.

84. *Inside the New Age Nightmare*, p. 38.

85. F. LaGard Smith, *What You Need to Know About the New Age Movement* (Eugene, OR: Harvest House Publishers, 1993), p. 106; and Kerry D. McRoberts, *New Age, Old Lie?*, p. 78. See also David Jeremiah with C. C. Carlson, *Invasion of Other Gods: The Seduction of New Age Spirituality* (Dallas: Word Publishing, 1995, pp. 67–68), where channeling is said to be drug-induced, or pure deception, or a form of possession by demons.

86. Dave Hunt and T. A. McMahon, *The Seduction of Christianity*, p. 117.

87. Anthony P. Stone, 'Astrology and other methods of divination', *Evangelical Review of Theology* 16 (1992): 404.

88. Randall Baer, *Inside the New Age Nightmare*, p. 41.

89. *Confronting the New Age*, p. 37; cf. Randall Baer, *Inside the New Age Nightmare*, p. 19; and John Ankerberg and John Weldon, *Cult Watch*, pp. 261ff.

90. *Ravaged by the New Age*, p. 26. To this list he adds psychedelic drugs, feminism, sodomy, sadism, unisex dress, and sorcery.

91. *The Gnostic Empire Strikes Back*, p. 97.

92. Constance Cumbey, *The Hidden Dangers of the Rainbow*, pp. 54 and 129–32.

93. *The New Age Cult*, p. 66.

94. *Ravaged by the New Age*, pp. 194ff., 219ff., and 243.

95. Amano J. Yutaka and Norman L. Geisler, *The Infiltration of the New Age*, pp. 7ff. See also John Eidsmore, *Basic Principles of New Age Thought*, p. 50, where the author states that the movie *Star Wars* portrays a distinctively New Age view of God, humanity, and the universe.

96. See, for example, Texe Marrs, *Dark Secrets of the New Age*, p. 206; Peter Jones, *The Gnostic Empire Strikes Back*, p. 7; and Constance Cumbey, *A Planned Deception: The Staging of a New Age 'Messiah'*, pp. 17–18.

97. *Satan's Evangelistic Strategy for This New Age*, where ch. 8 (pp. 113ff.) is dedicated to this theme. See also David Marshall, *The Devil Rides Out: New Age and the Occult: A Christian Perspective* (Grantham, UK: Autumn House Publishers, 1991), p. 120; and Florence Bulle, *The Many Faces of Deception* (Minneapolis: Bethany House Publishers, 1989), esp. pp. 175–94.

98. *Trojan Horse: How the New Age Movement Infiltrates the Churches* (Lafayette, IN: Huntington House Publishers, 1993). Cf. Madeleine L'Engle, *And It Was Good: Reflections on Beginnings* (Wheaton, IL: H. Shaw Publishers, 1983) and *An Acceptable Time* (New York: Farrar, Straus, Giroux, 1989).

99. Erwin W. Lutzer and John F. DeVries, *Trojan Horse: How the New Age Movement Infiltrates the Churches*, chs. 4–5, pp. 61–108. Cf. also David Marshall, *The Devil Rides Out*, p. 128,

100. Cf. Tony Higton in Michael Cole, Jim Graham, Tony Higton, and David Lewis, *What Is the New Age?* (London: Hodder and Stoughton, 1990), p. 52.

101. See also Dave Hunt and T. A. McMahon, *The Seduction of Christianity*, p. 12.

102. Elliot Miller, *A Crash Course on the New Age*, pp. 187–89. Cf. 'Under fire: two Christian leaders respond to accusations of New Age mysticism', *Christianity Today* (September 18, 1987), pp. 17–21.

103. See, for example, pp. 35, 68, 72, 77ff., and 256–57. Cf. also her work *A Planned Deception: The Staging of a New Age 'Messiah'*, p. 35.

104. *The Seduction of Christianity*, p. 7. Cf. Dave Hunt, *Peace, Prosperity, and the Coming Holocaust* (Eugene, OR: Harvest House Publishers, 1983, p. 203), where the New Age Movement is said to be 'a major factor in preparing for the antichrist'.

105. Ibid., pp. 36ff.

106. *Dark Secrets of the New Age*, ch. 9, pp. 31, 61, and 66ff.

107. See, for instance, Mary Ann Lind, *From Nirvana to the New Age*, p. 15; Randall Baer, *Inside the New Age Nightmare*, pp. 79 and 83; and Roy Livesey, *Understanding the New Age* (Chichester, UK: New Wine Press, 1986), p. 234.

108. There are some noteworthy exceptions to this. Kenneth R. Wade, in his book *Savage Future: The Sinister Side of the New Age* (p. 110), writes: 'Right now it [the New Age Movement] isn't even making strong inroads among nominal Christians ...'

109. *Understanding the New Age* (Dallas: Word Publishing, 1988), p. 229.

110. *A Crash Course on the New Age*, p. 197. For one of the better critiques of Constance Cumbey's views see pp. 193ff.

111. *Dark Secrets of the New Age*, p. 177.

112. *Unmasking the New Age*, pp. 33–35.

113. *New Age, Old Lie?*, p. 103. See also Kenneth R. Wade, *Savage Future: The Sinister Side of the New Age*, p. 81.

114. *Close Encounters with the New Age*, p. 32.

115. *The New Age Cult*, p. 20.

116. *Straight Answers on the New Age*, p. ix.

117. *New Age Movement*, p. 79.

118. *A Crash Course on the New Age*, pp. 21–27.

119. *Confronting the New Age*, pp. 58ff.

120. *Unholy Spirits: Occultism and New Age Humanism* (Tyler, TX: Institute for Christian Economics, 1994), p. 378. See also Douglas Groothuis, *Confronting the New Age*, pp. 211–12.

121. Ibid., p. 379.

122. *A Crash Course on the New Age*, p. 137.

123. *From Nirvana to the New Age*, pp. 137–39.

124. *Dark Secrets of the New Age*, p. 261.

125. *Cult Watch*, pp. 150–51. Cf. Judy Hamlin, *Shedding the Light on the New Age*, p. 37.

126. *Basic Principles of New Age Thought*, pp. 146ff.

127. *Thieves of Innocence* (Eugene, OR: Harvest House, 1993), pp. 212–13.

128. *The New Age Cult*, ch. 8, pp. 97ff.

129. Ibid., p. 102.

130. *Apologetics in the New Age* (Grand Rapids, MI: Baker Book House, 1990).

131. *New Age Movement*, pp. 79–82.

132. Kenneth R. Wade, *Savage Future: The Sinister Side of the New Age*, pp. 143ff.

133. *Dark Secrets of the New Age*, pp. 250ff.

134. Ibid., p. 257.

135. Ibid., p. 260. For comparable guidelines see Amano J. Yutaka and Norman L. Geisler, *The Infiltration of the New Age*, pp. 37–38; and Erwin W. Lutzer and John A. DeVries, *Satan's Evangelistic Strategy for This New Age*, pp. 178–80.

136. 'Christian books on the New Age: a review article', *Master's Seminary Journal* 1 (Fall 1990): 177–200.

137. 'A bibliography of conservative Christian literature on the New Age Movement' (Santa Barbara, CA: Santa Barbara Center for Humanistic Studies), Occasional Paper #2 (1989), p. 1.

138. Ibid., pp. 2–4.

139. 'The evangelical response to the New Age' in *Perspectives on the New Age*, ed. James R. Lewis and J. Gordon Melton (Albany, NY: State University of New York Press, 1992), pp. 152–63. See Francis A. Schaeffer, *The Complete Works of Francis F. Schaeffer: A Christian Worldview* (Westchester, IL: Crossway Books, 1982), vol. 1, pp. 59–90, vol. 3, pp. 381–401, and vol. 5, pp. 9–19 and 229–44.

140. 'The evangelical response to the New Age,' p. 155.

141. Ibid., p. 158.

142. Ibid., pp. 158–60.

143. *Worldviews in Transition: An Investigation into the New Age Movement in South Africa* (Pretoria: University of South Africa Press, 1994).

144. Buffalo, NY: Prometheus Books, 1988.

145. *Worldviews in Transition: An Investigation into the New Age Movement in South Africa*, p. 51.

146. *Understanding the Times* (Manitou Springs, CO: Summit Press, 1991), p. 850.

147. Michael A. Thalbourne and Peter S. Delin, 'A common thread underlying belief in the paranormal, creative personality, mystical experience and psychopathology', *Journal of Parapsychology* 58 (1994): 3–37.

148. John Rust, 'Schizotypal thinking among members of occult sects', *Social Behavior and Personality* 20 (1992): 121–30.

149. T. L. Brink, 'Personality factors related to disbelief in psychic phenomena', *Parapsychology Review* 9.4 (1978): 22–23.

150. Karla D. Carmichael, in her essay 'Counseling and the occult-involved student: guidelines and suggestions', *School Counselor* 41.1 (September 1993):

5–8, distinguishes between four levels of involvement in the occult: (1) fun and games; (2) dabblers; (3) serious involvement; and (4) criminal involvement.

151. Roger C. Burket, et al., 'Emotional and behavioral disturbances in adolescents involved in Witchcraft and Satanism', *Journal of Adolescence* 17 (1994): 41–54.

152. Cynthia M. Clark-Tennant, Janet J. Fritz, and Fred Beauvais, 'Occult participation: its impact on adolescent development', *Adolescence* 24 (1989): 757–72.

153. *Cult Watch*, pp. 133ff.

154. See, for example, Richard A. Crowe, 'Astrology and the scientific method', *Psychological Reports* 67 (1990): 163–91; and Uwe Hentschel and M. Kiessling, 'Season of birth and personality: another instance of non-correspondence', *Journal of Social Psychology* 125 (1985): 577–85.

155. T. S. Tyagi, 'Astrology and mental health', *Journal of Personality and Clinical Studies* 3.1 (1987): 63–66.

156. See, for instance, David Lester, 'Astrologers and psychics as therapists', *American Journal of Psychotherapy* 36.1 (1982): 56–66.

157. *Close Encounters with the New Age*, pp. 20–21.

158. *New Age Encyclopedia* (Detroit: Gale Research, 1990), p. 41.

159. *A Crash Course on the New Age*, p. 28.

160. *Larson's New Book on Cults*, p. 70.

161. Cf., for example, David S. Noss and John B. Noss, *A History of the World's Religions* (New York: Macmillan Publishing Company/London: Collier Macmillan Publishers, 8th ed., 1990), pp. 106ff.; and Ninian Smart, *The Religious Experience* (New York: Macmillan Publishing Company, 4th ed., 1991), pp. 140–44.

162. 'A bibliography of conservative Christian literature on the New Age Movement', pp. 2–3.

163. See, for example, Kevin Logan, *Close Encounters with the New Age*, pp. 25–26.

164. A good example is the view of sex and marriage expressed in Fino, *New Age Spirituality, New Age Sexuality* (Tucson, AZ: Silver Circle Press, 1994), pp. 135ff.

165. Cf. Dave Hunt and T. A. McMahon, *The Seduction of Christianity*, p. 213.

166. See, for instance, *Hindu Religion and Ethics*, ed. Kumar Pushpendra Sharma (New Delhi, India: Asian Publications Services, 1974), esp. pp. 258ff. For bibliographic references to extensive studies of Hindu ethics one can consult Austin B. Creel, 'Studies of Hindu ethics: a bibliographic introduction', *Religious Studies Review* 2 (1978): 26–33; and Barbara A. Holdrege, 'Hindu ethics' in *A Bibliographic Guide to the Comparative Study of Ethics*, ed. John B. Carman and Mark Juergensmeyer (Cambridge: Cambridge University Press, 1991), pp. 12–169.

167. Vishal Mangalwadi, 'The reincarnation of the soul', *Evangelical Review of Theology* 15 (1991): 143, states that reincarnation undercuts the philosophical foundations of morality, and then shows how Shirley MacLaine uses belief in reincarnation to justify homosexuality and adultery.

168. See, for example, Arthur L. Moody, *Faith Misguided: Exposing the Dangers of Mysticism* (Chicago: Moody, 1988).

169. Cf. Bernard McGinn, *The Presence of God: A History of Western Mysticism*, especially vol. 1: *The Foundations of Mysticism: Origins to the 5th Century* (New York: Crossroad, 1991).

170. *The Gnostic Empire Strikes Back*, p. 110. See Rosemary Rader, 'Asceticism' in *The Westminster Dictionary of Christian Spirituality*, ed. Gordon S. Wakefield (Philadelphia: Westminster Press, 1983), p. 24, who states: 'From its inception Christianity attached importance to ascetical ideals as the most effective means for living a Christian life.' Cf. also Samuel Rubeson, 'Christian asceticism and the emergence of the monastic tradition' in *Asceticism*, ed. Vincent L. Wimbush and Richard Valantasis (London: Oxford University Press, 1994), pp. 49–57.

171. James R. Lewis, 'A bibliography of conservative Christian literature on the New Age Movement', p. 1.

172. Cf., for example, Irving Hexham, 'The Evangelical response to the New Age', pp. 157–58.

3.

MAINLINE PROTESTANT AND EASTERN ORTHODOX RESPONSES TO THE NEW AGE MOVEMENT

The evangelical and fundamentalist responses to the New Age Movement are marked by one general distinguishing feature: they reject and condemn the New Age as an anti-Christian movement. Consequently their efforts are largely directed towards refuting its theological premises, attacking its religious and spiritual underpinnings, stressing orthodox Christian doctrines, and warning people of its infiltrating efforts in all aspects of modern culture. While they sometimes contain accurate descriptions of its predominant themes, they ignore, downplay, or fail to recognize any common ground between Christianity and the New Age. They make little or no effort to explore in depth the aspirations and beliefs that New Agers and Christians share in common.

Many Protestant commentators, like their fundamentalist counterparts, have also been preoccupied with New Age teachings. They have drawn attention to the gnostic elements of the movement and stressed their incompatibility with traditional Christian doctrine. The nature of God, the uniqueness of Jesus Christ, the nature of humanity and of the cosmos, and the stress on the irrational and the intuitive are often listed as the main areas that cannot be reconciled with traditional Christian teachings.[1]

Mainline Protestant reactions to the New Age, however, have been, in general, more varied and more insightful in their encounter with the New Age. This variety is exemplified by the manner in which Protestant writers explain the immediate causes of the movement's rise and success which they have been reluctant to attribute to human conspiracies. They do, however, occasionally lean to the explanation that satanic influences are at work. John W. Cooper,[2] for example, admits that the New Age is not a conspiracy in the sense that it aims at 'specific targeting, secret infiltration, and

a coercive conquest ...'. He suggests that its approach is rather subtle and fraudulent and that it uses attraction and gentle persuasion
and is thus more dangerous than an armed revolution. Philip H.
Lockhaas warns that conspiracy theories 'should be viewed with
caution, for they often prevent a rational assessment of the situation'. But he admits that there is a universal plot, but it is not of
human origin. Its roots lie in 'Satan's attempt to dethrone God and
bring to nothing the atonement of Jesus Christ'.[3]

Janet Bigland Pritchard adopts a slightly different position.[4]
While she rejects the opinion that there is an orchestrated con-
nivance to infiltrate and take over the churches, she does admit
'there is evidence of close cooperation/consultation between New
Age leaders' and that 'the hard core New Age is well-organized and
strongly anti-Jewish and anti-Christian'. And though she does not
mention the devil as the force behind these plans, she concurs with
the view that there is a 'spiritual conspiracy' to lead people away
from God.

This preoccupation with the part played by Satan in the rise and
success of the New Age Movement sometimes dominates the entire
Protestant response. Alan Morrison,[5] for example, writing from a
Baptist perspective, adopts the theory that the New Age is a new
form of Gnosticism devised by Satan on a global scale. He tries to
show in great detail how the mind sciences, Witchcraft, Eastern mysticism, and Christianized yoga are among the many strategies used
by Satan to corrupt the Church in the late twentieth century. The
New Age is the 'Gospel of Darkness', part of Satan's war against
God, a war which Morrison traces from its inception in the Garden
of Eden, through early Gnosticism, medieval sects, rationalism,
modern science, liberal theology, the rise of comparative religion,
and Theosophy. The twentieth-century roots of the New Age, which
include the works of Alice Bailey, Rudolf Steiner, and Teilhard de
Chardin, and various organizations, like the Liberal Catholic
Church, the White Eagle Lodge, and the Saint Germain
Foundation, are all part of Satan's master plot to pervert the
Church.

Many Protestants, however, spurn all conspiracy theories without
any reservation. Frank Whaling,[6] for example, rejects Constance
Cumbey's theory of a large, carefully-planned scheme as a mis-
placed attack, since New Age plans do not include secret
machinations to take over the world and New Age thought and
movements are too diverse to allow for collaboration on universal

plans. And Ruth Tucker, observing that both the New Age view of Jesus and its morality cannot be harmonized with Christianity, states unhesitatingly:

> For those who enjoy plotting suspense dramas with covert complicity and intrigue, the New Age Movement offers an abundance of raw material on which to fashion the scheme. But whether such a scenario would resemble the reality of a diffuse and ever-changing movement filled with self-serving prophets is another matter.[7]

A similar note of caution is sometimes adopted by smaller Christian denominations. The Salvation Army,[8] for instance, in a short list of guidelines for responding to the New Age Movement, notes that while various anti-Christian elements are certainly infiltrating Western culture, the belief that the New Age is plotting a worldwide conspiracy is an extreme theory. The guidelines advise church members that New Age beliefs might deceive human beings and lead them to deviate from God. They eschew, however, making references to satanic involvement and make it quite clear that the 'most important question is not whether we consider the New Age Movement to be a worldwide conspiracy or a disturbing trend with many independent sources, but whether we are grasping this unparalleled opportunity to declare the good news of the Gospel of Jesus Christ'.

Protestant responses can conveniently be divided into three main groups. The first borrows heavily from the fundamentalist/evangelical reaction and concentrates largely on refuting the movement's ideology and stressing the fundamentals of Christian doctrine. The second takes a diametrically opposite approach and accepts many of the ideals and practices of the New Age and tries to incorporate them into Christianity. The third attempts a balanced evaluation of the New Age, pointing out its strengths and weaknesses, comparing its teachings with major Christian doctrines, and sometimes hinting that not all New Age beliefs and practices should be condemned.

REJECTION OF NEW AGE WORLD VIEW

Depictions of the New Age

The influence of the evangelical/fundamentalist analyses of the New Age Movement can be seen in the works of many Protestants who have reacted with concern about its presence in the West and the challenge it poses to Christianity in an age of religious turmoil. The following reactions to the New Age are fairly representative of the Protestant literature.

A typical example of suspicion and rejection of all aspects of the New Age is provided by Eric K. Winkler, a Lutheran, who defines it as

> an eclectic, occult-based, evolution-promoting, man-centered, self-deifying, pervasive world view (philosophy of life) that seeks, through the transformation of individuals, to bring about a transformation of society in order to achieve the ultimate goal of a new world order of complete global harmony.[9]

He lists schematically seven major tenets of the New Age, all of which are in opposition to the world view of the Bible: (1) all is one; (2) everything is God and God is everything; (3) the human being is divine; (4) immortality and reincarnation; (5) a person can create one's own reality; (6) all religions are true; and (7) a new world is coming into being.[10] He detects New Age influence in all areas of Western life, including entertainment, education, business, and health care. Moreover he finds the New Age not only intolerant of Christianity but also anti-Christian. Like other commentators, he concedes, with apparent reluctance, that not 'all New Age emphases are bad'. Good nutrition, involvement with environmental issues, concern with nuclear disarmament, and working for peace are all certainly commendable. But he warns that vegetarianism could be deceptive and dangerous and other concerns of the New Age are built on spiritual philosophies that cannot be accepted by Christians.[11] 'Christianity', he writes, 'certainly can support some ideas of New Age Politics – environmental concerns, world peace, improving the lot of the impoverished, nuclear arms control, and others. But Christians are concerned about the spiritual roots of New Age politics as well as the effect of planetary consciousness on the freedom of religion.'[12] His suspicions about the New Age are encapsulated in his remark that the movement is a 'pervasive, deceptive, and diabolical movement in our society'.[13]

Another comprehensive effort to examine and denounce the New Age Movement has been attempted by Philip H. Lochhaas, also a Lutheran, who defines it simply 'as a network of otherwise dissimilar people intent on replacing the reality of a personal God with the idea that humanity is the center of all things'.[14] Lochhaas[15] distinguishes between two expressions of the New Age, namely, the occult and the humanistic, the former stressing channeling, reincarnation, and self-worship, the latter focusing on developing one's potential. Both sections offer salvation, a kind of personal transformation that human beings can obtain by their own efforts. The success of the New Age is attributed to human sinfulness and to deception, themes which occur repeatedly in Christian criticism of the New Age beliefs.

Lochhaas offers a slightly different version of the main principles of the New Age, principles which he thinks are given different inter- pretations by humanistic and occult New Agers and which he enumerates as follows:

> (1) '*All is one; therefore all is God*'; (2) '*Humanity, like all creation, is divine and has unlimited potential*'; (3) '*Humanity's basic flaw is its ignorance of divinity and oneness with all things*'; (4) '*Humanity's only need, therefore, is transformation – the awareness of divinity*'; (5) '*Transformation can be produced by a wide variety of techniques*'; (6) '*Personal transformation is the springboard to global transformation*'.[16]

He traces the beginnings of the New Age Movement back to the lies of Satan as recorded in Genesis 3:4–6 and attributes its more proximate origins to various sources, including Theosophy, New Thought, Eastern mysticism, and secular humanism. Lochhaas finds little difference between secular humanism and the New Age, since they both stress human potential and both are based on the assump- tion that human beings are self-sufficient or divine. And he suggests that many factors have contributed to its appeal. The New Age rep- resents a rebellion against science and technology. It is a symptom of the failure of secular humanism which denies or ignores the reli- gious dimension of life and an expression of the stress on sensual experience that pervades Western culture. The churches themselves are partly to blame for the popularity of the movement because they have to some degree succumbed to the secularizing tendencies that erode belief in God and the need for moral imperatives. But the leading component of the New Age's popularity is the strategy of Satan who deceives human beings into believing that they have the attributes of God.[17] The New Age is promulgated through many vehicles that are readily available in modern culture. These include psychic fairs, the entertainment industry, the 1993 World Parliament of Religions, metaphysical organizations, public educa- tion, and various psychologies.

The polarity between the New Age Movement and Christianity is sometimes dramatized by writers who draw lengthy contrasts between the two. Ronald H. Nash, for example, writing from a Reformed Church perspective, contends that the New Age is a hodgepodge of ideas meshed into a belief system. He maintains that:

> Almost every facet of the [New Age] movement is a renewal of a feature of ancient paganism or an element borrowed from modern religious aberrations such as Theosophy, Swedenborgianism, Transcendentalism, Spiritualism, Christian Science, and New Thought mixed in varied combinations with other elements of Eastern religions.[18]

He then draws up a chart showing how Christianity differs radically from the New Age and 'Naturalism'. He considers the following topics: God, metaphysics, epistemology, ethics, the human nature and condition, the human problem and its solution, death, and Jesus Christ. He ascribes to the New Age the following features: (1) it is pantheistic; (2) it holds that the world is divine; (3) it maintains that truth is relative and is attained through mystical states; (4) it adheres to a relativistic ethics; (5) it considers human beings as spiritual entities who are gods; (6) it defines the human problem as ignorance of the human potential; and (7) it proposes the transformation of consciousness as the solution to all human problems. Nash concludes that New Age thinking is in conflict with Christian belief in all the major religious, spiritual, and philosophical areas. In like manner Mark Bair[19] adopts an almost identical contrasting scheme and points out that the New Age is rooted in three world views, namely, naturalism, pantheism, and animism. He maintains that animism, which he defines as the pagan or primal religious view that sees the universe inhabited by many spiritual beings, might become the dominant thought in the New Age Movement.

Such authors encourage Christian opposition to, and rejection of, the New Age movement, not by having recourse to a human conspiracy theory, but rather by dwelling on the contrast between its teachings and those of Christianity. They argue that the New Age is dangerous because it borrows its vocabulary from Christianity and includes Christian themes which are given unorthodox interpretations. Christians can be easily misled and deceived into accepting New Age ideas while still maintaining their allegiance to the Gospel.

Peter Moore, an Anglican,[20] provides yet another negative analysis of the New Age which he prefers to call 'cosmic humanism'. He lists six distinctive beliefs of the New Age which are not compatible with Christian doctrine: (1) all is one; (2) all is God; (3) humanity is God; (4) we need a change in consciousness; (5) all religions are one; and (6) the cosmos is evolving into the New Age. In his view, the New Age is exceedingly 'seductive', since pantheism was the natural religion of humankind. It is a pervasive movement, influencing many aspects of social life. Its philosophical roots are in monism, while its most recent origins stem from the late 1960s. Its success is related to the decline of the influence of traditional churches.

The popularity of the New Age is related both to the ideas and ideals it rejects and to the positive goals it promotes. In schematic fashion Moore states that the New Age stands against (1) human domination of nature; (2) logical or 'either/or' thinking; (3) male supremacy and a masculine God the Father; (4) Newtonian or 'mechanistic' science; (5) transcendence; (6) the Bible; (7) Jesus but not Christ; and (8) Christians. On the more positive side, the New Age stands for (1) world order; (2) getting back to nature; (3) a rediscovery of mysticism; (4) reincarnation; (5) personal prosperity; and (6) discovering one's human potential. But even here Moore finds serious problems with the New Age quest. Thus, for example, he laments that the stress on globalism is made at the expense of patriotism and nationalism and that the desire for non-Christian mysticism includes 'Lucifer as a prime fascination'.[21]

For Moore, the fundamental flaw in the New Age Movement is that it has no basis for moral action. Even though New Agers talk about harmony, sharing, loving, nurturing and peace-making, their philosophy lacks the essential elements for distinguishing right from wrong and does not endorse any absolute standard. The conclusion that there is nothing in the New Age which can, even vaguely, coexist with Christianity is not hard to draw. Moore's approach typifies one broad section of Protestant reaction to the presence and perceived threat of the New Age Movement that is sometimes said to be Christianity's 'new rival religion'.

Many Protestant commentators on the New Age are concerned about its evolutionary perspective. Some highlight it since they believe that it is central to New Age thought. John W. Cooper, for example, offering a Calvinist point of view, characterizes its world view as 'evolutionary spiritual monism' and its goal as total transformation, a salvation gained by raising one's awareness of unity and harmony. He then goes on to explain how the New Age is essentially unbiblical and anti-Christian. He writes:

[The New Age] denies the personal nature of God, erases the creator–creature distinction, denies a stable creation order, blurs creation and fall, removes the difference between good and evil, lacks an abiding moral order, refuses to admit sin and guilt, relativizes Jesus Christ, believes in self-salvation, and in a hundred other ways directly contradicts truths essential to biblical Christianity.[22]

The Christian fundamentalist opinion that the New Age is making dangerous inroads in almost all branches of Christianity has also been embraced by several Protestant writers. Morag Zwartz, a Baptist, subscribes to a view that is very similar to the infiltration theories adopted by fundamentalist Christians and described in Chapter 2. She defines the New Age movement as a synthesis of the philosophical and religious thought systems opposed to the truth of the Lord Jesus Christ and His Word.[23] For her the New Age, in spite of its clever use of Christian terms like unity, peace, and brotherly love, is emphatically anti-Christian. In an appendix[24] she schematically compares the 'truth' of Christianity with the 'counterfeit' of the New Age.

Zwartz is suspicious of all kinds of meditation which seem to have roots in Hinduism. She willingly admits that Christians can and should meditate on the Bible, by which she means reflecting on God's works, commandments, and love. But she quickly adds that[25] 'there is no biblical basis for making a doctrine out of this [meditation], or conducting studies and seminars on the subject'. All New Age practices, like imaging, visualization, and yoga, have no place in Christianity. Far from being harmless, they manifest satanic influences and have evil goals; they should, therefore, be resisted at all costs.

The total disparity between the New Age and Christian doctrine is often highlighted even by those who make careful comparisons between the two religions. Jim Graham[26] notes that, notwithstanding the many differences, there is some common ground between the New Age and Christianity. He lists two major similarities, namely, nurturing the spiritual and providing a sense of purpose and meaning, both of which are important dimensions in human life. But he is quick to add that the methods used to enhance one's spirituality and the meaning given to human life differ radically in the two religious systems. He then outlines fifteen major differences between the two religions, differences which include teachings regarding the nature of God, the nature of the person, the goal of life, the afterlife, and the place of Jesus Christ in the history of religions.

Some writers attempt to avoid a blanket denunciation of the New Age by distinguishing between the more speculative New Age writers and the popular movement. Jane E. Stohl, a Lutheran, for instance, concedes that between the New Age and Christianity there are some clear points of contact. She points out that in some New Age passages

> there are echoes of the theology of the cross and of the divine hiddenness in what is weak, even shameful, in the eyes of the world. There is acknowledgment of human failure; there is repentance and then the commitment to a new life of discipline.[27]

But she concludes that the New Age world view cannot be harmonized with that of Christianity. For the former it is only human beings who, by their own efforts, can improve the human condition and achieve a better world and society. Central to the New Age is the denial of sin which consequently leaves human beings cut off from God's grace. The search for redemption is thus 'perilous and undermines its summons to hope and joy'.[28]

The New Age and the Interfaith Movement

Probably one of the most comprehensive denunciations of the New Age Movement is that of Herbert J. Pollitt, a Baptist, who advances the thesis that the Interfaith Movement is imbued with the ideas and goals of the New Age. Pollitt adopts the stance common among other Baptists who attack the Interfaith Movement and its approach of interfaith dialogue. He criticizes its pluralistic tendency which, he believes, negates the uniqueness of Christianity, and its syncretistic trend which incorporates non-Christian elements in Christian theology and practice. He dedicates three chapters to refute, respectively, the endeavors of the Catholic Church, the World Council of Churches, and the Church of England to establish better relationships with people of different faiths.

His main thesis is that the tenets accepted by those involved in the Interfaith Movement are found, in one form or another, in the New Age Movement. He lists the following eight principles that guide the Interfaith Movement:

(1) the denial that Christ is the only incarnation and the final and complete revelation of God;

(2) the refusal to acknowledge that the death of Christ is salvific;

(3) the rejection that the Bible is the supreme authority in matters of faith;

(4) the contention that unity of religions can be achieved by exploring the mystical element found in all of them;

(5) the deification of human beings as well as of nature and the universe;

(6) the acknowledgment that sex is a way in which human beings can reach transcendence;

(7) the tendency (especially in such writers as Pierre Teilhard de Chardin and Matthew Fox) to see the whole universe as one with little regard for God's creativity;

(8) the striving for global consciousness which cannot be realized unless religions abandon their claims to exclusive truth.[29]

These principles are, in his opinion, practically identical to the theology of the New Age, which, together with the Interfaith Movement, should be denounced as an insidious modern development that can undermine the very foundations of Christianity and that ultimately leads to the destruction of individual responsibility and the moral world order.

Many Christian writers who reject the New Age are suspicious of any kind of interfaith relations. Tony Higton, after attacking the New Age as a human-centered and manipulative religion, moves on to discuss the issue of Christians compromising their faith through interfaith events in cathedrals. He is careful to point out that he does not object to friendly relations between people of different faiths nor to cooperation between them on moral and social issues. He further asserts that he supports the freedom of religion and of individual consciences. But he insists that Christians should not compromise their faith, and favors an exclusive theology of religion which rejects all other religions without any qualifications. Reflecting on certain types of religious dialogue and faith sharing, he states:

> any action by Christians which states or implies that there are ways to God other than through Jesus is in serious error. If God has provided only one way of salvation, we do a great disservice to mankind (and also dishonor to God) by compromising this truth.
>
> So if non-Christian gods are worshiped on church property, or if Christians worship alongside people of other faiths, at the very least this is implying that Christians agree that there are other ways to God (or even other gods).[30]

The same thesis of Pollitt and Higton is endorsed by Alan Morrison, who commends what he envisages as the prime objectives of the Ecumenical Movement, namely (1) uniting all believers and (2) preaching the fullness of the Gospel. But he detects a hidden agenda which is more akin to New Age tenets than to Biblical doctrine. Morrison seems certain that ecumenism has degenerated into syncretism and universalism and suggests that both the Catholic Church and many Protestant denominations have succumbed to the false beliefs of the Interfaith Movement. He synthesizes the flaws of ecumenism into four major areas: (1) rejection of the Bible as the authoritative word of God; (2) rejection of the corruption of human nature; (3) rejection of the judgment to come; and (4) rejection of the uniqueness of Christianity. It is not difficult to see how many of the major beliefs of the New Age can be fitted into one of these errors.

The rejection of New Age ideas has also filtered into semi-official Protestant responses to its presence and influence. Janet Bigland Pritchard, in a study made for several Anglican Bishops, relies heavily on evangelical works on the New Age Movement.[31] She starts by showing how the search for altered states of consciousness lies at the heart of the New Age spiritual journey. Then she briefly describes basic New Age concepts, including those dealing with the divine, Christ, and ethical relativism, and observes that the New Age is closely allied with the occult. She advises Christian leaders to watch out for New Age beliefs and symbols which filter into liturgies, retreat programs, and healing ministries.

She does not, however, propose an assault on the New Age. Departing from the fundamentalist reaction, she admits that there are some parts of New Age ideology, such as the concern for the environment, the desire for peace, and the quest for spiritual experiences, which are in accord with Christianity and which should, therefore, be welcomed.

Rejection of the New Age on logical grounds

A different criticism of the New Age is pursued by Roger E. Olson[32] who, offering a Baptist perspective, points out that the movement is diverse and dynamic and can be distinguished in two major camps, namely, the intellectuals, like Marilyn Ferguson, David Spangler, and George Trevelyan, and the experiential seekers, like Shirley MacLaine and the channelers. Yet it promotes a common world view which he labels 'mystical-occultism' or 'cosmic humanism'. Olson, rather than dismissing the New Age for its un-Christian theology or berating its leaders for their conspiratorial efforts, attempts a critical assessment of its world view by using the universal criteria of truth called 'critical realism'. He examines the New Age for internal harmony and coherence and discovers three major inconsistencies that permeate New Age thought, namely, relativism (New Age epistemology), monism (New Age ontology), and humanitarianism (New Age ethics). Thus, for example, he is ready to admit that many New Agers are compassionate, caring people. But he then raises the question of whether their compassion is logically compatible with the New Age tenet that the individual creates one's own reality. The New Age is thus rejected on logical rather than theological grounds.[33] Though many writers refer in passing to the lack of logic and reason in New Age Thought, few base their rejection of it on rational arguments.

Another effort to discredit the New Age Movement by shifting the debate from theological to rational grounds has been made by Ernest Lucas.[34] Starting with the New Age claim to be in harmony with contemporary scientific developments and speculations, Lucas examines its metaphysical framework to test whether its basic assumptions can be supported by modern science. He gives an overview of the New Age which he sees rooted in the counter-culture movements of the 1960s, the religions of the East, and the occult. He limits the New Age's foundational axioms to four, namely (1) monism, (2) pantheism, (3) relativism, and (4) autonomy. These principles are behind many of the activities for which New Agers have been attacked and criticized. Thus, monism leads to the support of international peace movements and encourages environmental groups; pantheism supports involvement in various interfaith events and stimulates the revival of animistic religions; relativism tolerates diverse and opposed beliefs and moral principles; while autonomy underlies much of the practices of the human potential movement. Further, for New Agers, rationality is replaced with experience which means that subjective, rather than objective, criteria receive priority. Consequently, Lucas sees a great contrast between Christian and New Age beliefs and theologies.

Lucas starts by proposing a Biblical response to the New Age and, like so many other Christian writers, finds that the Bible does not support the New Age view of Jesus, its belief in reincarnation, its views of God and human nature, and its theory of salvation through the removal of ignorance. He points out that the New Age stress on mysticism is another area of contention, particularly when seen from a Christian evangelical viewpoint. He concedes that the mystic may have an experience of God or of the harmony and unity of God's creation, but he warns that the mystical experience of oneness should not be pursued for itself. And he thinks that true mystical experience does not lead to the loss of one's personal identity.

These derogatory reflections on the New Age are commonly found in many Christian responses. Lucas, however, also makes an effort to refute the scientific underpinnings of the New Age Movement. New Agers appear to be totally opposed to scientific thinking, even though they appeal to modern science to justify their view of truth and reality. They have criticized science for its reductionism, its mechanistic, deterministic view of the universe, its stress on the rational at the expense of intuition and feeling, its tendency to divorce mind from matter, and its promotion of materialism which ignores or denies the spiritual aspect of life. They have appealed to modern science to buttress their ideology which sees the material world as an illusion, the universe as a unified, interconnected whole, human consciousness as playing a key role in creating reality, and reality as a phenomenon which can be known through experience and not through logic. Lucas's rebuttal is to show that the contrast 'between classical and quantum logic is largely invalid'. He further adds that, as a Christian, he finds himself in agreement with many of the criticisms New Agers make of science. But he thinks that what they are criticizing is not science but 'scientism', which he describes as 'a metaphysical construct which takes as one of its basic assumptions the belief that the scientific method is the *only* valid route to truth and that it therefore potentially provides us with a *comprehensive* view of reality'.[35] He underscores what he maintains to be a central Christian stance, namely, that a metaphysical-reductionistic view of the human person is totally opposed to the Christian doctrine of the nature of the human person and its relationship to God.

Eastern Orthodox responses

Probably the most consistent and unified assault against New Age ideas and practices has come from the Orthodox Church in America. Bishop Chrysostomos, for example, admits that the New

Age is hardly new and then goes on to enumerate three major features that encompass its ideology. It is first of all a utopian movement. It draws from the aspirations found in all religions regarding human restoration, salvation, and attainment of immortality, all of which, however, must be sought within each individual and in this physical world. Secondly, it is eclectic and syncretistic, claiming that all religious philosophies are evolving towards a universal truth, the essentials of which are found in all religions. And thirdly, it stresses the need of a guru or spiritual master who manifests the essence of divinity to his or her devotees. Chrysostomos rejects the New Age claim that humans are divine because of internal contradictions and maintains that Christianity 'is diametrically opposed to the tenets of "New Age" religions and rests on a compelling theological response to the philosophical dilemmas and inconsistencies which comprise these religions'.[36]

Chrysostomos maintains that, because the New Age offers teachings that are judged to be completely opposed to Christian doctrine, it can be regarded as the future religion of the Antichrist or, at least, as a preparation for that religion. He declares:

> The spirit of Antichrist is all that which usurps the dominion of Christ, which stands in his 'stead'. . . . For what other reason, indeed, do we fear the Antichrist as a deceiver, as one who claims the power and dominion of Christ? What is inimical to Christ is not only or primarily what opposes him, but that which falsely presents itself as the universal truth which Christ alone is.[37]

Moreover, the New Age is demonic for the simple reason that it usurps Christ's divinity. He further argues that

> [O]ne need not worship the devil as such to be demonic. All that deviates from the Divine Will, which is fully contained in Christ, is demonic. And anything that we worship, aside from the Christian God, is the devil. One may not be fully aware of this devil-worship while engaged in it, but such worship is nonetheless just that: the worship of the antithesis of God, the devil. And if the devil is proud, then what greater devil is there than the one that the 'New Agers' worship: man as the 'essence of God'.[38]

For Chrysostomos, Christians should take the New Age Movement seriously because (1) it is dangerous, as shown by the tragedy of Jonestown which was influenced by New Age ideology, and (2) it points to what is wrong with contemporary Christian churches, which are not providing spiritual nourishment for their members. He sees the New Age as a challenge to Christians to delve into their rich heritage and to strengthen their commitment to their faith.

A more comprehensive and disparaging analysis of the New Age has been made by Seraphim Rose,[39] whose works have influenced other Orthodox writers on the subject. Like Pollitt, Rose rejects participation in the Ecumenical Movement as a betrayal of orthodoxy since it appears to respect and accept non-Christian religions. Denying that there is any substantial common ground between Christian and non-Christian religions, whose gods are demons, Rose is suspicious of Hinduism that prepares people for a new universal religion which is scientific, based on evolution, founded on eternal principles, and able to satisfy the spiritual needs of different types of people. He further laments the invasion of Eastern meditation into Christianity. For him, Eastern techniques, like yoga, Zen, and Transcendental Meditation, have nothing in common with Christian mysticism, prayer, or religious experience. New religious groups, which include beliefs and practices found within the New Age Movement, are incompatible with Christianity and should be avoided at all costs for three major reasons: (1) they have no foundation in Christian belief and practice; (2) the meditative experiences they promote are encounters with demons; and (3) the initiation into psychic experiences which they promote are dangerous because they open one to the attacks of fallen spirits.

This negative anti-ecumenical stance has a long history in some segments of the Orthodox Church. About thirty years ago, Metropolitan Vitay wrote:

> There is only God, there is His One, only Apostolic Church, and there is the whole human race all called to God through His Holy Church. All other religions, so-called Christian, monotheistic or pagan, all without the slightest exception, whether Catholicism, Protestantism, Islam or Buddhism – all are obstacles placed by the devil and his traps between the Church of God and the whole human race.[40]

New Age themes, like astrology, UFOs, and Witchcraft, are judged to be idolatrous or diabolical in nature.[41] Alexander Karloutsos, for example, states that it is sinful for a Christian to pay any attention to astrology, involvement in which is prohibited by the canon law of the Orthodox Church. He likens astrology to idolatry and labels it 'astrolatry'.[42] David Ritchie goes further and assures his readers that astrological symbolism is diabolical in character and will play a key role in the founding of the kingdom of the Antichrist. He warns that astrology encourages or tolerates involvement in more serious occult activities. Consequently it 'is anything but innocuous. It is one of the dark arts devised by the Devil for his servants; and serious involvement with astrology can mean only danger, both for the individual who practices and for the society that encourages its use.'[43]

The same interpretation is given to the flying saucer phenomenon. Rose[44] dedicates a whole chapter to the current interest and belief in UFOs and, after reviewing some of the main research on the topic, concludes that sightings of, and contacts with, flying saucers and alien beings are to be included with paranormal events which are considered by some to be miracles. Encounters with UFOs are likened to mediumistic techniques by which people are introduced to the occult realm of Satan and are judged to be a preparation for the coming of the Antichrist. Ritchie,[45] relying largely on Rose's analysis, is convinced that there are some definite similarities between extraterrestrial and demonic activities. Even the sexual acts described by abductees are 'essentially identical to the reported behavior of incubi and succubi' (which are respectively male and female spirits or demons who are believed to have sexual intercourse with men and women). He warns that there is a strong connection between UFOs and other occult activity. Extraterrestrials have the goal of introducing a social order based on occultism and the worship of the Antichrist.

None of the above-mentioned Orthodox writers reflects in any depth on the causes which lead people to join New Age groups or on the good and attractive qualities which the New Age might offer them. Hieromonk Damascene is a startling exception to this trend. In agreement with most orthodox writers he presents the Orthodox faith as the epitome of Christianity and of all religion, and admits that the Christian apologetical writings that refute New Age teachings are valuable in that they help Christians steer away from spiritual dangers. However, he goes on to point out that the New Age directs people to certain fundamentals of the spiritual life which the Orthodox Church has never abandoned but might have neglected. Referring to the many works that denounce the New Age, he states:

> What most of these books fail to mention, however, is that Eastern religionists and New Agers also have an important point. ... They have searched outside of Christian churches because these

churches have, in a sense, failed them. In substituting head-knowledge and emotional highs for experiential Truth, they are not teaching the basics, which the ancient Eastern religions have preserved. These basics are: 1) how to be free of compulsive think-ing and acquire stillness of thoughts; 2) how to cut off desires and addictions; and 3) how to conquer negative emotions.[46]

Practical replies to the New Age

Many Christian writers provide some practical suggestions for deal-ing with what is perceived as a threat or a challenge. Their responses are generally influenced by their rejection of New Age ideology and/or by their fears that anything connected with the New Age might taint the purity of Christian belief. Some, like Won Yong Ji,[47] follow the evangelical reaction and advise Christian pastors and mis-sionaries to engage in more systematic distribution of Christian literature, to develop means of better communication of the Gospel message, to give priority to a Christian lifestyle, and to restructure the theological curriculum in seminaries.

Others propose more elaborate means of counteracting the New Age. Winkler,[48] for instance, encourages Christians to: (1) grow in the knowledge of their faith; (2) learn about New Age ideas; (3) be alert as to how the New Age affects and infiltrates into their lives; (4) rely on the truth of the Gospel; (5) pray for strength to stand firm in their traditional beliefs. Lochhaas[49] divides the Christian response into three parts. First of all Christians must develop a per-sonal knowledge of the truth which will make them cognizant of the deceptions of New Agers who teach, for example, that reincarnation is taught in the Bible and that it provides them with hope for the future. Second, they should minister to people more positively by contributing to social, economic, and ecological programs and by fostering human development. And, finally, they should engage in evangelization. Moore[50] recommends that Christians should relate to the New Age (1) knowledgeably, (2) self-critically, (3) scrip-turally, (4) prayerfully, and (5) challengingly. He rejects the sensational approach to the New Age and admits that weaknesses in Christianity have contributed to the success of the New Age. He encourages Christians to study the scripture and to take a con-frontational approach to the New Age by pointing out its weaknesses and inconsistencies.

Because the New Age Movement is often conceived as a spiritual struggle between good and evil forces, many of the concrete responses to its presence rely heavily on scriptural references that deal with the conflict between God and evil. Thus, in typical fashion, Morrison[51] thinks that Christians should follow the example of Paul and put on the 'armor of God' which consists of the following items: (1) the belt of truth; (2) the breastplate of righteousness; (3) the preparedness of the Gospel of peace; (4) the shield of faith; (5) the helmet of salvation; (6) the sword of the spirit which is the word of God; and (7) prayer in the spirit. This, he believes, is 'the complete strategy for dealing with any demonic influence in the life of a Christian'.

In spite of the general negativity that characterizes these responses to the New Age, some writers are a little more cautious. Cooper, for instance, even though he totally rejects the New Age, urges caution and not a hysterical crusade. He warns that not all those involved in preserving the earth and in holistic health are necessarily evil in their intentions and that not all neopagans and Zen Buddhists are commited to the evolutionism of the New Age. In an implicit admonishment to many Christian responses, he asserts: 'We ought not to condemn mindlessly everything that resembles the New Age.'[52]

Others, like Winkler,[53] commend New Age ideals of good nutrition, concern for the environment, and work for peace and nuclear disarmament. But they maintain that these pursuits become dangerous when they are based on a New Age philosophy and spirituality. Still others agree that many of 'the concepts adopted by the New Age movement may provide mental and physical well-being in a limited way'.[54] Good nutrition, exercise, relaxation, and concern for the environment are mentioned as positive contributions by the movement. But their value is downplayed by the statement that the New Age can do nothing about sickness and death and that it 'does not really satisfy the spiritual vacuum in modern society'.

ACCEPTANCE OF NEW AGE IDEOLOGY

The negative reaction to the New Age is sometimes spurred on by the activities of some Christian churches that leave the impression that many New Age ideas can be easily incorporated into Christianity. Foremost among these churches are St. James's Church, in Piccadilly, London and St. John the Divine in Manhattan, New York City.

The open-arms approach of St. James is based on its pastor's view that the Church must treat in a friendly manner all those who are on a genuine spiritual quest, but are not prepared to accept a rigid Christianity that stresses dogma over experience. Without necessarily adopting New Age ideas, its rector, Donald Reeves, admits that the New Age can offer the Church many insights and that both Christians and New Agers can learn from one another. Creative spirituality figures prominently in St. James's programs, which do not limit themselves to Christian ecumenism but encourage interfaith dialogue.

The most controversial program at St. James is known as 'Alternatives', which is directed by William Bloom, a prominent British New Ager, and which covers a broad variety of New Age topics without any Christian input or evaluation. The brochure describing the 1996 Spring/Summer program makes it clear, if not explicit, that those who run it are simply using the premises of the church which is conveniently located in the heart of London. It states:

> Alternatives at St. James is dedicated to creative spiritual alternatives. Our purpose is to provide a friendly atmosphere in which to taste the best of these ideas. We are dedicated to the freedom of each individual to choose their own path of personal and spiritual growth. We are dedicated to exploring new consciousness. We warmly welcome people from diverse ethnic, sexual, religious, and agnostic backgrounds.

The offerings in their programs of talks and workshops contain typical New Age themes like Eastern meditation, channeling, psychic protection, personal transformation, and spiritual growth.

Some Anglicans hold that St. James has capitulated to the New Age and has become totally imbued with its spirit. Tony Higton,[55] for instance, contends that this Anglican church is heavily involved in the New Age. He complains that St. James has become 'a scandal of the first order' because it allows programs on Eastern religions, Paganism, and the occult to be offered on its premises. Morrison[56] concurs and accuses St. James of becoming a 'Model New Age Church' which aims at destroying the true Gospel of Christ.

Others, however, interpret the presence of Alternatives in the church more as a kind of coexistence than infiltration or even genuine dialogue. M. Perry writes that 'the arms' length policy which St. James Church operates towards Alternatives means that there is no meeting of minds between them on a Monday evening' and that 'Alternatives itself is organized and presented as frankly and completely New Age without any Christian veneer'.[57] Yet while Perry concedes that the principle of walking beside the New Age rather than firing shots at it is a good one, he fears that, in St. James's case, the Church might be going too far by hosting ideas which are quite incompatible with even the most liberal Christian theology.

Similar attacks have been made against the work done at St. John the Divine, an Episcopal church in New York City, which has played a host to diverse New Age groups and which is heavily involved in interfaith relations. St. John has been accused of harboring New Age themes and goals especially because it houses the Temple of Understanding, an interfaith organization. The Temple is an organization that has three major goals, namely, to promote understanding between the world's religions, to recognize the oneness of the human family, and to achieve a spiritual United Nations. It publishes a journal, *World Faiths Insight*, which deals with the relationship between different religions and organizes dialogue sessions between people of different faiths.

Other independent organizations look favorably on the New Age Movement and make efforts to promote dialogue between it and Christianity. Among these is Bethsheva's Concern, an organization based in Clifton, New Jersey, that publishes a magazine entitled *Christian*New Age Quarterly* which aims at expressing the voices of:

> Christians who wish to explore the spectrum of new age possibilities, but within the context of the Christian faith.
> New age visionaries who wonder at the Person of Jesus, are drawn toward an intimate relationship with Him, or simply wish to enlarge their understanding of Him free from proselytizing hints.
> Christian new agers who have discovered the wondrous unity of the Christian and new age paths – and that their walk with Jesus grows ever more vibrant as their new age vision expands!
> Anyone excited by unraveling the interconnectedness of spiritual understanding and courageously aware that essential diversity itself spawns spiritual growth.[58]

Bethsheva's Concern aims at improving the relationship between Christians and New Agers, a relationship which has been marked by distrust, and to establish one of healthy dialogue rather than one of mutual condemnation. It maintains that there is more affinity than contrast between those Christians and New Agers 'who touch and are touched by the Spirit'.

Catherine Groves, the editor of its magazine, has argued that there is a high degree of misunderstanding between Christians and New Agers. She admits that while 'most New Agers highly esteem all religious vantages, there festers a curious resentment toward conventional Christianity, which is typically dismissed as hypocritical and dictatorial'. Christians, on the other hand, often disparage the New Age Movement as a dangerous cult, a satanic deception, or a fad. In spite of the many diversities within the New Age Movement, there is, according to Groves, 'a centralizing integrity, a way of viewing life as intrinsically meaningful, sacred, and interconnected. Reminiscent in some ways of the mystic strain of our own Christian heritage, New Agers court the sublime in everyday experience, drawn into a dance with the divine.'[59] She thinks that, although many 'quasi-gnostic, monistic elements' permeate the movement, Christians can be renewed by its presence and vitality.

Several individual Christians are held responsible for promoting New Age philosophy. Among the most popular writers who are repeatedly criticized for their allegiance to the New Age are M. Scott Peck and Morton Kelsey.

Peck starts his comments on the New Age by rejecting the conspiracy theory. He explains that Marilyn Ferguson entitled her book *The Aquarian Conspiracy* with tongue in cheek, a kind of reaction against Christian fundamentalists who have declared the movement to be a satanic conspiracy to undermine Christianity. For Peck,[60] the New Age Movement is a reaction against the sins of Western civilization, particularly the sins of 'the emptiness of the spirit and the arrogance, narcissism, and blasphemy of the Christian Church', the sin of science, which has led us to 'technological inhumanity', and the sins of capitalism, imperialism, and the exploitation of the environment and people.

While lauding the New Age for its openness to new ideas and virtues and for leading people in the direction of wholeness and integration, Peck certainly does not think that it is an unmixed blessing. He berates it for going to extremes, thus creating 'a considerable amount of spiritual confusion', and dismissing Christian doctrine rather than the behavior of Christians who do not follow the teachings of their faith. He finds its refusal to admit the presence of evil unrealistic and its tendency to encourage 'adventuring without discernment' dangerous. Labeling Peck a New Age advocate is a misunderstanding of his carefully articulated and balanced approach, and designating him as 'the therapeutic high priest of the new spirituality'[61] is a gross exaggeration.

Another writer who has been targeted by Christian writers as an advocate of New Age themes is Morton Kelsey,[62] who was writing on New Age topics before the New Age movement reached its popularity in the 1980s. For Kelsey, the New Age is a reaction to the agnostic materialism of modern society which has found its way into Christian life and theology. Kelsey faults contemporary Christianity for ignoring the dimension of experience, for abandoning the practicing of meditation, and neglecting the importance of dreams. He finds that some New Age interests and practices, like channeling, ESP, and healing, need not be condemned and have a place in Christianity.

Kelsey's theory appears to be that the New Age is replacing Christianity in fulfilling the needs of the faithful and that its stress on experience, rather than on reason, was central among early Christians. He observes:

> Conventional Christianity that relies on authority and reason, rather than on human experience, has become unpalatable to many modern Western religious seekers. In its most vital days the Christian community laid great stress on the human experience of the risen Christ and on the gifts of the spirit, observable evidences of the spiritual dimension's influences on our ordinary human lives.[63]

Rather than condemn the teachings and practices of the New Age, Kelsey directs his attention towards the religious needs which acceptance of its ideology and participation in its activities are fulfilling. He suggests that the Christian Church can meet the religious needs of contemporary men and women. He urges the churches to stress the resurrection of Jesus and the effect it had on his followers, to provide classes in various forms of prayer, to create prayer groups where people can share their spiritual lives and religious experiences, and to show that the church is a healing, listening, and loving community.[64]

Other Protestant writers have also been interpreted as offering an uncritical acceptance of the New Age theology. Bruce Epperly, for instance, while admitting that there are some weaknesses in both New Age ideology and practice, maintains that there are good elements which Christianity can borrow. He starts with the assumptions that Christianity and the New Age need not coexist in conflict but rather in harmony and that both systems of belief can benefit from mutual interactions. 'The New Age', he writes, 'presents a significant and creative challenge to Christian faith. Today, Christians are called to listen prayerfully to the voices of truth and love within the New Age Movement and to hear in these strange and alien tongues messages that have been forgotten or repressed in our own heritage.'[65] Rather than being a diabolically inspired movement, the New Age is a catalyst for Christians to explore creative visions of spirituality, healing, revelation, and survival after death.

Epperly admits that the success of the New Age Movement is, in part at least, due to Christianity's failure to fulfill the needs of its adherents. Because of its inclusiveness and openness to culture, mainstream Christianity has emphasized the horizontal dimension of life and a commitment to social issues. But this has led to a partial neglect of the vertical dimension which includes the spiritual aspirations of the human heart.

There are, according to Epperly, four major components of the New Age with which Christianity can enter into dialogue: (1) the unity of all life, which is related to the Christian teaching about the Body of Christ; (2) the higher self, which bears resemblance to the Christian belief in the Christ within; (3) the power of the mind, or the process of sanctification in Christianity; and (4) spiritual technologies, or the methods of spiritual formation. He explores the New Age practice of channeling, which he compares to the Christian teaching on revelation and biblical inspiration; the stress on healing, which he believes is central also to the Christian Church; and the New Age thinking of Jesus, which he examines in the context of modern christology.

It would be a mistake to conclude that Epperly succeeds in reconciling Christianity with the New Age. It would be equally erroneous to insinuate that he is a New Age advocate. He has certainly attempted to build a bridge between Christianity and the New Age and offered some useful and insightful criticisms on central New Age themes. Thus, for example, he judges the New Age philosophical attitude that stresses self-healing to be rather simplistic, unaware of the complexity of human life, and neglectful of grace.[66] The New Age, according to him, has not really addressed the need of community nor has it developed greater social responsibility.[67]

A more tempered approach to the New Age is clear in several writers who believe that its presence has created opportunities for Christians to renew their faith. Typical of this approach are the reflections of Dan Wakefield,[68] a Unitarian/Universalist, who has pointed out that some 'age-old practices being introduced through non-church avenues of spirituality need not necessarily be seen as a challenge or diversion to either church or synagogue but as an opportunity to refresh, enliven, and strengthen one's own religious faith'. Wakefield[69] has in mind meditative practices and Christianized forms of yoga and mantra chanting. He argues that the borrowing of alternative practices from other traditions is healthy and invigorating. His approach gives qualified endorsement of some New Age beliefs and practices while stressing the need for Christians to return to the sources of their own rich tradition.

BALANCED EVALUATIONS OF THE NEW AGE

The majority of Protestant responses to the New Age Movement have attempted to steer a middle road between the confrontational and condemnatory approach and the more accommodating ones. They have, directly or indirectly, rebuffed the negative approach, even when they admit that it is difficult, if not impossible, to harmonize the major tenets of the New Age with traditional Christian teaching.

M. Perry, for instance, writes that the negative reaction to the New Age seems 'to have fallen into the trap of overestimating both the power and the ubiquity of New Age thinking, and on indiscriminately tarring with the New Age brush everything which does not accord with its own perception of acceptable Christian thought and behavior'.[70] And again: 'This whole approach is specifically designed to draw sharp lines between what its proponents regard as authentic Christianity and anything which can be remotely construed as having anything to do with the New Age.'[71] And Ernest Lucas, implicitly referring to some extremely negative Christian assessments of the New Age, cautions:

> There is need to avoid both paranoia and naiveté. It is paranoic to regard all those interested in international organizations or green issues as 'New Age'. However, it is naive not to recognize that there are some pressure groups and individuals involved in the areas that are inspired by the NAM.[72]

Many Protestant writers acknowledge that the New Age has positive things to offer. David Millikan, an Anglican, admits from the start that the New Age has an affirmative view of life, which is seen as neither tragic nor sad, but rather as full of hope and potential. The New Age, for him, is 'a product of the loss of power and influence of the middle class in contemporary society'. He explains

how in the midst of modern crises, like overpopulation, big business, environmental issues, and poverty, the New Age addresses
those who have 'lost their sense of potency and significance' and
'encourages the belief that we are not powerless pawns in the global
game'.[73] Hence the New Age stresses that human beings can control
their own destinies.

Another writer, Keith Innes,[74] while observing that the New Age
leads to involvement in occult and various forms of Witchcraft, to
the integration of good and evil, and to the belief in reincarnation
and in the immanence of God, does not dismiss its emphasis on the
paradigm shift since this metaphor does describe changes that are
actually taking place in contemporary culture. For him, directing
human beings to rely more on their intuitive thinking has its positive aspects which should be pursued.

The effort to reach a deeper understanding and a more balanced
appraisal of the New Age Movement has been pursued by several
authors. Philip Seddon,[75] for instance, echos the sentiments of
Lucas and seeks an assessment of the New Age that steers away from
both paranoia and naïveté. He suggests that it would be helpful not
only to see its historical roots, but also to consider it as being made
up of three levels. The first level is its variety, a variety that incorporates different movements and ideologies and which has no center.
The second level consists of a number of themes that pervade the
movement, namely, the quest for unity, the criticism of Christianity
as bankrupt, the desire for a higher consciousness, and the search
for genuine religiousness. The third level is a conscious embracing
of occultism as an alternative to Christianity which is thought of as
an exoteric, shallow religion.

The New Age, according to Seddon, can be summed up in four
basic themes and questions. The first deals with the questions of origins; the second with a new vision of wholeness and harmony; the
third with ecology; and the fourth with spirituality. It brings to the
fore certain vital concerns which are relevant to the problems
human beings face and which 'offer great opportunities for
Christian participation'. These concerns are: (1) the dehumanizing
effects of scientific reductionism; (2) the wasting effects of secular-
ism; (3) the deceptions of materialism; (4) the international rape of
the earth; (5) the threat of the end of history; (6) the search for
personal significance; and (7) religious jockeying for superiority.
In spite of these areas of contact, the New Age is rather ambivalent
and endorses beliefs and values which are unacceptable. Thus, its

monistic slant, its treatment of truth as relative, its acceptance of religious evolution as a central myth, its leaning towards totalitarianism, its feminist stress that leads to the worship of a goddess, and its Paganism are all seen as negative features that clash with Christian teachings.

Although Seddon makes some insightful comments on the New Age, he still leans towards the conspiracy theory. He advises Christians to respond to the New Age by being sober and vigilant lest they drift into syncretism or apostasy or succumb to the seduction of counterfeit spirituality and the spirit of the Antichrist. They should rely on God and be well grounded in their faith.

A more conciliatory tone is taken by Philip Almond,[76] who, writing in an Anglican magazine, starts by observing that the New Age is a religious movement that 'is playing a significant role in the construction of late twentieth-century Western consciousness'. He traces it to the Theosophical tradition and thinks it is more of a resurgence of the Western esoteric tradition that includes neo-Platonism, Gnosticism, Hermeticism, medieval magic, and alchemy, and that has sometimes existed in creative tension with orthodox Christianity. He holds that, while there are millenarian and apocalyptic trends in the New Age, it would be a mistake to conclude that all New Agers are expecting the end of the world, since there is a strong secularist ideology that pervades the movement. A utopian vision in which all creation exists in harmony and which underlies environmental concerns dominates New Age thought.

Almond's position is that, when seen as 'a reaction to the technological rationalism and materialism of late twentieth century culture', as 'a declaration of spirit over matter', and as a religious movement that 're-establishes the connection between the mundane and the transcendent',[77] the New Age has something to teach those Christians who have been swept away by the secularization process in Western culture.

Another Anglican commentator, Gavin McGrath, admits that the New Age eludes definitions and suggests that one would be more accurate in referring to New Age movements or expressions which are united by a world view of cosmic humanism. He identifies six aspects of the movement: (1) all is one; (2) all is God; (3) you are God; (4) the need for correct awareness; (5) all religions are one; and (6) things are progressing positively.

Like many other Christians, McGrath takes the New Age seriously. He states that it is possibly one of the significant cultural, intellectual, scientific and spiritual developments in Western culture since the Enlightenment. It is significant because the different expressions of the New Age movement or, as it is also called, the 'new consciousness', are not merely part of a passing fad meriting only a passing nod. In many ways they are a collective expression of our Western culture's intellectual, philosophical and spiritual zig zags over the past one hundred years.[78]

The New Age is often manifest in five modern trends or issues that can be found in daily life: (1) holistic health care; (2) certain expressions of radical feminism; (3) the ecology movement; (4) quantum science; and (5) global unity.

McGrath points out that Christianity differs from the New Age in its teachings on (1) the nature of God, (2) uniqueness of Jesus Christ, (3) the nature of humanity, (4) the nature of the cosmos, and (5) the possibility of knowledge. But he thinks that 'one should not be afraid to look for elements of God's truth in some of the New Age movement's manifestations'.[79]

He concludes by affirming that the Christian response to the New Age should not be one of panic, even though he seems certain that Satan is involved 'in a global and heavenly conspiracy'. He acknowledges that some elements in the New Age mirror the pains and confusion of modern men and women who want to respond to secular humanism with a spiritual alternative. And while he recommends compassion and witness, he also favors an intellectual response to the challenge of the New Age. He voices his concern with the irrational and anti-intellectual elements that are prevalent in New Age quarters and insists that Christians should not be influenced by these damaging tendencies. In line with many evangelicals he concludes:

> The New Age movement is ultimately based on a lie . . . New Age thinking misconstrues what is true and real. Accordingly, it actually minimizes the dignity of men and women. It blinds them from the truth, which in turn leads them to immorality and culminates in further rebellion and rejection of the one true God.[80]

Many writers are aware that Christians often find the teachings of the New Age rather confusing. Joyce Watson attempts to draw a picture of the New Age especially for those Christians who are both attracted to and baffled by its teachings. She traces three major sources of the New Age, namely, astrology, the cultural setting, and several spiritual roots. New Age spirituality, she holds, is based on a monistic world view which teaches that people should realize their own divine nature and which makes no clear distinction between good and evil. Gnosticism, Eastern religions, Paganism, humanism, Theosophy, the occult, creation-centered spirituality, and reincarnation are all components of the New Age, making it a different religion from Christianity. The New Age view of Jesus also departs from Christian orthodoxy.

The New Age has developed a practical spirituality that includes altered states of consciousness, prayer and meditation, and guidance through horoscopes, astrology, and channeling, all of which seem incompatible with Christianity. But New Agers, according to Watson, are looking for what can be readily found in Christianity. She writes: 'The tragedy is that many of those who look within the new age for power do so because they do not expect to find it in Christianity. Nothing can be further from the truth. From the very earliest days of the church up to the present day lives have been transformed and miracles have happened.'[81] She cites the Charismatic renewal as one example of the power within Christianity to change people for the better.

Watson[82] states that an individual can be led to involvement in New Age ideas and practices through many 'entry points', such as politics, interfaith dialogue, feminism, and concern for peace and justice. Two major New Age areas of concern, namely, healing and ecology, have been particularly responsible for attracting Christians to the New Age. Much of alternative healing, such as mind power, crystal power, faith healing, and yoga, draws on occult or psychic power to promote physical, psychological, and mental well-being. New Age healing techniques are based on philosophies of life and death that are not in harmony with the Gospel. While New Age healing is not necessarily always bad, it cannot be reconciled with Christianity, for Christian healing is based on the power of Christ and is complementary rather than opposed to orthodox medicine.

People are sometimes attracted to the New Age through their concern for ecology. New Age and Christianity approach the current ecological crisis quite differently. The former relies on the 'Gaia' theory which considers the earth to be a living organism, a kind of earth goddess, with the power to think and feel. Watson's opinion is that 'the Christian response to the "Gaia" theory is the recognition of a God-given balance of nature', a balance that has been upset by the fall of Adam and Eve. The solution to the ecological problem is not to treat the earth as a goddess but rather to restore the original relationship between God and human beings. Watson maintains that the New Age accusations that Christians are not really concerned with saving the planet are unfounded. She tries to show that various Christian organizations are dedicated to ecological issues without having recourse to New Age ideas or to the 'Gaia' hypothesis.

While she does not rule out the possibility that the New Age might be susceptible to satanic influences, Watson rejects the idea that the New Age is part of a satanic conspiracy to take over the world or that it is a sign of the end-times. She writes: 'There is a subtle danger in assuming that the New Age is inevitably the fulfillment of the Biblical prophecy regarding the end times – it can cause feelings of impotence and fatalism, and may hinder effective Christian witness and service.'[83] The New Age is, for her, a challenge for Christians to reexamine their own faith and to engage in evangelical endeavors. New Agers must be approached not through discussion, but rather through discernment and prayer.

Some writers have presented a rather broad definition of the New Age as an alternative religion. Philip L. Barnes, an Anglican, states that the 'New Age movement can be described as "an alternative spiritual tradition", that is, an alternative to the more familiar, and until recently in the West, the culturally dominant, Judeo-Christian tradition'.[84] He agrees with many other writers that the more recent roots of the movement lie in the counterculture of the late 1960s. He suggests that the following New Age terms and expressions are indicative of the movement's ideology and goals: self-realization, at-one-ment, personal and social transformation, cosmic consciousness, the Christ principle, the cosmic Christ, spiritual awareness, inner harmony, reconciliation, and the Higher Self within.

Barnes reiterates one of the most common criticisms of the New Age Movement, namely, its acceptance of some form of pantheism which is judged to be in direct opposition to the Christian belief in the transcendence of God. But in his analysis of the theology of the movement, he distinguishes between 'pantheism' and 'panentheism', a distinction that might be useful in understanding the New Age's view of God. The former refers to the belief that God and the universe are identical; the latter to the belief that, while the universe is a part of God, God consists of more than the universe. The latter leaves room for God's transcendence and seeks to combine the positive features of both theism and pantheism and has some similarities to the God of process theology.[85] Although Barnes ends up by rejecting panentheism as incoherent, his analysis of the New Age concept of God may lead to a better understanding of the New Age and open the door to dialogue.

Finally, Barnes proposes that the response of the Christian Church to the New Age should be two-pronged, intellectual and practical. The Christian Church should make a greater effort to demonstrate the credibility of its interpretation of reality and to show that it is able to satisfy the spiritual needs of individuals. He concludes by affirming:

> The New Age Movement witnesses to the longing of the human spirit for communion with God. The challenge of the Church is to show through its life and service that man's intellectual and spiritual needs are met in Christ in a way that cannot be met elsewhere.[86]

A slightly different approach to the New Age is provided by Frank Whaling, who provides a Methodist viewpoint. He speculates that the New Age religion should not be confused with living religious traditions, even though it might borrow several elements from them. Further, the New Age should be distinguished from the new religious movements because, unlike so many of them, it tends to be individualistic, flexible, and unstructured.

Whaling identifies six elements in New Age religion and thought: (1) the idea of moving into a new age or millennium; (2) the link it makes between new paradigms and the philosophy of science; (3) the focus on ecology and female issues; (4) a concern with healing; (5) a stress on the human potential and on the need not to undervalue human possibilities and potentials; and (6) an awareness of an inner voice which is seen as God's Spirit speaking from within and which is based on the immanent nature of God. He asserts that:

> Christians can largely affirm the elements that have been mentioned so far: the new science, holistic thought, a concern for ecology, a concern for women's rights, a concern for global issues, and a recognition of the power of healing, human potential and inward spirituality. Vibrant Christians can ally with New Age thought and sometimes are 'new age' in these matters.[87]

Whaling advises that the New Age should be taken seriously, though its influence should not be overstressed. He concedes that Christians can learn a lot from New Age thought, but warns that there are several areas of New Age involvement that the Christian should approach with caution. He highlights three aspects of the New Age about which one should be wary. Channeling is one area where great discretion is needed. While channeling might alert us to some spiritual needs, it can also cater to the gullibility of some New Agers who are taken advantage of by channelers. He objects to channeling not because, as many evangelicals claim, it has a dark side, but rather because it is a 'banal' practice and a diversion from direct contact with God.

Secondly, Whaling disagrees with the New Age tenet that psychic and spiritual power are similar if not identical. For him psychic power is neutral and devoid of moral content. He contends that the discernment of spirits is needed to determine genuine spiritual phenomena.

Thirdly, Whaling acknowledges that the New Age poses some challenges to certain Christian doctrines, such as the nature and role of Christ. He maintains that some New Age depictions of Jesus are sheer speculations with no historical foundation.

The understanding of the New Age in the light of the human yearning to be religious is echoed by other writers. Carol E. Becker,[88] an Evangelical Lutheran, argues that Christian criticism of the New Age Movement for its gnostic and pagan tendencies is fruitless. She prefers an approach that concentrates on the renewal of Christian faith 'in a meaningless, empty, and unhappy time'. In her opinion, the mainline churches are challenged by the New Age to be transformed. She adopts a position towards the New Age not common among Protestants. Rather than dwelling on those aspects of the New Age which cannot be harmonized with Christianity, she concentrates on the need for renewal within the Church. She proposes reforms along the following lines: (1) a development of a new religious consciousness in which we experience faith and learn to see the immanence of God in nature; (2) an effort to speak to the hearts of Christians in preaching and teaching; (3) a commitment to a faith system that is accessible to everybody and not just the elite; (4) an awareness that technology must be used to make life more personal and meaningful; (5) an understanding of the importance to communicate our faith in an attractive and meaningful fashion; (6) a dedication 'to address the public versus the private in our culture'; and (7) a striving for a new depth in our spirituality, art, and symbols.

One of the more comprehensive analyses of the New Age has

been provided by Ted Peters, a Lutheran, who avoids the condemnatory approach common in many Christian circles. He starts his reflections by looking at a number of areas, like astrology, holistic health, channeling, UFOs, and theosophy, all of which testify to the presence of the New Age in our midst. The New Age for him is not a cult, nor a business, nor a social or political movement. Rather 'it is best thought of as a phenomenon of cultural consciousness. It consists of a set of cosmological ideas and spiritual practices that nobody owns but that are widely shared by diverse groups and individuals.'[89] In spite of the wide variety of beliefs and practices in the movement, Peters maintains that a few common themes can be discerned:

> The direction is becoming clear: one moves into the direction of the inner life, but this eventually opens out onto the whole of the cosmos. It leads to identification of the self with the whole of the cosmos and with God. It also leads to the idea of transformation, of transforming oneself as well as the whole of society.[90]

With this short description in mind Peters draws up what he calls the 'Eightfold Path' of the New Age Movement: (1) holism; (2) monism; (3) the higher self; (4) potentiality; (5) reincarnation; (6) evolution and transformation; (7) gnosis; and (8) Jesus (sometimes). He concludes that the New Age 'is built upon gnostic foundations with a superstructure that combines Asian mysticism with some key Western ideas such as evolution and psychological wholeness'.[91]

Peters, further, thinks the movement's overall gnostic thrust is too naive and unrealistic and fails to acknowledge the presence of evil in human beings and in the cosmos at large. For Peters, the cosmic wholeness the New Age strives for is to be found in the future and not in the present by cultivating a higher consciousness. Further, a greater power, that is, God, is needed in our struggle against evil. At the same time Peters finds several good elements in the New Age spirituality, particularly its stress on integrating both the physical and spiritual dimensions of human life. In like manner he applauds some New Age practices and decries others. He writes:

> On the one hand, it appears to me that the new age is for the most part harmless and, in some cases, even helpful. Even if the theology is questionable, its ebullient optimism has a way of cheering up the downcast and making a damaged soul feel good about itself.

Nevertheless, there is an identifiable dark side to the new age. It can lead to abuse, to psychological damage, even to rape and death. This is not obvious when one looks only at the pacific ideals of unity and bliss. Yet there is danger. The danger arises when new age teachings take on a cult form.[92]

Peters examines the new cosmology as exemplified in the works of Fritjof Capra and David Bohm[93] and maintains that their works should be taken seriously. The modern world is indeed breaking down and theologians cannot ignore this cultural event. Systematic theologians should search for a philosophy which is both post-modern and still does not contradict the basic elements of the Christian faith.

Finally, Peters draws up a fourfold scheme for responding to the New Age. Unlike many Christian responses, his suggestions do not dwell exclusively on doctrinal issues and acknowledge some of the good elements in the movement's overall ideology and spiritual practices. In brief, he states that:

(1) *'Modest dabbling in new age spirituality is probably harmless; it may even be helpful'.*

(2) *'the new age vision is a noble and edifying one'.*

(3) *'pastors, theologians, and church leaders should take the new age movement seriously'.*

(4) *'the gnostic monism at the heart of new age teaching is dangerous because it leads to naiveté and to a denial of God's grace'.*[94]

One of the more thorough and schematic evaluations of the New Age is offered by Glenn A. Olds, a Methodist, who dwells on its enduring and constructive themes, its limits and liabilities, and its lessons. He commends the New Age for affirming the 'intrinsic integrity and inviolate authenticity of the *self's awareness of itself*', the 'primacy of *personal choice and responsibility* as uniquely human', and 'the intrinsic and personal access to the Divine' without any inter-mediary.[95] He endorses its stress on the wholistic nature of reality, on human potential, and on the power of positive thinking. And he approves of the New Age's quest for values, meaning, and goodness in nature and in humanity, its goal of restoring balance in human life, and its contribution to the development of a theology of the environment.

Olds, however, is aware of some of the problems that underlie both the philosophical and theological foundations of the move-ment. He finds that the New Age is seriously in danger of making the mind the sole constituent of reality, that it confuses potentiality with actuality and symbols with reality. Further, by overemphasizing immediacy, it hinders rational judgment and adopts a rather narrow viewpoint. Its rejection of anything transcendental and its pantheistic trends deprive it of any objective source of authentication of its own claims. It makes feeling the only criterion of truth, thereby leaving no opening for an evaluation of one's sentiments and desires. And, finally, it advances no theory of sin and evil, thus leaving itself open to the accusation that its claims are unrealistic since they do not take into account the human propensity to perversion.

Rather than rejecting the New Age because of its weaknesses, Olds prefers to dwell on the lessons one can learn from the movement. Thus, for example, the New Age's criticism of religion suggests that organized religion must be constantly challenged; otherwise it might lose its vitality. Its disapproval of modern science brings to our attention the need that scientific knowledge must be combined with a wider access to reality. Its concept of a 'global village' has the positive aspect of opening one up to a new awareness of cultural and cosmic diversity. Its call for spontaneity, wholeness, and interconnectedness should be welcomed because it could lead to better appreciation of the presence and mystery of God.

Several Protestant responses stand out as attempts not just to evaluate the New Age but also to promote mutual understanding between Christians and New Agers. David L. Moore, a Presbyterian, unlike the majority of Christian responses to the New Age, begins by asserting that both New Agers and Christians can learn from their respective religious commitments.

> The major purpose of this book is to provide some Christian teaching for the New Age practitioners who reject Christianity, so that they might start to see that the positive growth made over the past two thousand years is not to be rejected out-of-hand; while also providing enough New Age insight to the Christian practitioners so that they might see that there is something positive in the New Age which can be accepted without destroying their Christianity.[96]

Moore carefully draws up similarities and differences between the New Age and Christianity and points to the misunderstandings that are often the basis of mutual antagonism between Christians and New Agers.[97] Both religious systems believe in a supreme being who is the creator of all and who is present in the world and in people's lives. And although the two subscribe to different conceptions of

God, Moore thinks that the differences are comparatively minor. In like manner, both religions accept the existence and divinity of Christ or of a Christ consciousness, which is a major point of agreement that should not be overlooked or downplayed. Both religions have a sacramental system which is believed to impart grace. Further, both adhere to some kind of spiritual world that cannot be seen by the senses. Belief in angels, for example, is the norm in both religions. Finally, Moore points out that both Christianity and the New Age began as mystery religions or secret cults.

The differences between Christianity and the New Age are many. Christians and New Agers disagree about the nature and role of Jesus Christ, the former making him the only incarnate Son of God, while the latter maintaining that he is one of the many divine incarnations sent on earth to teach human beings. Belief in angelic and saintly beings plays a more important role in a New Ager's life than it does among contemporary Christians. The two religions adhere to different views of the cosmos. New Agers have a broader view of time, which they maintain is a fourth dimension. They tend to hold that other intelligent life exists in other planets and galaxies and that we are being visited by extraterrestrials. Moreover, a common New Age belief is that human beings have existed for a long period of time in physical, mental, emotional, and spiritual bodies and that they are reincarnated many times on their journey towards union with the divine. Unlike many Christian denominations, the New Age does not have clerical or priestly ordination after a period of training. And while Christians accept the Bible as the divinely inspired religious resource, New Agers accept a much wider and still growing body of spiritual books all of which are held to come from some divine source.

Moore tries to clear up some of the Christian misunderstandings of the New Age by examining its beliefs in detail. A good example of his efforts can be seen in his explanation of the New Age belief in God. The majority of Christian commentators simplify the New Age concept of God as being pantheistic and hence diametrically opposed to the Christian belief that human beings are creatures of God and hence separate and distinct from their creator. They fail to realize that the New Age view of God is much more complex and overlaps in several areas with the Christian position.[98]

Many of the accusations that New Agers and Christians have leveled at each other are based on inaccurate data and misconceived, stereotyped notions. On the one hand, Christians often attack the

New Age Movement for its shallowness and inconsistency and assume that it is (1) primarily concerned with mind control, (2) exists solely in esoteric cults that worship Satan, and (3) is Eastern in its thinking and thus non-Christian. On the other hand, New Agers consider Christians to be too narrow and exclusive in their religious beliefs. For Moore, the misunderstandings between Christians and New Agers are brought about largely by lack of communication.

A CRITIQUE OF THE PROTESTANT APPROACH

The various Protestant and Orthodox reactions to the New Age are based on different theological assumptions and on quite diverse views regarding the ways Christians should relate to people of other faiths. The theologies of religion[99] that interpret the major religious traditions are also operative in the understanding of the New Age Movement. Three main theories of non-Christian religions dominate current theological thought:[100] (1) an exclusive theology that maintains that only Christianity is the true religion and that salvation of non-Christians can only be achieved if they abandon their false religions and explicitly accept Christ and his teachings; (2) an inclusive theology which, while taking Christianity as the normative faith, allows for some truth and goodness in other religions and for the possibility of salvation outside explicit membership in the Church; and (3) a pluralistic theology that argues that all religions are equally valid paths to revelation and salvation. It is unfortunate that few, if any, of those who have responded to the challenge of the New Age have stated, much less examined, their own theologies of religions.

Critique of conservative reactions to the New Age

The responses of those Protestant and Orthodox Christians who adhere to an exclusive theology of religion reject the New Age lock, stock, and barrel and are very similar to the fundamentalist assault on the New Age and on anything which even remotely resembles it. Hence any dialogue or collaboration with New Agers is looked upon with suspicion and judged to be dangerous or threatening to the Christian's faith. However, the constant attacks on the New Age's false, un-Christian doctrines and denunciations of its practices add more to rhetoric than to a critical evaluation. They are more often directed to (1) deride New Age beliefs as 'blasphemous nonsense' for openly contradicting the biblical teachings on the nature of God and the place of Jesus Christ in God's plan for salvation and (2) attack its many practices as collusion with demonic forces. 'Every practice in which the New Age movement engages', according to Dennis E. Hensley, who offers a Church of God perspective, 'is in bold opposition to the commandments issued by God in the Old Testament and reinforced in the New Testament.'[101] He unhesitatingly urges people to abandon their involvement in the New Age practices by denouncing occult practices as evil and false, by confessing their sins and asking for forgiveness, and by accepting Christ as their savior. Blanket accusations, however, are rarely confirmed by hard evidence and vehement condemnations are not likely to achieve anything constructive, much less lead to the success of evangelical overtures. The first weakness of this type of Christian response to the New Age is that it is both unrealistic and futile.

A second flaw of the negative reaction to the New Age is that, although it correctly points to some of the major differences between Christian and the New Age beliefs, it does not promote understanding between people who obviously start with different religious premises. It rules out, rather than explores, the possibility of conversation and dialogue. Even in those areas, like mysticism, which might provide a link between Christians and New Agers, no effort is made to acknowledge similarities and points of contact. Further, the suspicion that New Agers are not sincere and the implication that their beliefs lead them to justify immoral actions are likely to elicit reciprocal negative responses, thus increasing the antagonism between people of different faith commitments. Accusations that New Agers indulge in evil and immoral behavior are, more often than not, sweeping generalizations that cannot be corroborated by hard data.

Equally misleading and counterproductive is the charge that the New Age is inherently anti-Christian. Peter Moore's statement[102] that much New Age literature 'breathes scorn and hatred of Christians' is both inaccurate and biased. One can find just as much, if not more, Christian literature that merits the same criticism. Sergei Ovsiannikov,[103] replying to a similar accusation by Seraphim Rose, remarks that Rose 'responds with as much thoughtless hatred as do evangelical and fundamentalist writers'. One would be more precise in distinguishing three types of New Age reactions to Christianity. The first, advanced largely by dissatisfied and/or disgruntled ex-

Christians, takes a negative approach and rejects Christianity as a bankrupt religion. The second simply ignores Christianity and pursues its own religious agenda without engaging in confrontation or dialogue. The third adopts an inclusive attitude and incorporates and/or reinterprets elements from Christian belief and worship. These reactions are very similar to the ways Christians themselves have reacted to the presence and influence of New Age thought.

Another weakness of this conservative approach is that it is too hasty in its judgment and too careless and shallow in its study of the issues involved. One flagrant example of this is the labeling of the New Age as being gnostic. It is customary among the majority of Protestant commentators on the New Age to see it as a resurgence of Gnosticism. There is no doubt a good measure of truth in this characterization of New Age thought. Little effort is spent, however, to examine the relationship between the Gnosticism and the New Age. Further, there seems to be the underlying assumption that anything which can be attributed to Gnosticism is evil and anti-Christian. Hence no real evaluation of Gnosticism is ever attempted. The New Age suffers the same fate. Those who denounce it outright never actually evaluate it. Everything connected with it is judged to be contradictory and opposed to Christian belief and practice. It is thus not difficult to reach the conclusion that New Agers are in league with the devil whose aim is to destroy Christianity. Such a position, however, cannot be substantiated by solid evidence. John Drane,[104] for example, rejects it not only because it does not conform to the facts, but also because it lulls Christians into a false sense of security.

The same method is also applied to those writers who are indiscriminately listed as proponents of the New Age. Teilhard de Chardin, Matthew Fox, Bede Griffiths, and Morton Kelsey are among the many authors who are repeatedly linked with the New Age. But again, there is very little effort to examine their writings in some detail and much less inclination to admit that not all the opinions expressed in their works can be classified as supportive of New Age thought. There is even more reluctance to concede that these writers have something positive (and orthodox) to offer to those seriously reflecting on their faith in an age of change and turmoil. While there is no doubt some truth in the accusation, since these writers are quoted by New Agers to support their ideology, even a cursory overview of their works would lead to the conclusion that listing them with New Agers is somewhat of an oversimplification.

Even if these authors can be associated with the New Age, their connections vary. One could hardly put together Teilhard de Chardin, Bede Griffiths, Morton Kelsey, and Matthew Fox in the same New Age camp.

There are some exceptions to these sweeping statements. David Rankin,[105] for example, while admitting that there are 'some clearly-discernable points of convergence' between Gnosticism and the New Age, correctly observes that the latter is not dualistic nor does it hold that human beings are innately imperfect or sinful. Consequently, calling New Agers modern gnostics without any qualifications may be both erroneous and misleading. Rankin also examines the works of Matthew Fox and Bede Griffiths, but he prudently abstains from condemning their writings *in toto*. He concurs with the New Age view that Matthew Fox's works stress the paradigm shift from redemption from sin to the blessings of creation, prefer the mystical to the rational spirituality, and emphasize the cosmic Christ at the expense of the historical Jesus. But he admits that Fox shares little in common with many of the popular New Age beliefs and practices. And he finds that Griffiths has been less influenced by the New Age, though he leans to a belief in God as depersonalized power and in redemption as a release from ignorance.

Rankin's analysis contains the germs for mutual exploration, but he fails to probe more deeply into the theology of either Fox or Griffiths. Thus, for example, he admits[106] that the latter does not entirely repudiate the classic Christian concepts of sin and redemption. But if he does not, then salvation, for him, cannot mean simply a release from ignorance. It would be probably easier to harmonize Griffiths's thought with more traditional Christian rather than New Age theology.

The lumping of the New Age Movement with the Interfaith Movement is another flaw shared by both Protestant and Orthodox writers who fail to realize that the Interfaith Movement has a solid base in Christian theology. It is a serious error to equate the Ecumenical Movement with the Interfaith Movement. Since the former is concerned with the relationship between the Christian Churches, the latter with the relationship between different religions, their theological assumptions and ways of proceeding differ. While the Ecumenical Movement starts with explicit Christian theological presuppositions, the Interfaith Movement does not. The nature of the latter's discourse demands a broader and vaguer set of principles designed to be inclusive of a variety of religions, including Shamanism and Wicca.

Thus, for example, one major interfaith organization on the Internet[107] affirms the following six axioms designed to embrace diverse religious commitments and to facilitate exchanges between people who adhere to different faith perspectives: (1) the truth in all faiths and religious paths; (2) the seeking of attunement to Spirit is the highest goal of conscious living; (3) an inclusive vision of 'We'; (4) the essential goodness of human beings; (5) the belief that each person is part of the healing of the world; and (6) the value of interfaith interactions as enriching awareness of the Spirit in the world.

Other interfaith organizations are based on similar inclusive principles that are meant to help people of different religious traditions work together for commonly shared goals. Thus, the Interfaith Alliance,[108] in its mission statement, specifies its aims as (1) to promote 'the positive role of religion as a healing and conservative force in public life' and (2) to offer hope and renewal in an age when family values are being undermined and threatened. It stresses the dignity of the individual and the importance of community in an age of irresponsible individualism. Similarly, the International Interfaith Centre at Oxford[109] states that its aims are (1) to develop inter-religious understanding, cooperation and respect for religious freedom; (2) to facilitate cooperation between, and provide information for, those people involved in interfaith work; and (3) to make available opportunities for learning about the world's religions. The World Congress of Faiths,[110] also headquartered at Oxford, describes itself as 'a pioneering fellowship dedicated to bringing people of different faiths together'. Its statement of belief is inclusive: 'The World Congress of Faiths believes that understanding between people of different religions is important for good community relations, for moral and spiritual renewal and for world peace. WCF by its educational work encourages interfaith understanding and co-operation at all levels of society.' None of these interfaith organizations was founded with the intention of creating a syncretistic religion or promoting particular religious views or theologies.

Those Christians, like Pollitt and Rose, who reject these principles of the interfaith movement as either false or as misinterpretations of the Christian faith, appear unaware of the many interreligious issues which multiculturalism has brought to the fore. Interfaith principles and goals are neither false nor anti-Christian. They are more fundamental declarations and are not meant to express Christianity as it is distinct from other religions. Rather, they are intended to find common ground in order to enable members of diverse ideologies to come together and work for commonly shared, religious, social, and sometimes political aspirations which are purposely couched in terms not appropriate to one particular theological discourse. Their goals are to avoid or minimize conflicts and misunderstandings. Members of interfaith organizations maintain their distinct religious identity and theology. While there are examples of the unification of Christian Churches[111] there are no instances of Christian churches merging with non-Christian religious bodies.

Hesitancy in accepting the principles of the Interfaith Movement might be understandable in an age when religious pluralism has raised issues about the integrity and identity of one's faith and its relationship to the many religions of humankind. Misrepresenting the attitudes of Christian churches who participate in interfaith dialogue is not. Pollitt,[112] for example, attacks the Catholic Church for establishing a relationship of dialogue with people of other faiths. He finds Vatican II's document on non-Christian religions unacceptable because it not only ascribes holiness to other religions but it also abandons the mission of the Church. He fails to take into consideration that the Council's 'Declaration on Non-Christian Religions' must be seen in the context of the other documents of the Council, particularly those on the Church and on Mission.[113] He ignores the many documents by the Pontifical Council for Interreligious Dialogue that refine and clarify the Vatican's initiative in dealing with non-Christian religions and that explore at some depth the issue of the relationship between dialogue and mission.[114] None of the principles he ascribes to the Interfaith Movement is even remotely applicable to the Catholic approach of dialogue with people of other faiths. Moreover, he decries all efforts to adapt Christianity to the cultural setting in which it is implanted as syncretism. For him, it appears that the only valid Christianity comes tailored in a very particular Western cultural garb.

Critique of liberal responses to the New Age

Those organizations and individual Christians who have embraced the New Age with open arms have contributed to the understanding both of the current religious scene as well as of Christianity's inner resources. Their efforts at collaboration, rather than confrontation, are more likely to help Christians cope with the issues that the New Age might have brought to the fore. The criticisms which have been directed against them, however, have some justification. Whether the teaching of New Age tenets and the performance of its rituals in Christian churches actually contribute to dialogue and mutual understanding is debatable. Some churches can sometimes be criticized for allowing a one-way conversation between Christianity and the New Age, a conversation in which the latter does most of the talking, while the former plays a passive role. In some of the New Age programs that are sponsored by Christian churches, there is little mutual interaction or influence. Moreover, it is unrealistic to proceed as if the New Age is beyond any critical assessment. The responses of both those who denounce the New Age as evil and those who indiscriminately accept all that it offers clamor for a more balanced and thoughtful Christian reaction to a current religious movement that has caught the imagination of many people on several continents.

Critique of balanced responses to the New Age

The efforts of those Protestant writers who have pointed out both the weakness and strengths of the New Age are a step in the right direction. These writers are prepared to accept both that there are some good religious elements in the New Age Movement and that its adherents are sincere in their spiritual quest. But the concession that some truth can be found in New Age teachings is granted reluctantly and there is little effort to delve into what exactly are the New Age's good components and how Christians could benefit by them. And again one does not find detailed and concrete examples showing how one can understand New Age beliefs in such a way that they can be related to Christian doctrine. Besides, praising the New Age for its ecological concerns is not enough. One must also show how respect and care for the environment can be supported by Christian theology.[115] Similarly, New Age practices, like yoga and Zen, are not to be superficially rejected as unsuitable and damaging to Christian spirituality. The real question is whether these and other New Age practices can be imbued with the Christian spirit, whether they can become a legitimate mode of Christian prayer and/or spirituality.

Similarly, many writers draw attention to the fact that Christians can learn from the New Age, but the examples given are vague, if at all present. Areas like the care for the environment, the holistic approach to health, and collaboration rather than confrontation in business and politics, which figure prominently in New Age discussions, are acknowledged as topics that Christians should reflect on. But there is a fear that New Age ideas have so permeated these areas that Christians might be contaminated by false doctrine. Many Christian responses have been so intent on insisting that the New Age is absolutely incompatible with the Bible that they have neglected to dwell on the Christian theological basis for environmental concern, for a less mechanistic treatment of health issues, and for an endorsement of harmony rather than discord.

More thoughtful evaluations of the New Age, however, have led several commentators to abandon the idea that it epitomizes the antithesis of Christianity. Almond,[116] for example, considers the New Age Movement to be a revival of the Western esoteric tradition which has sometimes existed in creative tension with orthodox Christianity. The New Age's concern for the environment is based not only on its pantheistic slant, but also on a millenarian vision of a world in which all living creatures exist in perfect harmony. When seen as 'a reaction to the technological rationalism and materialism of late twentieth century culture', and as a religious movement that 're-establishes the connection between the mundane and the transcendent', the New Age has something to teach those Christians who have been swept away by the secularization process in Western culture.

CONCLUSION: CONFRONTATION OR ENCOUNTER

The issues which Protestant and Orthodox commentators on the New Age have brought to the fore are in many ways the same as those discussed in fundamentalist and evangelical writings. The majority seem to opt for some kind of theological confrontation. But several Protestants, while admitting that the New Age is largely incompatible with Christian doctrine, make an effort to avoid a confrontational approach. Instead they favor an encounter in which Christianity clarifies its belief system and learns from the presence of the New Age. And they realize that many of the goals, aspirations, and beliefs of New Agers overlap with Christian teaching and practice.

Attempts to find some contact between the New Age and Christianity may lead not only to a better understanding of the New

Age, but also to a more pastoral response to its presence. It may, moreover, be more evangelical. Vehemently denouncing New Age beliefs and practices, accusing its adherents of immorality, and berating them as collaborators in a grandiose satanic conspiracy is not likely to increase their esteem of Christianity. Surely, the preaching of the Good News has to be more positively oriented.

Efforts to explore the common ground between the two religions are sometimes found among Protestant writers. Thus, to cite one example, Melvin Dieter,[117] writing from the perspective of the Church of God, which follows the Wesleyan tradition, explores points of contact between the two movements. He begins by admitting that the 'New Age movement is able to gain a hearing because it is giving vent to contemporary religious concerns that the churches have often ignored or misunderstood'. He believes that the Wesleyan Church's understanding of Scripture and salvation is similar to the spiritual potential that the New Age ascribes to men and women. Three of the hallmarks of the New Age, namely, optimism, holism, and synergism (the latter meaning that human beings have to take responsibility for getting things done), are also central to the Wesleyan Church. Dieter sees these points of contact as an opportunity for Christians to evangelize New Agers.

In like manner, George Braswell,[118] giving a Baptist point of view, notes that there are some areas central to the New Age which bear some resemblance to Christianity. He starts by providing a standard analysis of the New Age, listing its many themes, tracing its past and present roots, and describing the works of the many gurus who carry its message. He considers New Age teachings about God, creation, humanity and its predicament, Jesus Christ, and history and eschatology and concludes that they differ radically from Christian Biblical teachings. Yet he observes that many of the assumptions underlying spiritualism and related psychic phenomena are closely linked. Christians and New Agers, in spite of their disagreements, can come together and share religious experiences, thus minimizing their mutual distrust and antagonism and develop ways of collaborating on agreed-upon goals.

Many Protestant commentators on the New Age are worried that it might replace Christianity as the main religion of the Western world. But challenges to Christianity might actually reinvigorate the Christian faith. Rankin admits that the New Age offers one of the greatest challenges to Christianity at the end of the millennium. He adds:

Whether one chooses to regard this challenge as a grievous threat to orthodoxy and Christian truth or as a precious opportunity for spiritual growth depends very much, as they say, on one's point of view.[119]

The real issue which the presence of the New Age Movement has raised is not whether Christianity will survive its ubiquitous presence and apparent influence. Rather, the New Age has drawn attention to a set of more complex questions that most Protestant and Orthodox writers have not even begun to ask. The first is whether the direct doctrinal confrontation with the New Age is ultimately self-defeating. John Drane, for example, has remarked that New Agers 'will not be won over to Christ by confrontation'.[120] The second is whether the continued restatement of Christianity in traditional terms is doing a disservice both to Christianity and to those who are seeking spiritual nourishment at the beginning of the twenty-first century. And the third is whether the Christian theology of religions is to remain dominated by the exclusive mentality or whether it can broaden its horizons to include other religions in God's plans for the salvation of the human race.

NOTES

1. Gavin McGrath, 'The significance of the New Age Movement', *Churchman: A Journal of Anglican Theology* 105.1 (1991): 37–38.

2. 'Testing the spirit of the age of Aquarius: the New Age Movement', *Calvin Theological Journal* 33 (1987): 302.

3. *How to Respond to the New Age Movement* (St. Louis: Concordia Publishing House, revised ed., 1995), pp. 47–48.

4. 'The New Age Movement: report of research done for the Anglican bishops of Bath and Wells', mimeographed copy, 1992.

5. *The Serpent and the Cross: Religious Corruption in an Evil Age* (Birmingham, UK: K & M Books, 1994).

6. 'Christianity and New Age thought' in *St. Andrews Rock: The State of the Church in Scotland,* ed. Stewart Lamont (London: Bellew Publishing, 1992), pp. 120–21. See also Keith Innes, 'Looking at the New Age', *ANVIL: An Anglican Evangelical Journal for Theology and Mission* 8.1 (1991): 25.

7. *Another Gospel: Alternative Religions and the New Age Movement* (Grand Rapids, MI: Zondervan Publishing House, 1989), p. 326.

8. Campbelltown Salvation Army, 'Guidelines for Salvationists: New Age Movement', http://www.pastornet.net.au/salvcamp/newage.htm [date modified: 01/27/97; date downloaded: 06/29/97].

9. *The New Age Is Lying to You* (St. Louis: Concordia Publishing House, 1994), p. 16.

10. Ibid., pp. 16ff. Cf. William Watson, *A Concise Dictionary of Cults and Religions* (Chicago: Moody Press, 1991), p. 162, who gives an identical list of the main themes in the New Age belief system. See also Richard D. Thompson, 'A look at the New Age Movement', *Military Chaplain's Review* (Fall 1989): 13–29.

11. *The New Age Is Lying to You*, pp. 49–50.

12. Ibid., p. 125.

13. Ibid., p. 197.

14. *How to Respond to the New Age Movement*, p. 8.

15. See also, for example, Michael Cole, 'Defining the New Age' in *What Is the New Age? A Detailed Candid Look at This Fast Growing Movement*, by Michael Cole, Tony Higton, Jim Graham, and David C. Lewis (London: Hodder and Stoughton, 1990), pp. 12–13.

16. *How to Respond to the New Age Movement*, pp. 10–12. [Italics in original.]

17. Ibid., pp. 18–20.

18. *World-Views in Conflict: Choosing Christianity in a World of Ideas* (Grand Rapids, MI: Zondervan Publishing House, 1992), pp. 103–31.

19. 'The postmodern phenomena of New Age spirituality: examples in popular literature', *Ashland Theological Journal* 27 (1995): 60–63. Cf. James Sire, *The Universe Next Door* (Downers Grove, IL: InterVarsity Press, 1988), pp. 165–66.

20. 'The challenge of the New Age Movement', http://206.1.24.2/TESM/missmini/Moorenew.htm [date modified: 04/16/96; date downloaded: 01/3/97]. See also Kevin McGrath, 'The significance of the New Age Movement', pp. 31–34, where the same six beliefs are listed and briefly explained.

21. 'The challenge of the New Age Movement', p. 4.

22. 'Testing the spirit of the New Age of Aquarius: the New Age Movement', p. 302.

23. *The New Age Gospel: Christ or Counterfeit? A Warning to the Churches in Australia and New Zealand* (Melbourne: Paranesis Publishing, 1987), p. 4.

24. Ibid., pp. 162–67.

25. Ibid., p. 50.

26. 'Comparing Christianity with the New Age' in Michael Cole et al., *What Is the New Age?*, pp. 146–64.

27. 'The New Age: called to grace', *Word and World* 12 (1992): 271.

28. Ibid.

29. *The Inter-Faith Movement: The New Age Enters the Church* (Edinburgh: The Banner of Truth Trust, 1996), pp. 149ff. Cf. also Won Yong Ji, 'The challenge of the New Age to theology and mission', *Missio Apostolica* 2 (November 1994): 86–87.

30. 'New Age as religion' in Michael Cole et al., *What Is the New Age?*, pp. 54–55.

31. 'The New Age Movement: report of research done for the Anglican bishops of Bath and Wells'.

32. 'Christianity, coherence, and the New Age Movement', *Christian Scholar's Review* 20 (1991): 350–61.

33. The theme that the New Age is irrational and incoherent is often repeated in Christian literature. See, for example, Ronald H. Nash, *World-Views in Conflict: Choosing Christianity in a World of Ideas*, pp. 140ff.

34. 'A short introduction to the New Age Movement', *Science and Christian Belief* 4 (1992): 3ff.

35. 'Scientific truth and New Age thinking', *Science and Christian Belief* 4 (1992): 21–22.

36. 'The "New Age" movement in the light of traditional Christian theology', *Ashland Theological Journal* 35 (1993): 33.

37. Ibid., pp. 34–35. See also Fr. Damascene, 'A pilgrimage to old Valaam today', *Orthodox World* 25 (1989): 409.

38. 'The "New Age" movement in the light of traditional Christian theology', p. 35.

39. *Orthodoxy and the Religion of the Future* (Platina, CA: St. Herman of Alaska Monastery Press, 1996), pp. xxii–xxxii.

40. 'Ecumenism', *Orthodox World* 19 (July–August, 1969). This position has more recently been endorsed by Michael Woerl, 'Ecumenism, the New Age, and the parliament of the world's religions', *Orthodox Life* 44.3 (May/June 1994), pp. 7–21.

41. For a rejection of modern Witchcraft see Sr. Anastasia, 'The rising acceptance of Witchcraft', *Orthodox Life* 42.3 (May/June 1992): 19–24.

42. 'Astrology is astrolatry', http://www.goarch.org/access/orthodoxy/astrology [date modified: 03/06/96; date downloaded: 08/28/97].

43. 'The astrology trap', *Orthodox Life* 43.3 (July/August 1993): 10.

44. *Orthodoxy and the Religion of the Future*, pp. 109–11.

45. 'UFOs: the demonic connection', *Orthodox Life* 43.2 (March/April 1993): 23.

46. 'The sunrise of the East: from Eastern religions to Eastern Orthodoxy', *The Orthodox World* 32 (September/October 1996): 209–19.

47. 'The challenge of the New Age to theology and mission', p. 91.

48. *The New Age Is Lying to You*, pp. 198–99.

49. *How to Respond to the New Age Movement*, pp. 49ff.

50. 'The Challenge of the New Age Movement'.

51. *The Serpent and the Cross*, p. 523.

52. 'Testing the spirit of the age of Aquarius: the New Age Movement', p. 303.

53. *The New Age Is Lying to You*, pp. 59–61 and 127.

54. See the anonymous article, 'The New Age – will it come?', *Awake* (March 8, 1994): 10.

55. 'New Age as religion' in Michael Cole et al., *What Is the New Age?*, p. 52.

56. *The Serpent and the Cross*, pp. 415–19.

57. *Gods Within: A Critical Guide to the New Age* (London: SPCK, 1992), pp. 133–34.

58. Taken from promotional materials distributed by Bethsheva's Concern, P.O. Box 276, Clifton, NJ 07011–0276.

59. 'The New Age: a call for dialogue', *Word and World* 12 (1995): 268–70.

60. *Further Along the Road Less Traveled* (New York: Simon and Schuster, 1993), pp. 196–98.

61. Mark Bair, 'The postmodern phenomena of the New Age spirituality', p. 68.

62. See, for example, his *The Church and the Supernatural* (Minneapolis: Augsburg, 1976) and *The Other Side of Silence: A Guide to Christian Meditation* (New York: Paulist Press, 1976).

63. 'The former age and the New Age: the perennial quest for the spiritual life' in *New Age Spirituality*, ed. Duncan Ferguson (Louisville, KY: Westminster/John Knox Press, 1993), p. 35.

64. Ibid., pp. 56–57.

65. *Crystal and Cross: Christianity and New Age in Creative Dialogue* (Mystic, CT: Twenty-Third Publications, 1996), p. 27.

66. Ibid., p. 104.

67. Ibid., p. 187.

68. 'New Age, new opportunities', *Theology Today* 51 (1994): 143.

69. Attempts to incorporate such prayers have been made by many Christians. See, for examples, Basil Pennington, *Centered Prayer: The Way of Centering Prayer* (New York: Doubleday, 1986) and Nancy Roth, *A New Christian Yoga* (Cambridge, MA: Cowley Publications, 1989).

70. *Gods Within: A Guide to the New Age* (London: SPCK, 1992), p. 129.

71. Ibid., p. 131.

72. 'A short introduction to the New Age Movement', *Science and Christian Belief* 4 (1992): 5.

73. 'Religion in the New Age', *St. Mark's Review*, no. 144 (June 1991): 6–7.

74. 'Looking at the New Age', *ANVIL: An Anglican Evangelical Journal of Theology and Mission* 8.1 (1991): 19–33.

75. *The New Age – An Assessment* (Bramcote, Notts: Grove Books, 1990).

76. 'Towards an understanding of the New Age', *St. Mark's Review*, no. 144 (Summer 1991), pp. 2–3.

77. Ibid., p. 5.

78. 'The significance of the New Age Movement', p. 30.

79. Ibid., p. 37.

80. Ibid., p. 39.

81. *A Guide to the New Age: For Confused Christians* (Bramcote, Notts: Grove Books, 1991), p. 12.

82. Ibid., pp. 15–16.

83. Ibid., p. 21.

84. 'The New Age Movement: an outline and assessment', *Churchman: A Journal of Anglican Theology* 107.1 (1993): 54–69.

85. The God of process theology is a little more complex than Barnes apparently thinks. See, for example, Bowman L. Clarke, 'Two process views of God', *International Journal for the Philosophy of Religion* 38 (1995): 61–74.

86. 'The New Age Movement: an outline and assessment', p. 66.

87. 'Christianity and New Age thought' in *St. Andrews Rock: The State of the Church in Scotland*, ed. Stewart Lamont, p. 124.

88. 'In any age: can we hear God?' in *New Age Spirituality: An Assessment*, ed. Duncan S. Ferguson, pp. 20–34.

89. *The Cosmic Self: A Penetrating Look at Today's New Age Movements* (New York: HarperSanFrancisco, 1991), p. 4.

90. Ibid., p. 51.

91. Ibid., p. 91.

92. Ibid., p. 101.

93. See, for example, Fritjof Capra, *The Web of Life: A New Synthesis of Mind and Matter* (London: HarperCollins, 1996); and David Bohm, *The Undivided Universe: An Ontological Interpretation of Quantum Physics* (London: Routledge, 1991).

94. *The Cosmic Self*, pp. 194–97. [Italics in original.]

95. 'The New Age: historical and metaphysical foundations' in *New Age Spirituality: An Assessment*, ed. Duncan S. Ferguson, pp. 59–76.

96. *Christianity and the New Age Religion: A Bridge Toward Mutual Understanding* (Atlanta, GA: Pendulum Plus Publishers, 1992), p. 17.

97. Ibid., pp. 23ff.

98. Ibid., pp. 140–41 and 164ff.

99. See, for example, Gavin D'Costa, 'Christian theology and other faiths' in *Companion Encyclopedia of Theology*, ed. Peter Byrne and James Leslie Houlden (New York: Routledge, 1995), pp. 291–313.

100. For a brief exposition of these theories see Christopher Sinkinson, 'Questions people ask: is Christianity better than other religions?', *The Expository Times* 107 (June 1996): 260–64.

101. 'Old or new?: understanding the New Age Movement', *Journal of Vital Christianity* 3 (July 1991): 23.

102. 'Significance of the New Age', p. 39.

103. 'New Age and the Orthodox Church', *Sourozh: A Journal of Orthodox Life* 59 (February 1995): 17.

104. *What Is the New Age Saying to the Church?* (London: Marshall Pickering, 1991), p. 212.

105. 'The New Age and the old Gnosticism', *Lutheran Theological Journal* 26 (August 1992): 98ff.

106. Ibid., p. 105, footnote 7.

107. See 'www.interfaith.org', http://www.interfaith.org/principles.html [date modified: 11/17/97, date downloaded: 01/04/98].

108. http://www.tialliance.org/ [date modified: 12/18/97; date downloaded: 01/03/98].

109. http://www.interfaith-center.org/oxford/ [date modified: unknown; date downloaded: 01/03/98].

110. http://www.interfaith-center.org/oxford/wcf [date modified: unknown; date downloaded: 01/03/98].

111. One of the best-known examples is the Church of South India. See Stanley J. Samartha, 'Vision and reality: personal reflections on the Church of South India', *Ecumenical Review* 49 (1997): 483–93.

112. *The Interfaith Movement: The New Age Enters the Church*, pp. 69ff.

113. For these documents, cf. *The Documents of Vatican II*, ed. Walter M. Abbott (London: Geoffrey Chapman, 1966).

114. Francis Cardinal Arinze, *The Church in Dialogue: Walking with Other Believers* (San Francisco: Ignatius Press, 1990).

115. There is a growing literature on this topic. See, for example, Celia Deane-Drummond, *A Handbook in Ecology and Theology* (London: SCM Press, 1996); and James A. Nash, 'Toward the ecological reformation of Christianity', *Interpretation* 50 (January 1996): 5–15.

116. 'Towards an understanding of the New Age', *St. Mark's Review*, no. 144 (Summer 1991), pp. 2–5.

117. 'The Gospel and New Age thought', *Journal of Vital Christianity* 3 (July 1991): 27.

118. *Understanding Sectarian Groups in America* (Nashville, TN: Broadman and Holman Publishers, 1994), p. 196.

119. 'A Gospel of the New Age?', *Ministry, Society, and Theology* 5.1 (July 1991): 13.

120. *What Is the New Age Saying to the Church?*, p. 212.

4.

CATHOLIC RESPONSES TO THE NEW AGE MOVEMENT

Like many of their Protestant counterparts, Catholic commentators on the New Age have been rather slow in becoming aware of, and responding to, the New Age phenomenon. And again, like the Protestant reactions to the movement, many Catholic responses have been, somewhat heavily at times, influenced by the fundamentalist/evangelical criticisms of the theology and practices of the New Age.

It is useful to distinguish four strands of Catholic responses to the New Age Movement. The first follows traditional Catholic theological approaches in that it assumes an apologetic stance and concentrates on dogmatic issues. In general it is both critical and suspicious of many of the theoretical underpinnings of the movement and of the practices that it endorses. It sees the New Age Movement as a sign of dangerous spiritual and political trends which, if not checked, could have drastic consequences on both religion and society. It also suspects that the devil might be involved in the rise and spread of New Age ideas and rituals.

A second approach starts with the traditional assumptions of the first, but is willing to look at the positive side of the New Age and to admit that there are some good elements in the movement. While it criticizes the New Age for constructing a syncretistic theology that warps Catholic teachings, it concedes that something can be learned from its success and influence. It consequently avoids a blanket condemnation of the New Age. It even suggests that the New Age may have unearthed some of the problems Christian spirituality is currently encountering. Moreover, it traces the origin of the New Age to human historical factors and eschews the diabolical interpretations so readily accepted by fundamentalist and evangelical writers.

The third response is the official Catholic reaction to the movement. Though not very original in its content, since it largely incorporates materials from the first two methods, this approach is important both because it influences Catholic pastoral practice and because it endeavors to lay down some practical guidelines for Catholics in their encounter with New Age ideas and practices.

The fourth response is more innovative. It attempts to delve into the theological and philosophical principles that underlie the New Age and to note the similarities that exist between the New Age and the Catholic world views. It is ecumenical in scope. Unlike the traditional response, it tends to emphasize the good elements of the New Age. And unlike the previous approaches it is inclined to locate these positive aspects, when possible, within the Catholic tradition. It finds in the New Age some positive and stimulating trends that might be beneficial to the spiritual life of Christians, even though it is at times critical of some of its practices.

Like other rebuttals of the New Age, Catholic responses are based on different theologies of religions. The conservative Catholic reaction rests on an exclusive approach to non-Christian religions. The more moderate approaches and most of the official ones have been, in varying degrees, influenced by an inclusive theology of religion which has been officially sanctioned by the Second Vatican Council and by the work of the Pontifical Council for Interreligious Dialogue. The more creative responses to the New Age are guided by one of the several pluralistic theologies of religions which have been proposed both within and outside Catholic theological circles.[1]

TRADITIONAL CATHOLIC RESPONSES TO THE NEW AGE MOVEMENT

Many Catholic reactions to the New Age are concerned with the question of orthodoxy. They consequently concentrate on the differences between New Age teachings and Catholic theology and see little, if anything, in the New Age that can be recommended. They often end up condemning New Age beliefs and practices as antagonistic to Catholicism. Their advice to Catholics is to beware of New Age beliefs and to shun any practice linked with it.

The influence of Constance Cumbey's denunciation of New Age ideology, goals, and practices is prevalent. Cornelia R. Ferreira, for example, starts by defining the New Age Movement as an occult socio-political movement that is the synthesis of, or umbrella for, all heretical and seditious movements. Calling itself a revolution, its aim is a complete cultural transformation, to be obtained by occultism replacing Judeo-Christianity, and totalitarian socialism instead of the Judeo-Christian system of government.[2]

Ferreira identifies three major 'cornerstones' of the New Age: (1) occultism, (2) secular humanism, and (3) Theosophy, from which the more recent revival of the New Age stems. She dismisses Blavatsky's views on the evolution of human (divine) consciousness and on the coming Messiah, both of which are central to the New Age, as 'drivel' that bear the influence of Freemasonry.

Like several fundamentalist Christians, Ferreira finds the goal of a new world order somewhat threatening. Any attempts to look on the planet as whole are interpreted as endorsing a new socialist dictatorship or a tyrannical globalism that deemphasizes or rejects patriotism which, according to her, 'is a Christian virtue'. She ends up denouncing the United Nations and the European Common Market as supporters of globalism and consequently, of the New Age Movement. In her opinion the Church is sometimes used to promote the same ideas. Bishops preaching 'a more just and fraternal world *rather than* the Kingdom of God' are indirectly promoting the New Age world view. The New Age, she believes, 'through brainwashing workshops and seminars' has penetrated deeply into the Church hierarchy, since its ideas and goals have been adopted by, for instance, the Pontifical Council for Justice and Peace, the Jesuits, and the Leadership Conference of Women Religious.[3] Such opinions are hardly new; they are frequently expressed in conservative Catholic circles.[4]

The New Age beliefs that Ferreira briefly refers to are monism and pantheism which, in her view, are incompatible with personal responsibility. She prefers to stress the political rather than the religious dimensions of the movement. She identifies the political aspirations of the New Age with the communism of Russia which is bound to lead to wars and destruction.

Ferreira's assessment of the New Age naturally leads her to conclude that Satan, who initiated the New Age in the Garden of Eden, is responsible for its current revival and dissemination through a network of organizations. Though she does not seem to accept the human conspiracy theory, she certainly leans to a satanic one in which human beings, organizations, and even the Church are used as tools to further the one world religion of Satan.

In spite of Ferreira's pessimistic analysis of the present situation which is heading towards the establishment of Satan's kingdom on earth, she sees a ray of hope. Human beings can save civilization by returning to God's plans as set out by our Lady of Fatima, plans which also require 'the Rosary and the scapular, the First Saturday devotion, and sacrifice – especially that of one's daily duty'.[5]

Another example of how the New Age is completely rejected is provided by John Carlo Rosales, who has also strongly been influenced by Cumbey's views, even though he succeeds in avoiding the hysterical tone found in many fundamentalist writings. Rosales begins by locating the roots of the New Age in the Theosophical Society and dedicates a substantial part of his essay to describing its teachings which are a form of modern Gnosticism. He maintains that Theosophy's four key doctrines, namely, the immanence of God, the evolution of the human soul, karma, and reincarnation, deny basic Christian concepts. The New Age has incorporated and adapted Theosophy's teachings. The importance it places on holism leads to a shift in emphasis from rational thinking to intuitive knowledge. Its tenet that all is one (monism) leads to the collapse of all ethical values.

Rosales thinks that the New Age is a religion with its own scriptures, prayers and mantras, spiritual centers (such as Findhorn and Esalen), and priests and gurus. Its God is a neutral force that can be manipulated. Its spirituality is based on faith in human potential and in the divine energy that pervades the cosmos. The use of certain psychotechnologies (such as meditation, yoga, and Zen) comprise an essential part of the New Age religion. In spite of the diversity within this religion, Rosales finds a unifying theme:

> What is common among many New Age groups is a counterfeit religious experience such as contact with demons through drugs, meditation, psychotechnologies, and other ventures.[6]

Echoing, once again, some of the more extreme fundamentalist writings, Rosales concludes that the New Age favors the introduction of a universal credit card system, the creation of a global food authority, the adoption of a political dictatorship, and the promotion of Aryanism, abortion, artificial insemination, and genetic control.

Rosales specifies four major criticisms of the New Age from a Catholic viewpoint: (1) its goals are too worldly and cannot be harmonized with the Catholic view, expressed in several documents of

Vatican Council II and in the *Catechism of the Catholic Church*, both of which teach that, while there is a need to make this world a better place, one must not lose sight of the ultimate end of human beings, namely God; (2) it incorporates many of its ideals and concepts from Theosophy and thus shares in the condemnation of Theosophy by the Holy Office;[7] (3) its involvement in the occult runs counter to Catholic practice as expressed in the *Catechism of the Catholic Church*; and (4) its view of suffering is deficient and faulty and contradicts Catholic thought on the subject as can be seen by referring to Pope John Paul II's Apostolic Letter on the subject.[8] He concludes by dismissing as superficial any similarities between Catholicism and the New Age.

One of the harshest Catholic evaluations of the New Age Movement is probably that of George W. Rutler,[9] who adopts the stance found in many fundamentalist writings. He sardonically refers to the New Age as an 'antique' and states that its world view can be identified as gnostic (just as the Nazi, Marxist, and Fascist world views are gnostic). Like the Gnosticism of old, the New Age was preceded by several conditions: the breakdown of the family, the growth of wealth, the decline of educational standards, too much travel without purpose, and the desire for instant gratification. Its lure is compared to that of the serpent in the Garden of Eden. The New Age promises the dawning of a new era, encourages one to become a superperson, and incites the individual to 'get high' on drugs, promiscuity, and greed. Like all religions, with the exception of Judaism, Christianity, and Islam, the New Age is ultimately pessimistic and self-destructive.

Several Catholics have expressed the fear that the New Age has penetrated the Catholic Church and has led many to adopt New Age beliefs and practices that are not compatible with their faith. Randy England's[10] analysis of how the New Age is affecting the Catholic Church seems to draw heavily on those evangelical writers who advance an infiltration theory to demonstrate that the New Age has plans to take over the Christian Church. He detects the presence of New Age in practically all spheres of Catholic life, including parochial schools.

He doesn't see anything particularly novel in the New Age, which is guilty of the same sin committed by the first human beings in the Garden of Eden (Genesis 3:2–5). He points out that the Catholic Church experienced the impact of the New Age in its confrontation with Modernism in the late nineteenth century. He does not accept the human conspiracy theory but believes that there is a real conspiracy orchestrated by the devil himself.[11]

Similarly, England is suspicious of anything associated with the New Age. He acknowledges the influence of Eastern religions on the New Age Movement and dwells on several of its beliefs, like the immanence of God, reincarnation, the divinity of the human being, and evolution, none of which are compatible with Catholic doctrine. He dedicates a section to New Age practices, especially yoga, Transcendental Meditation, and visualization, which, he claims, are dangerous forms of occultism that cannot be 'safely appropriated by Christians'. Some New Age practices,[12] like the use of crystals, are interpreted as a rejection of God since they seek the solution of spiritual problems elsewhere.

Underlying England's approach is a theology of religions shared, though not always clearly articulated, by other Catholic commentators on the New Age Movement. Whether other religions contain elements of truth which are similar to Christian belief is, apparently, not relevant to him. He denies that Christians can learn anything worthwhile from other religions:

> Many teachers are convinced that we have much to learn from the East, especially when Eastern meditation offers techniques and experiences which traditional Christianity apparently lacks. Does oriental religion really offer value which Christianity does not?[13]

It follows that any attempt to adopt and transform non-Christian elements into Catholic practice is frowned upon. Catholic writers on spirituality, like Anthony de Mello,[14] are repudiated for encouraging dangerous practices that are not congruous with, and hence cannot, even in modified form, be incorporated into, Catholic devotional life. He complains:

> It would seem that the thrust is to 'baptize' non-Christian behavior with sacred trappings in order to make them acceptable to Christians. Occult practices cannot be so sanctified, but rather the Holy Name is profaned instead.[15]

The only kind of meditation he accepts as genuinely Christian is discursive prayer where reasoning plays the major role. Beyond which, there is the mystical experience of contemplation which cannot be achieved by the 'mindless techniques of bearded gurus'. Unlike Christian meditation, which has God as its object, occult meditation endeavors to turn one's mind into an empty and open receptacle, thus making it subject to satanic influences.

The same alarm about the influence of the New Age is raised by Peter Kreeft,[16] who is also concerned with the inroads it has made into Christianity by the subtle means of infiltration. He identifies the movement with a new Paganism that differs from the old which had (1) a sense of piety, 'the natural religious instinct to respect something greater than yourself', (2) an objective and absolute morality, and (3) the awe of the transcendent that led to the worship of the pagan gods. By joining the forces of humanism, polytheism, and pantheism and by endorsing a relativistic, subjective, and pragmatic morality, the New Age Movement presents a formidable enemy. Kreeft denies that there is a conspiracy on earth and proposes instead a conspiracy in hell to account for the revival of Paganism in its new form. Unlike many fundamentalists and evangelicals, he concludes with a positive and hopeful note: the enemies of the Church cannot win and the new Paganism will one day be as dead as the old.

Among the most articulate and comprehensive Catholic conservative assessments of the New Age Movement is that of Ralph Rath, who relies heavily on and adopts the fundamentalist/evangelical understanding and condemnation of the New Age described in Chapter 1. He starts by providing an evaluative description of the New Age which colors his interpretation of both its beliefs and practices. In his opinion the New Age 'is a noxious mixture of pantheism and occultism that is spreading like a virulent plague throughout the country'.[17]

Rath locates the roots of the New Age in Eastern religions as well as in Gnosticism, occultism, Paganism, and pantheism. While he strongly denies the human conspiracy theory, he credits Satan with the emergence and successes of the New Age. From the very start he warns his readers that the vitality of the New Age comes from powerful demonic spirits and urges those who study it to pray for God's protection. For him this is necessary, because those students who encounter New Age beliefs and practices, like reincarnation, near-death experiences, channeling, astrology, healing by crystals, and pyramid power, run the risk of becoming directly under diabolical influence.

Almost half of Rath's book is dedicated to a description of the inroads the movement has made in the fields of cults, religion, education, politics, science, health, business, and entertainment. The rest outlines a Christian rebuttal that is aimed largely at those New Age doctrines that are in conflict with Christianity. He mentions the

Catholic Church's position on dialogue with the world religions, but seems to think that such dialogue is not applicable to the new religious movements (or cults) including the New Age Movement. 'The New Age is false and it is banal. Christianity is infinitely beautiful. There is no comparison between the two.'[18]

A similar, though much more personal, approach to the New Age is that of Mitch Pacwa, who appears to have embarked, for a while at least, on a conversion career[19] from involvement in drugs, to Jungian psychology, astrology, the Enneagram, and other New Age fads. His final conversion to the charismatic movement led him to realize that all his previous experiments were completely opposed to Christian doctrine.

Pacwa is among the few Catholic commentators who propose a precise definition of the New Age Movement which he describes as 'a loosely structured, eclectic movement based on experiences of monism that lead people to believe in pantheism, with a tendency to hold millenarian views of history'.[20]

In spite of the growing influence of the New Age, Pacwa denies that it is a cult. He rejects the idea that the New Age is a conspiracy. He locates its roots in the counterculture of the 1960s and its sources in Eastern religions, Western occultism, modern science, and humanistic psychology. He does not explicitly endorse the satanic theory, though he warns Catholics not to read New Age materials unless they need to do so in order to refute the errors they contain.[21]

The way Pacwa deals with Jung is a typical example of the application of the doctrinal approach. He finds Jungian teachings incompatible with Christian doctrine. He identifies three aspects of Jungian thought that are more compatible with Gnosticism: (1) faith is a blind acceptance of doctrines; (2) personal experience of God is better than dogmas; and (3) archetypes provide real knowledge. Examining more in detail Jung's view on Christianity, Pacwa concludes that his concepts of God, of Christ and his mission, of the Holy Spirit, and of the Church are colored by gnostic and mythic interpretations and by his own personal rejection of, and antipathy towards, the Christian faith.

Pacwa rejects astrology not only because it is not based in fact, but also because it is repudiated in the Bible and by the Church. He finds it theologically unacceptable since it teaches human beings to rely on the planets and the stars rather than on God and hence cannot be harmonized with Christianity. He himself gave up using the Enneagram because it poses serious theological problems. It is based on the mystic and mythic aspects of the teachings of occult writers and it espouses a notion of salvation inconsistent with Christian doctrine.[22]

In union with several other Catholic commentators, Pacwa[23] also directs his critical assessment towards the creation spirituality of Matthew Fox. He questions his scholarship, world view, and theology. He finds his interpretation of scriptural texts and of the medieval mystics, like St. Hildegard and Master Eckhart, sloppy and faulty. He denounces Fox's ideology because it is dominated by the new paradigm which incorporates 'the right hemisphere of the brain with its emotion, connection-making, mysticism, cosmic delight, maternity, silence, and darkness'.[24] Even though Fox rejects pantheism in favor of panentheism ('everything is in God and God is in everything'), the statements he makes on the cosmic Christ sound, according to Pacwa, pantheistic.

Pacwa[25] argues that the best response that Catholics should give to the New Age Movement is to live better Christian lives and to strengthen their intellectual knowledge of their faith. Among his suggestions for evangelizing New Agers are to listen to them and question their values and to look for their good ideas and relate them to the truth. He proposes various traditional evangelizing methods to deal with efforts being made to introduce Catholics to New Age teaching. He favors confrontation, on both the individual and communal levels.[26]

One of the most scathing debunkings of the New Age is provided by Christopher Lasch who, in a series of articles on Gnosticism, starts his comments on the New Age with a statement that sets the tone for everything he says about the movement:

> The New Age movement – the latest contribution to our long history of bizarre fads and panaceas – invites a mixture of ridicule and indignant alarm. Not just the degradation of piety but its blatant commercialization prompts the suspicion of large scale fraud.[27]

He thinks that the New Age phenomenon, like mesmerism, spirit rapping, and many nineteenth-century fake cures, cannot last because it mixes a large variety of ingredients that cannot hold together and that cannot provide coherent explanations of, or answers for, those personal difficulties that attracted people to join its ranks in the first place. In fact, he dismisses New Age techniques as useless in bringing about a genuine religious and intellectual conversion, since the movement lacks a 'spiritual discipline'.

Lasch admits that the discontents addressed by the New Age are important, but the spirituality it offers does not provide solutions to the problems people face. He concedes further that New Age spirituality does furnish some genuine insights, but it seeks its answers from a gnostic philosophy which denies the limits imposed on human beings by nature. Its attitude corresponds to the mystical tradition of the East which made its way to the West in Hellenistic times and remained an undercurrent of thought ever since. It has also, according to Lasch, been repeatedly censured by the Catholic Church in its condemnation of many religious movements which, over the centuries, espoused it. The New Age can be seen as a continuation or revival of this mystic tradition. Lasch writes:

> The New Age movement is best understood, then, as the 20th-century revival of an ancient religious tradition; but it is a form of Gnosticism considerably adulterated by other influences and mixed up with imagery derived from science fiction – flying saucers, extraterrestrial intervention in human history, escape from the earth in a new home in space.[28]

Lasch finds no redeeming qualities in the New Age Movement. He makes no effort to explain its success or to make sense out of its alluring features. He thinks that its theology is muddled and its spirituality deceptive. Unlike so many critical commentaries on the movement, he does not waste time refuting its false doctrines. He cannot possibly conceive how anything can be learned from it.

MODERATE CATHOLIC RESPONSES TO THE NEW AGE MOVEMENT

Not all Catholic responses to the New Age have been as negative as the ones just described. Several authors make an effort for a more balanced assessment of the New Age Movement. Ralph Martin,[29] for instance, concurs with many commentators when he observes that the New Age is not an organized or unified entity. For him it is rather a broad term that 'describes a certain psycho-spiritual worldview'. Relying on one particular evangelical Christian author,[30] he divides its ideology into six major components: (1) God is an impersonal force; (2) monism and pantheism; (3) human beings are god; (4) the need for a change of consciousness; (5) there is no right or wrong; and (6) great optimism. Like most Catholic writers, he observes that these teachings are hardly new or original and that they are incompatible with the teachings found in the Gospels. He faults the New Age, among other things, for reducing Jesus to just one of many spiritual masters, ignoring evil in the universe, denying heaven and hell, and encouraging practices condemned in scripture.

But Martin is more cautious about ascribing the emergence of the New Age to any kind of conspiracy. He rejects the human conspiracy theory and is doubtful about the satanic influences that are so readily adduced to account for its rise and success. Even though for him the New Age is a false spirituality, he interprets it as 'yet another expression of humanity's need for God and its desire for the spiritual life'. And although he sees New Age influences on both culture and religion, he does not promote the attitude of paranoia which detects the New Age everywhere. Unlike Rosales, who sees the New Age symbol of the rainbow as a bridge between human beings and Lucifer,[31] he reminds his readers, for example, that the rainbow is also a powerful Christian symbol and, consequently, should not be rejected because New Agers have adopted it.

In a similar vein Andrew Miles argues that the popularity of the New Age Movement raises serious questions for Christians. 'Is it compatible with Christian belief and practice? Is it totally opposed? Or is there perhaps a certain amount of overlapping?'[32] He compares briefly Christian and New Age beliefs regarding God, Jesus, the nature of the human person, salvation, and nature and finds New Age beliefs opposed to those of Christianity. While he agrees that the goodness of nature is a common tenet in both systems, he warns of the dangers of falling into the worship of nature or its forces, which is Paganism. And again he finds New Age concerns for holistic health compatible with Christianity, but he warns Christians to avoid psychic healing or healing through higher spiritual beings. And he observes that there is also some similarity between the Christian and the New Age concepts of the spiritual world. Though he does not attribute the emergence of the modern New Age to Satan, he suspects that evil spirits may be involved in some of its practices. Because of the New Age denial of evil, the influence of evil spirits is generally not acknowledged and hence little effort is made to discern them. Divination, channeling, Witchcraft, the attribution of magical powers to various objects (such as crystals) are recognized as being the activity of evil spirits and are rejected because they are condemned in the Bible.

Finally, Miles sees the New Age Movement as a challenge for Christians, many of whom find themselves in a spiritual vacuum. In spite of his reference to the influence of the devil, Miles leans towards ascribing the origin of the New Age to some basic trends in human nature, namely the desire and quest for true religiosity and spirituality which Christians have ignored. Indirectly, the movement is forcing Christians to a self-reexamination and a rediscovery of neglected aspects of their traditional faith. Among these are listed: (1) an awareness of the sacredness of all creation; (2) the holistic healing ministry of the Church; (3) the mystical teaching and practice of the Church; (4) the awareness of the unity of the human race; and (5) the ability to discern what comes from evil spirits. Indirectly, he concedes that these areas have not played an important role in Western Christian spirituality. Consequently he does not dismiss the movement as a whole and admits that there are some overlapping areas between the New Age and Christianity. The New Age may not be reconcilable with Catholic doctrine, but it could serve as a lesson to those Catholics whose spiritual life is in dire need of nourishment.

For some, the New Age Movement is the most important religious event in the second half of this century. Aidan Nichols,[33] for example, thinks that the movement, in spite of its 'impressionistic quality', is having an effect on both culture and religion. Rejecting both secular humanism and the Judeo-Christian world view, the New Age advances an evolutionary monism and proposes several 'techno-psychologies' (such as meditation, mood-changing music, and the martial arts) for the expanding of one's consciousness. The movement's ideology is an amalgamation of several trends taken from Eastern religions, spiritualism, relativity theory and quantum physics, feminism, and the 1960s hippie movement.

Nichols lists three main results that have flowed from the success of the New Age. The first is the revival of Paganism with the consequent worship of Mother Earth. The second is the increase in occult practices, such as Witchcraft, Satanism, and astrology. The third is the spread of the idea that religion consists of self-empowerment or of fulfilling human potential, rather than of the traditional goals of worshiping God, recognizing a savior, and working for one's sanctification. By so doing, the New Age rejects several basic tenets of Christianity and reduces Jesus to an ascended master whose Christ consciousness human beings should strive for.

Finally, Nichols offers a Catholic critique of the movement. He starts by denying that the Vatican Council's treatment of world religions can be applied to the New Age Movement. He does, however, recognize that the movement has several positive features, namely, its 'rejection of materialism, its concern for the created order (not under that name), its enthusiasm for world peace, its commitment to meditation, its belief in the creativity of the human spirit, and its call for a transformation of human beings as they are now'.[34] But he mentions several negative trends in the movement that cannot be reconciled with Christianity, particularly its denial of a God who is the creator, redeemer, and sanctifier, its exaggerated view of human nature and its capabilities, its irrationalism, and its ethical relativism and sexual permissiveness.

Nichols rejects the idea that the networking between New Agers forms some kind of conspiracy. He mitigates the polemical tone used by evangelical and fundamentalist Christians to condemn the movement. And he commends the optimistic goals of the New Age which can resemble Christian teaching, even though they are diametrically opposed to the main Christian doctrines about God, Christ, the human condition, and the need for salvation. But he still thinks that the evangelical Christian view that the New Age can be identified with the Antichrist is not far fetched.

The impact of the New Age is taken seriously by many Catholics, some of whom attempt to understand it in the light of its historical and cultural contexts. Jack Finnegan,[35] for example, ignores the evangelical theories that have been adduced to explain the presence of the movement and acknowledges that the New Age Movement 'is part of the cultural landscape the Gospel must dialogue with if the Christian story is to remain at the heart of European culture and spirituality'.

Finnegan traces the origins of the New Age to the late 1960s and early 1970s, and describes it as:

> an extremely widespread but loosely structured mega-network of individuals, groups and organizations who tend to share common values characterized by mysticism and monism, and a common vision of a coming new age of peace and mass enlightenment.[36]

New Agers, who belong to 'the *neo-Gnostic, neo-pagan, neo-Pelagian,* religious-mystical-metaphysical revival', share five basic philosophical themes and adhere to six fundamental religious concepts. From a philosophical perspective, they stress (1) a holistic perspective of life; (2) the importance of holistic health; (3) the concern for ecology; (4) the role of astrology as indicative of the Age of Aquarius; and (5) personal responsibility. Theologically, New Agers accept the following beliefs: (1) reincarnation; (2) the doctrine of karma; (3) human beings are divine; (4) avatars; (5) the coming of the new messiah, Lord Maitreya; and (6) God as an impersonal consciousness and power.

Finnegan offers two main critical reflections on the New Age. The first is that its beliefs lead to a complete moral breakdown in which evil does not exist. The second is that its view of Christ reduces Jesus to another saintly teacher, a view that contradicts that of orthodox Christianity.

An interesting approach has been taken by Rosino Gibellini,[37] writing in a popular Italian magazine. Like many other Catholic writers, this author acknowledges that the New Age has a long history, but places the birth of the movement in California and traces its more immediate roots to Alice Bailey. The goals of the movement are a paradigm shift leading to a transformation of consciousness. Gibellini admits that there is a conspiracy, though he does not specify whether he thinks it is the product of human or satanic forces. But he qualifies his assertion by stating that it is 'a conspiracy without a political doctrine, without a manifesto'. He further maintains that the New Age should be dealt with differently from other religious movements because it is global and comprehensive, it brings together several currents of thought, and it influences both culture and religion.

Gibellini observes that Constance Cumbey's link between the New Age and Nazism has also been made by other Catholic writers,[38] but he finds no justification for it. He prefers to follow another more promising line of interpretation that distinguishes between the popular level of the New Age, where astrological and esoteric elements prevail, and a superior level, which is instructive and open to dialogue. He surveys several Catholic responses to the New Age and distinguishes two trends, which correspond roughly to the first two approaches outlined in this chapter. The first is somewhat cautious, more interested in the discernment of spirits, and more likely to stress the differences between the New Age and Christian spirituality; the second is more positive and is open to understanding and to discovering similarities between the New Age and Christianity.[39]

Another comprehensive treatment has been provided by Jean Vernette, who lists 'ten commandments' of the New Age which can be summarized as follows: (1) await eagerly the Age of Aquarius; (2) believe strongly in the new paradigm; (3) reawaken your awareness through yoga and meditation; (4) pay special attention to your own body; (5) follow your guru with respect; (6) believe faithfully in the irrational and develop your hidden psychic powers; (7) worship religiously the goddess Gaia; (8) reject traditional religions, since direct communication with the divine is possible; (9) communicate naturally with spirits; and (10) do not fear death, since reincarnation is in store for all according to the laws of karma.[40]

He traces the ancient roots of the New Age from the works of Immanuel Swedenborg (1688–1772) and Franz Anton Mesmer (1733–1815) to the nineteenth-century popularity of spiritism and to the contemporary revival of the occult. The more recent origins of the movement are to be found in centers like Esalen and Findhorn, in the hippie movement of the 1960s, in oriental philosophy, and in the new psychology. Because of the many elements that make up the New Age, the movement is open to a variety of definitions. It was born out of the perilous condition in which the human race currently finds itself. Its main message is that human beings form part of a whole and that change is essential if society is to become peaceful and loving. It proposes an ecological, mystical, and religious (or spiritual) vision. For Vernette, the New Age is made up of three main elements: syncretism, Pantheism, and a search for knowledge outside revelation.

Vernette sees the New Age as a challenge to the Church because it proposes an alternative spirituality and also because its millenarianism presupposes that Christianity should be superseded or supplanted by a new religious climate. It clashes with major Christian doctrines since it denies grace and the need of redemption. It further reduces Jesus to one manifestation of the cosmic consciousness. Therefore, it cannot be reconciled with Christianity. He is also critical of the New Age because sometimes it lacks common sense and honesty and takes advantage of the vulnerability of those who are looking for true spirituality and spiritual healing. However, he concedes that there is something valid in the movement which has provided insights and valid practices in such areas as medicine, education, ecology, spirituality, and human potential. He seems willing to learn from the movement and to adopt practices that can be harmonized with the Catholic faith.

Several French commentators have followed Vernette's approach. André van Raemdonck[41] thinks that the New Age attracts people because it addresses three areas of concern: possession of material things, power over individuals, and knowledge of hidden wisdom. He concedes that the New Age contains some positive values, among which are the human quest for the absolute (God), the holistic approach, and the stress given to intuition. But it mixes these with elements that are incompatible with Christianity. Gnosticism, Pantheism, belief in reincarnation, and divinatory practices are New Age elements which must be weeded out before any effort is made to adopt its positive contribution.

Another French theologian, A. Fossion, in line with many other Catholics and Protestants, acknowledges the 'seduction' of the New Age and opts for a critical appraisal of its beliefs and practices. He describes the New Age as a combination of many theories and practices taken from various religious traditions, the physical sciences, astrology, ecology, depth psychology, and the mental therapies. He identifies three major 'deviations': (1) belief in esoteric wisdom and hidden revelation and acceptance of occult practices; (2) syncretism; and (3) an escape from the realities of life and its moral challenges. He notices that Christian identity is built on the following elements which are, apparently, lacking in the New Age: (1) the Christian faith recognizes a personal God who gives life and calls people to enter into a covenantal relationship with him; (2) it also invites us to build a more just and more fraternal world, in the concrete situations of our history; and finally (3) it calls for critical exercise of reason, in order to understand oneself and enter into dialogue with others.[42]

Another writer, William Kent Burtner, who is known for his anticult sentiments, has expressed a surprisingly moderate view in a book which rates as one of the most negative Catholic anticult publications. Burtner calls the New Age a 'conflation of a variety of non-traditional religious organizations, self-help programs, modern witches, large group awareness training, and esoteric satanist groups'.[43] Unlike so many other writers, he does not provide a comprehensive list of New Age beliefs, nor does he show how these conflict with Christian doctrine. He dismisses some New Age ideas, such as the belief that life is illusion and that the human soul is reincarnated in future lives, and then describes very briefly some New Age groups and activities, including channeling, psychic readings, healing by crystals, awareness training, and modern Witchcraft, which, he holds, has been influenced by Satanism.

Although Burtner thinks that the practices of some New Age

groups could lead to pathological states of mind, he admits that not everything in the New Age is inherently evil. Neither can it be dismissed as irrational. He points out that the promotion of altered states of consciousness through a set of exercises is hardly a New Age invention. What the New Age has done is to promote these techniques (such as meditation and visualization) as if they were new and to use the experiences they create to validate the authority of the group itself. The techniques themselves are not harmful. On the contrary, some could be beneficial. 'But within the New Age movement, they are too often used by persons unfamiliar with the context from which they are derived. The results can sometimes be quite hazardous.'[44]

Burtner refuses to identify the movement with Hinduism (or any other Eastern religion) and dismisses the satanic theory of cult formation. He thinks that the New Age is successful because people are constantly seeking to find meaning in the world around them. Besides, alienation from the Catholic tradition and the impersonality of large congregations have led people to seek more personal and spiritual experiences elsewhere. Not everything in the New Age is threatening. It should be approached with caution and discernment.

One of the more insightful evaluations of the New Age Movement has been that of William Dinges, who avoids the harangues that have been usually directed at the movement but stops short of suggesting dialogue. For him, the New Age flows from the religious consciousness of the 1960s and 1970s. It is made up of a large assortment of religious, psychological, and scientific theories and practices. Dinges[45] thinks that some New Age beliefs and practices are not authentically religious when they fit more easily into 'the murky realm of sorcery, superstition, and pseudo-science'.

The reasons Dinges gives to account for the rise of the New Age are mundane. Its roots are, first of all, historical, particularly in the nineteenth-century American interest in the occult and Eastern traditions. Secondly, the culture crisis of the last 30 or 40 years has provided a fertile ground for religious experimentation. Thirdly, Dinges[46] lists several other causes not often mentioned by Christian commentators to account for the success of the movement. Among these are: (1) the growth of the study of comparative religion; (2) the increase of Asian immigrants to the US; (3) the work of 'spiritual entrepreneurs' who profit by a pluralistic society that includes religion in its market economy; and (4) the influence of the mass media, especially some Hollywood celebrities who advertise the movement's beliefs and practices.

While Dinges thinks that the New Age Movement is an important phenomenon in contemporary Western culture, he does not include it with a number of more significant religious trends of the latter part of this century, such as the rise of the religious right and the spread of neo-Pentecostalism. He thinks that the New Age points to three major religious and cultural developments, the 'signs of the times' as he calls them:

(1) The rise of the New Age Movement is an indication that people do not abandon religion when faced with new problems and that secularization is not an inevitable consequence of modernity. The New Age indirectly points to the religious nature of humankind.

(2) The tendency in Western society to compartmentalize religion and science into separate, distinct, and almost incompatible areas of human endeavor. The New Age call for a holistic and integrative way of looking at life is, according to Dinges, 'a creative and contemporary response' to Western 'mind/body/spirit cultural schizophrenia'.

(3) The New Age challenges and makes a judgment of mainline religion. Its stress on experience, rather than dogma, and its interest in mysticism and meditation may lead to spiritual renewal of the Christian Churches, but it may also result in great disagreements between those who favor the incorporation of insights from the New Age and those who reject it *in toto*.[47]

Finally, Dinges enumerates both the positive and negative aspects of the New Age. Among the former he lists the stress on freedom and human solidarity, the concern for ecology, and the need for a creation-centered spirituality. Among the latter he includes the latent Gnosticism, the use of magic, the inability to face the problem of evil, the inclination to self-glorification, and, sometimes, the fraud which underlies the marketing of New Age gimmicks. Discernment, for Dinges, is essential to any evaluation of the New Age.

Like Dinges, Kathy Walsh attempts a balanced assessment of the New Age. She sees the phrase 'New Age' as an umbrella term which comprises different and sometimes conflicting beliefs and activities. The New Age is syncretistic in that it combines beliefs and practices from Eastern religions, from the occult and metaphysical traditions, and from 'native' traditions in the West (like 'Wicca' and American

Indian religions). She pinpoints the fundamental belief of the movement as one which sees the human race 'on the verge of a radical transformation of consciousness (the Age of Aquarius) which will improve dramatically the way human beings relate to each other and to the rest of reality'.[48]

Walsh lists as endemic to the movement several dangers including the uncritical acceptance of Eastern concepts. Thus, she argues:

> The concept of karma, for example, or a belief in the power of the mind to control matter, or both, can give rise to the belief that individuals are totally responsible for creating their own reality. Taken to extremes, this is tantamount to blaming victims for evils or misfortunes that befall them, and becomes a justification for gross inhumanity or injustice.[49]

In like manner she labels as dangerous those trends within the movement that claim that diseases can be cured by mental power, overstress emotion and experience, and put so much emphasis on the individual that empathy, altruism, and communitarian values are discouraged, personal culpability and responsibility downplayed, and reason rejected.

However, in spite of these problems, she does not think that Catholics should respond with fear. She states:

> Nevertheless, Catholics should not unthinkingly accept some of the more alarmist Christian condemnations of the New Age Movement. Indeed, many of the accusations made by fundamentalist Protestants against it are similar to the criticisms they make of Catholicism itself, especially accusations of employing alternative sources of revelation, of superstition and of magical practices.[50]

Moreover, she believes that there is much to learn from the movement. The fact that the Catholic tradition allows for the wider use of the senses in worship and confirms the presence of miracles, angels, and visions should help Catholics accommodate some New Age ideas, for instance, those regarding creation spirituality, and ritual practices. Walsh prefers to apply the approach to non-Christian religions adopted by Vatican Council II to the New Age Movement and to engage in dialogue with its members.

The effort to balance critical assessments of the New Age with an acceptance of its good trends is fairly common. James Wheeler, for instance, finds fault with the movement for advancing a 'spiritual sensuality' which the mystics always found suspect. He, moreover,

thinks that the movement denigrates human individuality by teaching an amorphous union of all. But he points out:

> So it is welcome to see a movement appearing on the horizon that
> emphasizes contact with the spiritual, with prayer, with the life
> hereafter, rather than the consistent and compulsive message of
> how something physically sensual is a panacea.
>
> A movement that embodies the spirit of light and peace, that
> places the material secondary to the spiritual, that stresses the
> development of spiritual powers and presence, is something that
> we would need. It is also heartening to see people begin to search
> on the spiritual plane who have never sought there before.[51]

The more moderate responses to the New Age realize that, even
though its ideology cannot be fully harmonized with tradition, it has
provided a stimulus for theological reflection which might in the
end be beneficial. In the words of two scholars who include the creation spirituality among the movements within the Catholic
Church:

> There is a rule of thumb in classical Catholic theology that no
> movement, not even a heresy, is without some core-truth which
> energizes it and attracts disciples, but which is exaggerated and
> out of balance with other truths. It seems clear enough that
> Catholic Tradition cannot transform itself into Creation
> Spirituality. Too many aspects of biblical revelation would not fit
> that model. But it may well be that some elements of Creation
> Spirituality might, in a nuanced or modified form be assimilated
> to Catholic Tradition.[52]

OFFICIAL CATHOLIC RESPONSES TO THE NEW AGE MOVEMENT

The official Catholic response to the New Age Movement has been,
at best, sporadic and conflicting. Probably one of the most negative
analyses of the New Age Movement in North America has been that
of Francis Cardinal Stafford, former Archbishop of Denver. In his
view the movement is a return to Paganism and a 'perversion of the
Christian faith'. He traces its immediate source to the Age of
Aquarius which was ushered in the West in the early 1960s and
which was typified by an anti-Christian mentality, a fascination with
Eastern religions, and a counter-cultural political ideology. Those
who identified themselves with the New Age fitted comfortably with

the trend of the 1960s that rejected organized religion and hence exalted secularity.

Stafford traces back the New Age Movement to the early Gnosticism, the various gnostic sects (like the Cathars) of the Middle Ages, and more recently to the Rosicrucians, the Theosophical Society, Christian Science, and Transcendentalism. All these he dismisses as promoting nihilist and pessimistic philosophies which, together with cultural anarchy, 'have coalesced in the New Age Movement'. Other characteristic marks of the New Age are its regard of the Church as an obstacle to human progress, its rejection of sacramental realism, and its acceptance of a pagan morality which rejects personal responsibility. Stafford opts for a complete rejection of the New Age and anything vaguely connected with it. He concludes by stating:

> In the end, the New Age is no more than one more pagan soteriology: it looks to the extinction of the good creation that is in Christ, the image of God, in order that one may image Nothing.[53]

Equally negative is the assessment of the New Age made by Archbishop Norberto Rivera Carrera of Mexico City in a 1996 pastoral instruction. In contrast to Stafford's superficial analysis of the New Age, Carrera's pastoral is a lengthy, comprehensive, and well thought-out exposition of what is held to be a dangerous and malicious movement in contemporary culture. Starting with some reflections on the end of the millennium, Carrera[54] calls the New Age Movement 'the most attractive, but also the most ambiguous and questionable expression of this millenarist tendency'. The New Age adheres to an optimistic belief in a forthcoming golden era in which human beings will take a great evolutionary step that will change their consciousnesses.

Carrera lists four major factors that have helped the New Age to expand: (1) the rapid process of globalization; (2) the aggressive commercialization in all areas of human life; (3) the spread of rationalism which has relegated faith to subjective feeling or personal opinion; and (4) the human thirst for transcendence. Against this cultural background, the New Age is seen as a movement that unites people by a common world view or mentality and by fluid communication. And though the movement is not a sect or a religion and has no single directive organization, it can be discerned by four basic beliefs: (1) environmentalism, which fosters the worship of mother Earth; (2) pantheism, where the notion of a personal God,

who is distinct and separate from the created world, is discarded;
(3) Gnosticism, which looks for a superior intellect, esoterism, and
occultism; and (4) pseudo-science, which includes interest in astrology and UFOs.

Without much hesitation the pastoral letter judges the New Age
to be incompatible with the Gospel. Its religious, spiritual, and
moral relativism, its evolutionary perspective which sees the merging with the divine, rather than salvation, as the ultimate human
destiny, its claim that human beings are divine, its acceptance of
many enlightened teachers to guide humanity rather than Jesus
Christ as its sole savior, its belief in reincarnation, and its endorsement of non-Christian meditation techniques place it in direct
confrontation with basic Christianity. In schematic form the following twelve major elements of the New Age are said to be most
opposed to the Christian message: (1) 'it depersonalizes the God of
Christian revelation'; (2) 'it disfigures the person of Jesus Christ,
devalues his mission, and ridicules his redeeming sacrifice'; (3) 'it
denies the unique, unrepeatable event of his Resurrection by affirming the doctrine of reincarnation'; (4) 'it empties the Christian
concepts of creation and salvation of their contents'; (5) 'it rejects
the Church's teaching authority and its institutional forms'; (6) 'it
relativizes the Gospel's original, unique, and historically based content'; (7) 'it deforms language, giving a new meaning to Christian
and biblical terms'; (8) 'it falsely bases its opinions on the writings
of Christian mystics and turns their true meaning upside down'; (9)
'it irreversibly waters down the practice of Christian prayer'; (10) 'it
discards the human person's moral responsibility and denies the
existence of sin'; (11) 'it misleads children and young people in
their religious formation'; (12) 'it divides Christian families and
exploits them for financial gain'.[55]

In what appears to be an attempt to soften this outright and
uncompromising denunciation of the New Age, the pastoral adds
briefly a note of caution:

> Of course, it would be an error to label as harmful everything
> [the] New Age provides and offers. Its spirit of openness and dia-
> logue, its insistence on the human need for a deep religious
> experience, its deep concern for preserving the environment, its
> confidence in the creative power of the human being, its healthy
> recommendations for dieting and physical fitness, and its attitude
> of optimism in the face of grave ills afflicting the world are but a
> few of its positive points that spontaneously come to mind.[56]

The pastoral ends with the task Catholics have 'in the face of the *New Age* confusion'. They are urged to be well-informed about this movement and to defend their faith and values. Members of the clergy are urged to provide instructions in matters of doctrine.

Negative assessments of the New Age are sometimes buttressed by papal statements. Thus, for example, Pope John Paul II, in an address to several American bishops, warned:

> New Age ideas often open up a way for themselves in preaching, catechesis, congresses, and retreats, and thus come to influence even practicing Catholics who may not be aware of the incompatibility of those ideas with the faith of the Church.[57]

Less condemnatory is Archbishop Edward A. McCarthy of Miami in his pastoral instruction entitled 'The New Age Movement', which, he thinks, began in California in the 1960s with the spread of Eastern religions. He describes it as:

> a quasi-religious subculture that is widespread but not in any way sharply defined. It is said to aim at making individuals come in touch with the light of their inner selves and all manifestations of the divine inside and around them through a variety of exercises or techniques involving the mind.[58]

Like Stafford and Carrera, he finds that 'many of the elements of the New Age Movement are altogether incompatible with Christianity'. Its roots lie in a variety of sources, like the Enlightenment, Swedenborgian thought, and Mesmerism, that veered from the Christian tradition. It leaves out completely such basic Christian beliefs as the existence of a personal God, the incarnation, and the redemption offered by Jesus Christ. Pivotal beliefs and practices of New Agers, like astrology, reincarnation, and spiritualism, are not reconcilable with Christianity. But he explicitly recognizes many of the movement's positive features. He writes:

> It does reflect a commitment to the sacred and spiritual, a rediscovery of the transcendent that is a reaction to the scientific rationalism and the secularism of our day. It does reflect the seeking in our time of a living, feeling experience of spirituality through signs and symbols, as do the sacraments. It nourishes self-esteem as a necessary ingredient in the search for truth. It is committed to peace, human happiness, good will and obedience.[59]

He observes 'that actually the Catholic Church offers many of the answers which New Agers are seeking'. The New Age's reaction to scientific rationalism, its integration of matter and spirit, and its stress on mystical experiences are solidly based in the Church's tradition. Spiritual seekers need not look outside the Church in their quest for peace, harmony, and union with God. Parish communities should be challenged by the New Age to reflection, improvement, and reform.

Another comprehensive official response to the New Age Movement can be found in a pastoral letter by Godfried Cardinal Danneels.[60] Danneels begins by giving an overview of new religious movements (sects) which are seen as satisfying genuine human needs that the traditional churches are neglecting. Following the 1986 Vatican document on New Religious Movements,[61] he sees the New Age as a challenge to the Church to strive for greater pastoral effectiveness and a more solid ongoing program of religious education.

Danneels is aware that it is not easy to come up with a clear definition of the New Age. He writes:

> It [the New Age] is not a religion, but it is religious; it is not a philosophy, yet it implies a vision of humankind and of the world and provides a key to the interpretation of this vision; it is not a science, but it makes use of 'scientific' laws, even though these belong to the realm of the stars. New Age is an amorphous amalgam of the esoteric and the occult, of myths and magic about the secrets of life, mixed in with a touch of Christianity and a few ideas derived from astro-physics.[62]

He places its origin in California and links its main ideology to Alice Bailey's publication of *The Reappearance of Christ*.[63] In spite of the fact that it has no founder, no headquarters, no scripture, and no dogmas, the New Age espouses a popular spirituality which has neither God or grace. It is built on four pedestals: (1) a scientific base; (2) oriental religions; (3) a new psychology; and (4) astrology. It is an expression of that gnostic faith which has been around since the early centuries of the Christian era.

While criticizing the New Age for its egocentric world view and its syncretism, Danneels does not link it with Satanism and much less with a satanic conspiracy. And while he states that the New Age is a challenge 'because it directly attacks Christianity', he concurs with McCarthy that

> there are some good things about the New Age. It stresses universal brotherhood, peace and harmony, greater awareness, involvement in making the world a better place, greater mobilization for good,

etc. Moreover, the techniques it promotes are not always bad: yoga and relaxation can have excellent effects.[64]

The letter's tone suggests that the New Age gives alternative answers to the religious quest that is endemic to human nature. It hints that there are several points of contact, such as mysticism, between the New Age and Christianity. It concedes that the New Age criticism of Christianity may not be completely unfounded:

> [t]here may well be some truth in the accusations of New Age against Christianity with respect to the lack of lived experience, the fear of mysticism, the endless moral exhortations and the exaggerated insistence on the orthodoxy of doctrine.[65]

The pastoral's stress, however, is still on those doctrinal issues that make the New Age incompatible with Christianity. It argues that the contents of the Christian faith must be clearly enunciated and the New Age evaluated in the light of true doctrine.

Some official guidelines for dealing with the New Age can also be gleaned from the recent *Catechism of the Catholic Church*, even though no explicit reference is made to the New Age Movement. Regarding reincarnation, the *Catechism*, in a section that deals with the meaning of Christian death, quotes from the letter to the Hebrews (9:29) and from Vatican II's Dogmatic Constitution on the Church,[66] and summarily dismisses the belief with a simple statement: 'There is no "reincarnation" after death.'[67] In like manner, pantheism is declared to be a response to the question of origins that differs from that provided by the Christian faith.[68]

In a section entitled 'You Shall have No Other Gods Before Me', the *Catechism*[69] makes concise statements on superstition, idolatry, divination, and magic. The attribution of magical power to certain practices, including also sacramental signs, is said to be 'a deviation of religious feeling'. Polytheism is a form of idolatry and contradicts the injunction of the first commandment by divinizing what is not God. It is 'a perversion of man's innate religious sense' and thus 'incompatible with communion with God'.

Many of the popular practices of the New Age Movement, such as channeling, divinatory practices like astrology, and magical rituals, are summarily condemned:

> All forms of *divination* are to be rejected: recourse to Satan or demons, conjuring up the dead or other practices falsely suppose to 'unveil' the future. Consulting horoscopes, astrology, palm reading, the interpretation of omens and lots, the phenomenon of

clairvoyance, and recourse to mediums all conceal a desire for power over time, history, and, in the last analysis, other human beings, as well as a wish to conciliate hidden powers. They contradict the honor, respect, and living fear that we owe to God alone.

All practices of *magic* or *sorcery*, by which one attempts to tame occult powers, so as to place them at one's service and have a supernatural power over others – even if this were for the sake of restoring their health – are gravely contrary to the virtue of religion. These practices are even more to be condemned when accompanied by the intention of harming someone, or when they have recourse to the intervention of demons. Wearing charms is also reprehensible. *Spiritism* often implies divination or magical practices; the Church for her part warns the faithful against it. Recourse to so-called traditional cures does not justify either the invocation of evil powers or the exploitation of another's credulity.[70]

The *Catechism*[71] also dedicates several paragraphs to vocal prayer, meditation, and contemplation. Discursive prayer is stressed, even though there is reference to the part played by the imagination and to the need to involve the senses. It is admitted that there 'are as many varied methods of meditation as there are spiritual masters', though there is no attempt to specify what these are and no reference to Eastern meditation techniques that have been popular among New Agers and have, in some cases, been adopted by Catholics to enhance their spiritual lives.

INNOVATIVE CATHOLIC RESPONSES TO THE NEW AGE MOVEMENT

The responses described above have a common interest, namely, that of responding to the challenge the New Age makes to Catholic doctrine and devotional practice. They all find that New Age teachings are in conflict with Catholic doctrine. They differ, however, in that some shun any kind of contact with the New Age and are reluctant to find positive elements in its teachings, while others are more open to listening and learning and hence more willing to recognize the positive contributions that it can make to Christianity and religion in general.

Several Catholics have, however, pursued alternative approaches to the New Age. Some maintain that the New Age contains the ingredients for a renewal or reform of Catholic theology. Others detect an overlapping between New Age and Catholic teachings and conclude that dialogue, rather than confrontation or condemnation, is a better way of dealing with various New Age beliefs and practices that are often rejected as the antithesis of the Christian faith. Still others stress that Catholics have a lot to learn from the New Age.

Probably the most controversial figure in the Catholic response to the New Age is Matthew Fox,[72] who represents the view that some of its major tenets can be accepted by Christians and that its roots can be traced to traditional Christian sources, particularly medieval mysticism. Though other Catholic theologians, notably Thomas Berry,[73] have espoused creation spirituality, particularly as it applies to ecology, feminism, and world religions, Fox has been the focal point of the Catholic debate because of both his writings and his prolonged, public confrontation with the Catholic hierarchy.

Fox is known for a theology which he labels creation spirituality and which, in the words of Rosemary Radford Ruether, can be briefly described, somewhat eclecticically, as follows:

> Creation spirituality starts with original blessing, rather than with original sin. It regains the understanding that our original and true nature, the original and true nature of all things, is 'very good'. Although this good original self has been obscured and distorted by alienation and sin, it is still our authentic self. Redemption comes to us, not as a power alien to our natures, but as an 'aha' experience that puts us back in touch with our authentic natures. Redemption also reconnects us with our relational nexus. We reconnect with the relationship of reason and intuition, consciousness and embodiment, ourselves and others – humans, animals and plants.[74]

In one of his major works,[75] Fox develops at some length the theology of creation spirituality which he believes was the original Christian theology. He elaborates its main concepts by contrasting it with the traditional theology which is centered on the fall and redemption of the human race. This latter theology starts with the assumption that faith is an intellectual assent to doctrinal propositions. It is patriarchal and emphasizes the fatherhood of God. It is further ascetic, with mortification and control of passions as the path to holiness. Its starting point is sin, especially original sin. Human beings are first and foremost sinners who must repent and whose spiritual life is dominated by a quest for personal salvation. Obedience, righteousness, duty, guilt and redemption, and purity from the world are the constant recurring themes. It is, moreover, theistic, underlining a rigid dualism between God and creation. Its christology focuses on the divinity of Christ.

Creation theology takes quite a different stand. It starts by seeing faith as trust. It dwells on the feminist aspect of life and sees God not only as father, but also as mother and child. It celebrates, rather than condemns, the body. It is hopeful rather than pessimistic. It looks for the salvation of the people of God and the cosmos. It acknowledges the presence of a divine quality in humanity. Its virtues are sensuality, justice, beauty, and hospitality. Its concept of God is panentheistic. Its view of Christ is cosmic.[76] Jesus is a prophet, an artist, a storyteller, and Son of God who calls people to their divinity.

Such a theology calls for a paradigm shift and underlines many of the theological and practical underpinnings of the New Age. The concern for the environment, the stress that human beings are basically good with a spark of the divinity embedded in their natures, the effort to stress the cosmic Christ rather than the historical Jesus, the tendency to see all religions as paths to holiness, and the goal of mystic union are common themes in both creation spirituality and in the New Age.

In spite of the fact that New Agers list Fox as one of the sources of their theology, he cannot be completely identified with the New Age Movement. Thus the common accusation that the New Age is a revival of Gnosticism can hardly be applied to Fox, whose view of nature differs radically from that of Gnosticism. Further, Fox does not encourage some New Age practices, like channeling and the use of crystals, that have been the hallmark of many New Agers.

Although many Catholics find Fox's creation spirituality incompatible with Catholic teachings and spirituality, others think that it promotes a change in emphasis rather than a denial of traditional doctrine. Alexandra Kovats, for instance, points out that creation spirituality starts 'by affirming creation and human beings as good and unique expressions of God's creative energy and love'. While she admits that this is in sharp contrast with the fall/redemption spirituality that stresses sinfulness, she insists that creation spirituality does not abandon or deny sin. She writes:

> Creation spirituality acknowledges that the fall happened. We experience the results in our broken relationships with God, with the natural world, with one another and within ourselves. However, before the fall there was a blessing. And blessing is still

with us. The idea is that all of creation – life itself – is a gift from our life-giving, life-sharing creator. As such all creation is meant to be experienced as good. The idea echoes the 'and God saw that it was good' refrain in the creation story in Genesis.[77]

Kovats enumerates several basic insights of creation spirituality. First of all, it celebrates the fact that human beings are made in God's image. Second, it draws attention to the theme that all reality is related and thus promotes compassion. It rejects the dichotomies, such as spirit and matter, male and female, and natural and supernatural, which have dominated Western religious thought. Further, Kovats believes that creation spirituality has also five practical applications to daily Christian living: (1) it invites Christians to see all of life as holy; (2) it sees human beings as blessings; (3) it stresses that life is a gift; (4) it deals with sin, suffering and death (even though it has often been criticized that it ignores them); and (5) it gives importance to the major problems human beings face, namely those relating to ecology, economics, peace, and justice.

The influence of Fox's creation spirituality has been felt in both academic and popular circles. Fox, in spite of the condemnation from church authorities, has continued his teaching and publishing. He has founded 'The University of Creation Spirituality', which offers doctor's and master's degrees and certificates and which includes in its curriculum of courses topics like medieval creation myths, creative spirituality culture, universal themes in myths and dreams, feminism, ecology, and ecumenism. The interest in creation theology and spirituality has also spilled into more traditional Catholic theology, as seen by the number of articles published in Catholic periodicals.[78]

Other Catholics, while not endorsing the theology of the New Age, have maintained that dialogue with it is both necessary and fruitful. One of the most comprehensive Catholic treatments of the New Age Movement has been that of Ronald Quillo, whose dialogical approach stands in sharp contrast to the blanket denunciations and dire warnings of many Christian writers. Quillo starts by observing that a 'major feature of the New Age is its pronounced interest in consciousness'. He then compares and contrasts New Age consciousness with that found in the Bible. His main thesis is that there is more harmony than discord between the two and that they can coexist, even though there are some major disagreements. Christians, therefore, need not feel threatened by the New Age which can provide a new appreciation of biblical teachings.

Quillo finds it hard to give a precise definition of the New Age. He suggests that a common thread of the New Age is 'a renewed and intensified enthusiasm for the nonempirical or spiritual dimensions of reality insofar as they are thought to hold all reality in relatedness, unity, and in a dynamic movement toward improvement'.[79] He then enumerates eleven principles held by New Agers: (1) 'Everything is divine, including human consciousness'; (2) 'Truth is constituted from within'; (3) 'Growth in consciousness or overcoming faulty consciousness is the key to blissful living and the immediate goal of all enlightened persons'; (4) 'Death leads to reincarnation'; (5) 'There are numerous valid paths to divinity'; (6) 'The attainment of bliss involves concern for the good of all'; (7) 'Health means wholeness and unity of body, mind, and spirit'; (8) 'The unity of all requires closeness to and respect of nature'; (9) 'We need to trust intuition, imagination, and feeling'; (10) 'We need to trust paranormal phenomena'; (11) 'We need to trust the divine'.[80]

Quillo next examines selected biblical texts to point out parallels between Christian teachings and New Age principles. Thus, for instance, he finds God's covenant with Abraham in accord with New Age pluralism that respects all religions. Even the manner in which God made the covenant is reminiscent of the New Age belief that dreams and other altered states of consciousness provide contacts with the divine.[81] He quotes various psalms to show that both the Bible and the New Age enjoin human beings to treat nature and the environment with responsibility. And he suggests that God's willingness to forgive, to give human beings a second chance after they had sinned, is based on the same principles that are involved in the theory of reincarnation which provides human beings with renewed opportunities here on earth. He thinks that the biblical teachings of retribution and forgiveness can be linked to the idea of reincarnation.[82]

Parallels between the New Age and the New Testament are also detected by Quillo. The importance of forgiveness, for example, is stressed in both. So also is holistic health. The use of stories by Jesus is not that different from visualization. On several instances in the Gospels Jesus manifests paranormal powers, such as when he calmed the winds and the waves (Luke 8:22–25). Moreover, the use of divination is not unknown in the New Testament. Zachariah, the father of John the Baptist, was chosen to be officiating priest in the temple by the casting of lots (John 1:9) and the apostles adopted the same method to select Matthias as one of the twelve apostles (Acts 1:26). Quillo also interprets references to the return of Elijah and John the Baptist and to Jesus' claim that he will come back as somewhat similar to reincarnation.

Quillo mentions also some of the major differences between the Bible and the New Age. He states, for instance:

> But New Age monism, or belief in the divinity *of* all, differs from a biblical view whereby God is *in* all as a benevolent creator or whereby persons originally created in the image of God can additionally resemble God by grace.[83]

So also, while he argues that both resurrection and reincarnation are forms of rebirth or new life, he admits that the belief in multiple reincarnations on earth differs from the Christian hope in the resurrection. But in spite of the difference, Quillo is able to direct attention to the point of contact between the two beliefs, namely, both 'recognize a solidarity between the living and the dead, either as members of Christ's body or as a community of benevolent spirits'.

With regard to Catholic involvement in the New Age, Quillo holds that Christians can be led away from their institutional church when they discover a spiritual home elsewhere. However, the Christian can 'find certain elements of the New Age attractive – prayers or meditation, perhaps – and use them profitably without diminishing essential Christian beliefs and practices'.[84] He, consequently, advises Christians to be cautious in adopting New Age beliefs and practices: '. . . the prudent Catholic will distinguish between amusement from journalistic astrology and serious faith in a system whose foundations are questionable'.[85]

Quillo also tackles directly the question of whether a Catholic can participate in the New Age Movement. He lists several typical, and not necessarily universal, characteristics of New Agers and thinks that Catholics 'may support and adopt any New Age supposition, perspective, and practice not at odds with Catholic teachings'.[86] Thus, to give one example, Quillo points out that the New Ager usually adopts an ecumenical spirit and respects the sincere and reputable beliefs of other people. Catholics can subscribe to such an attitude provided they do not lose sight of the fact that their spiritual lives revolve around the faith of Jesus Christ and his Church.

A somewhat similar approach is advanced by George Maloney,[87] who favors an ecumenical perspective in his examination of New Age thought. He concentrates on some of the basic ideas that characterize the New Age rather than on its more popular aspects, such as channeling, healing with crystals, and occult practices. He is willing to learn from the movement. Rather than advocating a total rejection of the New Age, he looks for areas of agreement with the Christian tradition. He thinks that the New Age's holistic vision of the universe and the role of humanity in it can be harmonized with Christian thought. He explicitly states that the new paradigm which has been employed to understand and deal with global change in the twentieth century can and should be accepted by Christians, 'insofar as it is compatible with the basic truths of Christian revelation'. And he maintains that the New Age offers a complementary vision to the heavily rationalistic spirituality which has dominated Western Christianity. He favors the development of an Earth spirituality, 'a spirituality that will restore for us the sense of the sacred immanence of the divine in all of God's creation, including ourselves, in our vital relationships with our world'.[88]

According to him several factors have contributed to our lack of harmony with the universe. Both philosophy and theology have tended to separate human beings from nature, the former by stressing human control over nature, the latter by overemphasizing God's transcendence, thereby neglecting the mystical experience of union with God. Maloney[89] attempts to outline what he labels a 'logos mysticism' which stresses the process of interpersonal relationships between God and all creatures. Jesus, the logos, becomes the bridge that spans the nothingness between God and human beings.

Maloney[90] observes that, throughout Christian theology, efforts have been made to present Christ in his relationship to the world and that a theology of the cosmic Christ, more recently revived by Teilhard de Chardin, can be found in the letters of St. Paul, in John's Gospel, and in the writings of the Greek Fathers. Unlike many New Agers, Maloney stresses the cosmic nature of Christ without losing sight of the historical Jesus and his resurrection which is a new beginning.

In sharp contrast to some Catholic writers, such as Mitch Pacwa, Maloney does not dwell on the negative aspects of Jung's religious thought and his rejection of organized Christianity. Rather he accepts some basic insights from Jungian psychology on which, he believes, a Christian spirituality can be built. 'Of the various schools of psychology, I believe the Jungians provide the most insights that are compatible with Christianity.'[91] For him there is much to be gained by recapturing the language of the unconscious, myth, symbols, and sacraments, all of which are central in Jung's religious psychology. Individuals can 'find the divine presence positively working out of the unconscious to bring forth creative, individuated persons with a cosmic sense of belonging to the universe and contributing to its rich development in terms of highest moral values'.[92]

While Quillo and Maloney tackle the problem of relating the New Age to Christianity on a popular level, Michael Fuss presents a more deeply theological approach.[93] Fuss offers a uniquely European perspective and begins by delineating four European roots of the New Age: (1) the Judeo-Christian tradition; (2) secularization and science; (3) gnosis, heresies, and esotericism; and (4) oriental religion. He traces the New Age, with its key concept of an emerging new consciousness, to Swedenborg, who is the 'main inspirer of New Age philosophy'. And he observes that transformative communities, like those of Esalen and Findhorn, have been motivated by the modern neo-gnostic circles.

Fuss centers his remarks on the New Age on six of its key concepts: (1) holism, the new paradigm which 'pretends to offer a theoretical frame to integrate the entire worldview of modern man' and which implies that the divine pervades the whole universe; (2) transformation, which is more than a reformation, for it aims at a radical change of consciousness and not just an improvement, and which is equivalent to the Christian idea of redemption; (3) ecology, the concern for which is based on the new mythology of the Mother Goddess and is hence a revival of cosmic religion; (4) reincarnation, which indicates an individualistic approach to salvation and presents a radical change from belief in the resurrection; (5) a new Christology, where the cosmic Christ becomes the solar Logos and ceases to be the biblical Jesus and in which 'the entire revelation of the historical Jesus is an applied oriental wisdom'; and (6) the network, which diffuses New Age ideas through the different methods of mass communication prevalent in modern society. Fuss locates this medium on the level of mass communication which promises immediate satisfaction and tends to manipulate religious and ethical values.[94]

Finally, Fuss works out several elements that must guide a theological evaluation of the New Age. The first is to consider 'European theology of liberation based on the option for dialogue'. Fuss maintains that the presence of the New Age reveals the need for a liberating Messiah who is not to be found either in human reason or in gnosis. He finds Christian salvation and holistic healing incompatible since the latter assumes that the human being is part of the divine nature. Next, he proposes that the European capacity for synthesis (not syncretism) can create a new balance in bringing together different religious strands. And finally he believes that the new situation demands a 'radical preferential option for dialogue' which goes beyond ecumenism and which reaches out to non-Christian communities. He suggests that cosmic religion should become 'a common basis for theological discourse' and that the 'trinitarian mystery of the Christian God contains the key for a meaningful theological discourse in a changing culture'.[95]

In contrast to several superficial handlings of and responses to the New Age, David Toolan's erudite and highly sophisticated analysis[96] is in a class by itself. Toolan, like Pacwa, though probably to a lesser degree, was personally involved in the New Age scene, but on a deeper and more intellectual level. He considers the quest for meaning and healing, which are central to New Age consciousness, as being rooted in both Eastern and Western contemplative and mystical traditions. He, therefore, sees a continuity between Christian thought and some philosophical and theological trends in the New Age. Uniting modern developments in philosophy, psychology, physics, and cosmology, Toolan looks towards future developments in Christian theology that would incorporate the best elements of the New Age.[97] He faults the New Age for its idealism and self-centeredness and accuses the movement of having a 'claustrophobic, inbred quality characteristic of sects concerned only with saving club-members' own skins'.[98] In agreement with many Christian and non-Christian critics, he dismisses the crystal gazers and psychic channelers as 'the lunatic fringe'.[99]

Many Catholics who have responded to the New Age have pointed out that a lot can be learned from its presence. Richard Woods is one of the most articulate writers who have specified more precisely what the New Age can teach. Rather than interpreting the New Age as an unorthodox religious system which should be opposed at all costs, he states:

> I am convinced that New Age beliefs are a thoroughly Christian phenomenon. As such it has its origins in the late Jewish apocalyptic and early Christian expectations. And just as it is the product of a Christian view of the world, its history, and its destiny in relation to God, how we speak about God in the light of today's New Age spiritualities, as well as how we look on the New Age 'movement' itself will reflect our Christian vision and attitudes.[100]

Woods treats the New Age as a millennial movement and briefly outlines the Christian belief in the advent of a New Age. Relying on sociological and psychological studies on religion, he points out that when organized religions lose their credibility, people turn to more satisfying belief systems. In so doing they run the risk of reverting to more primitive forms of religions and to superstition which is 'a lucrative enterprise of rather vast proportions and often tragically destructive consequences'. He avoids condemnation, but favors a critical approach to New Age. He writes:

> Not all New Age Spirituality is dangerous, very little is destructive, some is positively beneficial. It is wise to be generous in sifting the wheat from the chaff, given the human propensity toward prejudice. But it is also wise to test the spirits. Uncritical and enthusiastic endorsements of New Age spiritualities are as unhelpful as uncritical and blanket condemnations.[101]

He finally lists four lessons one can learn from the success of the New Age. The first thing that the New Age teaches us is to be critical of the way we usually talk about God. The Christian view of God has been, in his opinion, so academic and conceptual that it has become divorced from life. It has assumed that mainstream Christians have a copyright on what to say about God. It has also been too moralistic and too negative. Secondly, the New Age directs our attention to the mystical dimension of Christianity. It is the ignorance, on the part of Christians, of their rich mystical tradition that accounts, in part at least, for the success of New Age spiritualities. Thirdly, the New Age directs our attention to evangelization which must be characterized by honesty, openness, and attractiveness. It must also be discerning. 'In some respects', he adds, 'such as involvement in astrology, reincarnation, nature-worship and the like, Christians must distance themselves from what have been recognized consistently and properly as blind alleys and superstitions.'[102] Finally, the New Age is an opportunity for dialogue with different religious traditions, a dialogue which requires respect between partners.

A recent, if less intellectual, addition to the religion resources on the Internet offers another imaginative Catholic approach to the New Age.[103] Under the leadership of Lavinia Byrne, those who contribute to this Web site, which is still under development, declare that they are Christians and yet feel very much part of New Age hopes and aspirations. They confess:

we acknowledge the relationship of spirit and matter.
we are concerned for our environment.
we respect what is valuable in all truly spiritual traditions.
we believe that salvation affects the whole person in body and soul.

The aims of this Web site are: (1) to answer questions dealing with New Age thought. Among the topics taken up so far are the belief in reincarnation, especially among Catholics, the reasons behind such a belief, the questions which reincarnation raises in ministry, and some recent Catholic writings on the subject; and (2) to provide courses, such as one on 'Mystic Meditation', that deal with various aspects of spirituality.

The more open Catholic approaches to the New Age differ among themselves in the extent to which they accept New Age ideas and in the criticisms they offer of its beliefs and practices. To all, however, encountering the New Age can be a learning experience and adopting some of its spirituality can be enriching. The whole tenor of this Catholic response to the New Age echoes Vatican II's approach to non-Christian religions, that is, one not of condemnation or rejection, but rather of exploration of whatever good they have to offer.

THE PROMISE AND PERIL OF THE CATHOLIC RESPONSE

Catholic commentators on the New Age offer a variety of irreconcilable responses to the religious issues raised by a movement that is, beyond any doubt, leaving its mark on Catholic theology, spirituality, and devotion. They start from diverse theological assumptions and adopt different theologies of religion. They share, however, several things in common: (1) they show little interest in giving the New Age an apocalyptic interpretation; (2) they are much less pessimistic than fundamentalist Christian writings about the possible outcome of the New Age; and (3) with few exceptions, they are less hysterical in tone than many of the responses that have stemmed from fundamentalist and evangelical sources. Moreover, in many reactions to the New Age one can detect an ambivalent theology of religions. Even official or semi-official statements, while eager to promote the approach of dialogue adopted by Vatican Council II, frequently end up taking an apologetical and condemnatory stance which does not contribute to dialogue.

The first approach, which adopts a traditional standpoint and advances a total rejection of the New Age, is, from a theological standpoint, the weakest. Its condemnation rests on the identification of false doctrines conceived as static propositional statements and assumes that theological speculation and development have already come to an end. It is entirely defensive of the status quo and is concerned that variety within the Church is likely to destroy its unity. The results are theological stagnation or fossilization and religious conflicts, since little attempt is made to discover similarities and build on common ground. Mutual exchange of ideas becomes impossible and participation in ritual is frowned upon as an implicit denial of one's belief or as an act which endangers it. This Catholic approach is against any form of dialogue and, at best, gives only lip service to the 'Vatican Declaration on Non-Christian Religions'. It fits into the ideology of fundamentalist Catholic groups and sects which have proliferated since Vatican II.[104]

Moreover, this approach not only makes theological discourse between Christians and New Agers virtually impossible, but also creates serious obstacles to human discourse and communication. Thus, to cite a fairly typical example, Ferreira's arguments against the New Age are, from a theological point of view, of poor quality. She displays little knowledge of history and Catholic theology. Her theological method seems to consist of selecting and stressing certain aspects of Catholic tradition that fit into her preconceived religious and political agenda. A clear instance of this is her view that the New Age stress on globalism is satanic and goes against patriotism which is a Christian virtue. But she fails to observe that the 'charity of patriotism, while being preferential in its practical object, is at the same time universal in its ultimate aims'.[105] She forgets that, while patriotism may indeed be a virtue, provincialism is not. Her tendency to ignore the global picture is, moreover, unrealistic because it leaves out contemporary changes in society and culture. The castle mentality she betrays fits more comfortably into a medieval framework than in a situation where barriers between nations are crumbling and where contact with religious pluralism is becoming part of the average person's daily experience. Another example is her comment that the New Age proposes a new form of government which is at odds with that of the Judeo-Christian tradition. She never specifies what this Judeo-Christian government really is. Nor does she bother to ask the question whether there is indeed a specific type of government that fits into this tradition. Moreover, she seems completely oblivious of Catholic teachings on social justice. Added to this, she is unaware of the move toward inculturation,[106] which assumes that at least some indigenous and non-Christian customs can be imbued with the Christian spirit and become part of the variety that pertains to a universal faith which is not inextricably linked to one particular historical period or cultural context.

The same tendency to reject everything that is not traditionally Catholic can be detected in Pacwa's analysis of the New Age. Some of his critical remarks – for example, those on astrology, Jungian psychology, and Matthew Fox's creation spirituality – are valid. They are, however, deficient for the precise reason that they make no mention of their attractive features that can be reconciled with Christian doctrine. He does not follow the official procedures of dialogue that the Catholic Church has adopted since Vatican II. The way he deals with Jung is typical of the method that builds walls of separation rather than bridges to understanding. Pacwa rightly reminds his readers of Jung's personal antipathy to Christianity and mythological interpretation of the major Christian articles of faith. He then adds: 'My problems with Jung do not necessarily stem from the psychological insights he offers. In the hands of a professional, these can be useful for personal growth.'[107] Surely, this is the very area that requires further study and elaboration.[108] Catholics are not attracted to Jung because of his anti-Christian sentiments. It is Jung's original psychological insights, his appreciation of spiritual matters, and his sensitivity to the individual's religious quest that account to a large extent for the revival of interest in his works. Moreover, Jung's psychological insights are not necessarily inseparable from his rejection of Christianity.

In like manner Pacwa's approach to Fox's creation-centered spirituality is not only defective but also reflective of the same sloppy scholarship of which he accuses Fox. First of all, although he dedicates a whole chapter to the topic, he never quite explains what Fox's view is. Consequently he never advances a proper theological critique of his theology. Moreover, the average reader, for whom the book is intended, is never informed of creation theology, which is a respectable branch of theology in traditional circles.[109] A dialogical approach would have started with a brief and accurate exposition of Fox's theology based on his original works. This would have been followed by an outline of the traditional theology of creation with its application to spiritual life. Then an evaluation of Fox's views would have been attempted while noting the similarities and differences between the two systems. Finally, the good elements in Fox's view which can be harmonized with, and possibly enrich, Christian spirituality would have been duly noted. To assume, from the beginning, that Fox's theology is heretical and cannot teach us anything violates the basic laws of dialogue as well as the fundamental rules of human relationships. It further ignores the claim that creation spirituality has enhanced the spiritual lives of many Christians.

Another example of the way in which this stagnant approach to spirituality is manifested is seen in the treatment of parapsychological topics. There is a tendency to dismiss all ESP phenomena as dangerous and anti-Christian. The criteria for reaching such a judgment are not always clear. Telepathy, clairvoyance, paranormal healing, out-of-body and near-death experiences, apparitions, and contact with the saints or spirits of the dead are all treated with suspicion or simply denounced because of their connection with the occult and with the New Age. The fact that such phenomena are not unknown in Christianity and have been observed in many saints is ignored. While the incorporation of many of these occult topics, some of which have become magical fads, into Christian spirituality may indeed be out of the question, it does not mean that they all should be denounced as dangerous and satanic.[110] On the contrary, some have even suggested that extra-sensory perception can be useful in pastoral ministry.[111] Others think that the interpretation of dreams, which is not unknown in the Bible, can play a part in the development of one's spirituality.[112]

Rath is one of the few conservative commentators on the New Age who refers to interreligious dialogue. Yet he exhibits little understanding of the requirements of dialogue and even less appreciation of the fact that dialogue is basically a relationship between individuals who are deeply committed to their respective belief system. At one point he states that 'the New Age is based on deception. This is certainly allied to the satanic.'[113] Such statements reiterate the familiar anticult rhetoric that indiscriminately lumps together all non-Christian movements (such as Transcendental Meditation, Yoga groups, contemporary Paganism, and satanic cults). They are a form of demagoguery and definitely are not conducive to dialogue. Rath, moreover, fails to find any points of contact between the New Age and Christianity. In his final two chapters on basic Christian teachings and evangelization he relies completely on fundamentalist literature. Although he correctly draws attention to the fact that the New Age religion differs from Christianity in doctrine, he overstresses the pantheistic element in the former and fails to make any reference to Christian teachings on the indwelling of the Holy Spirit and divinization. And he omits any reference to the rich tradition of Christian mysticism. Apparently unaware of the changing cultural and religious world view of the late twentieth century, he responds to the New Age unconstructively and ineffectively. In the end his remarks are unproductive; they only succeed in buttressing the convictions of those who already share his opinions.

A common feature that dominates this Catholic approach is fear. Those Catholics who subscribe to it are apparently afraid that Christianity is under attack, that it runs the risk of being overrun and becoming a minority religion with little influence on people's lives. This attitude is not founded on accurate knowledge on the New Age, which is too diffuse and unorganized to mount a real threat. The New Age is made up of too many incompatible beliefs and magical practices to become a world religion. It does not threaten the survival of Christianity, which is certainly not bankrupt, but rather presents a creative challenge to Christians in an age of change and turmoil.

The second approach to the New Age is characterized by some openness with hesitation. It is less fearful and less concerned with the success of the New Age. Its willingness to recognize some good qualities in the movement is a move in the right direction. But it is slow in developing these qualities. It lacks imagination. Like the previous approach it does not realize that many Christian customs and practices became traditional over many centuries and were borrowed from pagan sources and 'Christianized' in the process.

Official and semi-official reactions to the New Age are, like the previous two approaches, still concerned with Christian doctrine and suspicious that any contact with the New Age might lead to the loss of one's faith. Responses like those of Stafford and Carrera can easily be classified with conservative and fundamentalist literature which adds little to understanding and even less to dialogue. Other responses, like those of Danneels and McCarthy, seem more favorable to dialogue and are more in harmony with the 1986 'Vatican Statement on New Religious Movements', which acknowledged that these religions are satisfying some basic human and spiritual needs and which was more interested in the Catholic Church's task to see that such needs are satisfied within the framework of Church teaching and practice. They are also more open to admit that Christians can learn from the New Age, even though many of the elements of its spirituality and teachings cannot be harmonized with Christian doctrine.

The final Catholic approach described above is the most promising. It contains some insights into New Age philosophy and theology. It fits more comfortably with the contemporary efforts at interreligious dialogue and with the inculturation processes now at work in Africa and Asia. It can also lead to the discovery and appreciation of certain neglected elements of the Christian faith. Among its weaknesses and difficulties are the dangers of syncretism, that is, of adopting some New Age beliefs and customs without reflecting whether and to what degree they can be harmonized with Christianity. In many cases there is little discernment and one is left with the impression that the New Age is more or less another Catholic movement. There is also insufficient awareness of the difficulties in interreligious dialogue and of additional problems and obstacles brought about by the presence of new religious movements, including the New Age.[114]

Some Catholic commentators appear to be too inclined to accept and Christianize any New Age belief and/or practice. Matthew Fox is a good representative of this method. While his approach may be better suited at establishing a relationship of dialogue with the New Age, his dichotomy between creation spirituality and redemption spirituality is overstressed. Margaret Atkins,[115] for example, has remarked that St. Augustine, who doesn't fare well in Fox's assessment of current Catholic theology, 'provides certain valuable insights for a balanced and properly theocentric theology of nature'.

Ronald Quillo's interpretation of the New Age and his efforts to find common ground between New Age and Christian beliefs are more promising. But several of the similarities between the New Age and Christianity on which he dwells at length are rather far-fetched. His own analysis shows that the differences are profound and unreconcilable. In the final chapter of his book he places together in schematic form the eleven principles of the New Age and the corresponding biblical teachings.[116] Even a cursory reading would show that fewer than half these principles have parallels in Christianity.

A good instance of Quillo's ambiguous approach is the way he handles the New Age belief that everything is divine, a belief that has led many commentators to dismiss it outrightly as a heretical, pantheistic system. Quillo points out that it is a basic Christian tenet that the divine presence (God) is in all creation, especially in human consciousness. But then he seems to equate the New Age principle that everything is divine, including human consciousness, with the Christian belief that human beings are made in God's image and participate in the life of Christ. Again, while he affirms that New Age monism is difficult to reconcile with the personal God of the Bible, he is apparently unaware that this monistic premise colors practically all New Age beliefs and practices.

In like manner his efforts to draw parallels between New Age involvement in ESP and the paranormal powers mentioned in scripture are interesting. However, he omits to mention that in the New Age there is a stress on the individual's need to develop and use such powers, a stress which is not in the Bible. How one deals with such practices as channeling, divination (by astrology or the use of the tarot), and healing by crystals is left unanswered. One really wonders whether the New Age reliance on the paranormal and on the divine is ultimately an acknowledgment of the person's own inner strength rather than an act of trust in a saving God.

Quillo[117] admits that his conclusion, namely, that scripture and the New Age contain more similarities than differences is controversial. Less debatable, however, is his view that both New Agers and Christians can learn from each other. And one can hardly argue with his efforts to carry on a healthy conversation with people who hold diverse beliefs. In spite of its shortcomings, Quillo's method can lead to a better understanding of the New Age and impel Christians to delve more deeply into their own rich traditional heritage.

These more favorable evaluations of the New Age, however, seem too reluctant to fault the New Age. Dinges was correct when, reflecting on the New Age, he remarked: 'Nonsense, farce, and sin must be called by their proper name.'[118] A good example can be taken from Shirley MacLaine's New Age experiences. On one occasion, having heard of a death of a friend in a car accident, she remarked: 'why did he choose to die that way?' The answer is simple: the individual did not choose to die in a car crash. Death is the common lot of humankind and people do not determine how and when they die, unless they opt for suicide. MacLaine's tenet that a person can choose whether and when to get sick or die is, to say the least, unrealistic. It can also be quite dangerous and harmful to those who go about believing that positive thinking can automatically influence the course of events. It is assertions like these that have elicited negative reactions not just from Christian commentators but also from social scientists.

The danger of some Catholic responses to the New Age is that they might easily degenerate into all-out attacks against anything even vaguely resembling the New Age or else accept New Age principles and endorse its practices without discriminating between what is valuable and truly compatible with Catholic teaching and what is not. While the promise of other responses is their willingness to start with a theology of religions that is more in tune with Vatican II's 'Declaration on Non-Christian Religions' and the work of the Pontifical Council for Interreligious Dialogue and that allows room for both theological development and spiritual growth. The challenge of the New Age for Catholics is to determine whether, while remaining faithful to their tradition, they can treat the New Age as a genuine religious movement and apply to it the same theology of religions that official Church documents have used in the treatment of other faiths. The questions that need to be answered are whether the New Age contains any truth and revelation and whether Catholicism can be enriched by its contact with the religious expressions and spiritualities generated by a movement that has probably already left a lasting impact on popular religion at the end of the second millennium.

NOTES

1. For a brief summary of the main forms of pluralistic theologies of religions, see James C. Livingston, *Anatomy of the Sacred: An Introduction to Religion* (New York: Macmillan, 3rd ed., 1998), pp. 425ff.

2. 'The New Age Movement: the kingdom of Satan on earth', *Homiletic and Pastoral Review* 91 (August/September 1991): 10.

3. Ibid., p. 15.

4. See, for example, *The Fatima Crusader*, a North American publication by the National Committee for the National Pilgrim Virgin of Canada.

5. 'The New Age Movement: the kingdom of Satan on earth', p. 18.

6. 'A closer look at the New Age Movement', *Christ to the World* 40.1 (1995): 65.

7. Ibid., p. 68. Cf. *Acta Apostolicae Sedis* 11 (1919), p. 317 and Henricus Denzinger, *Enchiridion Symbolorum* (New York: Herder, 1965), no. 3648.

8. 'Salvifici Doloris' ('On the Christian meaning of suffering', Feb. 11, 1984), *The Church Speaks: The Church Documentary Quarterly* 29.2 (1984): 105–39.

9. 'The New Age fun house', *Homiletic and Pastoral Review* 91 (October 1991): 17–21.

10. *The Unicorn in the Sanctuary: The Impact of the New Age Movement on the Catholic Church* (Rockford, IL: TAN Books and Publishers, Inc., 1991), especially ch. 7, pp. 135ff.

11. Ibid., p. 153.

12. Ibid., pp. 42–43 and 67–77.

13. Ibid., p. 100.

14. See his book *Sadhana, A Way to God: Christian Exercises in Eastern Form* (St. Louis: Institute of Jesuit Resources, 1979).

15. *The Unicorn in the Sanctuary*, p. 106.

16. *Fundamentals of the Faith: Essays in Christian Apologetics* (San Francisco: St. Ignatius Press, 1988), pp. 102–6.

17. *The New Age: A Christian Critique* (South Bend, IN: Greenlawn Press, 1990), p. 5.

18. Ibid., p. 303.

19. See, for instance, James Richardson, 'Conversion careers', *Society* 17.3 (1980): 47–50. Pacwa's own religious journey seems to fit in Richardson's description of those individuals who go through sequential conversions to quite different belief systems.

20. *Catholics and the New Age* (Ann Arbor, MI: Servant Publications, 1992), p. 13.

21. 'When the New Age comes to your parish', *New Covenant* 21 (March 1992): 9.

22. *Catholics and the New Age*, pp. 121ff.

23. Ibid., pp. 173ff. See also Mitch Pacwa, 'Catholicism for the New Age: Matthew Fox and creation-centered spirituality', *Christian Research Journal* 15 (Fall 1992): 14–16, 18–19, 29–31.

24. *Catholics and the New Age*, p. 181.

25. Ibid., pp. 192–203.

26. 'When the New Age comes to your parish', pp. 9ff.

27. 'The New Age Movement: no effort, no truth, no solutions', *New Oxford Review* 58 (April 1991): 8.

28. Ibid., pp. 11–12.

29. 'Discerning the New Age', *New Covenant* 19 (March 1990): 6–7.

30. Douglas Groothuis, *Unmasking the New Age* (Downers Grove, IL: InterVarsity Press, 1986).

31. 'A closer look at the New Age Movement', p. 65.

32. 'The New Age Movement and Christianity', a leaflet published by Dove Publications (Pecos, NM).

33. 'The New Age Movement', *The Month* 25 (March 1992): 84–89.

34. Ibid., p. 88.

35. 'The New Age Movement – a new religion?' *The Furrow* 43 (1992): 352.

36. Ibid., p. 353.

37. 'New Age: la dolce vita', *Il Regno* 37, no. 665 (July 15, 1991): 425–29.

38. He refers specifically to Marie-France James's book *Les Précurseurs de l'ère du Verseau: jalons du renouveau de l'ésotéro-occultisme de 1850 à 1960* (Montréal: Editions Paulines, 1985).

39. 'New Age: la dolce vita', pp. 428–29.

40. 'New Age: l'alba di una nuova era', *Sette e Religioni: Rivista Trimestrale di Cultura Religiosa* 1 (1991): 410–29.

41. 'Pourquoi le Nouvel Age fascine-t-il?', *Lumen Vitae* 48 (1993): 255.

42. 'Christianisme et Nouvel Age', *Lumen Vitae* 48 (1993): 262.

43. 'New Age Movement. What is it? Is it really new?' in James LeBar et al., *Cults, Sects, and the New Age* (Huntington, IN: Our Sunday Visitor, 1989), p. 152.

44. Ibid., p. 165.

45. 'Aquarian spirituality: the New Age Movement in America', *Catholic World* (May/June 1989): 138.

46. The issue is discussed at length by Winston L. King, in his essay 'Eastern religions: a new interest and influence', *The Annals of the American Academy of Political and Social Science* 387 (January 1970): 66–76.

47. 'American spirituality: the New Age Movement in America', *The Catholic World* (May/June 1989): 141.

48. 'The Age of Aquarius', *The Tablet* 249 (May 20, 1995): 629.

49. Ibid., p. 630.

50. Ibid.

51. 'Reflections on narcissism, the "New Age" movement and intimacy with God', *Journal of Christian Healing* 13 (Fall 1991): 28.

52. Robert L. Fastiggi and Charles Stinson, 'New Religious Movements within the Catholic Church', *Jeevadhara* 20 (1990): 387.

53. 'The "New Age" movement: analysis of a new attempt to find salvation apart from Christian faith', *L'Osservatore Romano* (English edition), N. 4 (January 27, 1993): 11.

54. 'A call to vigilance: pastoral instruction on New Age', *Catholic International* 7 (August/September 1996): 408.

55. Ibid., p. 414.

56. Ibid., p. 415.

57. Address to the Bishops of Iowa, Kansas, Missouri, and Nebraska, *L'Osservatore Romano* (English edition) (May 28, 1993).

58. 'The New Age Movement: pastoral instruction', *Catholic International* 3 (April 1–14, 1992): 334.

59. Ibid., p. 335.

60. For an English translation see *Christ or Aquarius?: Exploring the New Age Movement* (Dublin: Veritas, 1992). Excerpts from this pastoral have been published in *Catholic International* 2 (May 1991): 480–88.

61. 'Sects or New Religious Movements: pastoral challenge' in *New Religious Movements and the Churches*, ed. Allan R. Brockway and J. Paul Rajashekar (Geneva: WCC Publications, 1987), pp. 180–97.

62. *Christ or Aquarius?*, pp. 24–25.

63. New York: Lucis Trust, 1978 [first published 1948].

64. *Christ or Aquarius?*, p. 35.

65. Ibid., p. 27.

66. *The Documents of Vatican II*, ed. Walter M. Abbott (London: Geoffrey Chapman, 1966), p. 48.

67. *Catechism of the Catholic Church* (Liguori, MO: Liguori Publications, 1994), #1013, p. 264.

68. Ibid., #285, p. 74.

69. Ibid., #2110–2117, pp. 512–14.

70. Ibid, #2116–2117, pp. 513–14.

71. Ibid., #2700–2719, pp. 648–52, where several principles are included under the heading 'Expressions of prayer'.

72. For a short biographical account of Fox's career see Mitch Pacwa, 'Catholicism for the New Age: Matthew Fox and creation-centered spirituality', *Christian Research Journal* 15 (Fall 1992): 16. Matthew Fox's troubles with the Catholic hierarchy and with his religious superiors have been reported in many newspapers. See, for example, Jane Gross, 'Vatican orders a year of silence for a "new age" Catholic priest', *New York Times* 138 (October 9, 1989): 21.

73. See, for instance, his book *Befriending the Earth* (Mystic, CT: Twenty-third Publications, 1991).

74. 'What is creation spirituality'. This short excerpt, which can be found on the Creation Spirituality Home Page on the Internet (http://www.csnet.org/), is adapted from her essay published in the November/December 1990 issue of *Creation Spirituality* magazine.

75. *Original Blessing: A Primer of Creation Spirituality* (Santa Fe, NM: Bear and Co., 1983), pp. 316–19.

76. See Matthew Fox, *The Coming of the Cosmic Christ: The Healing of Mother Earth and the Birth of a Global Renaissance* (San Francisco: Harper and Row, 1988).

77. 'Creation spirituality', *Praying*, no. 25 (July/August 1988): 5.

78. Thus, for instance, the November 1990 issue of *The Month* (vol. 23) was dedicated to 'creation theology', while the Spring issue 1989 of *Listening* (vol. 24) and the January 1993 issue of *The Way* (vol. 29) were devoted to creation spirituality.

79. *Companions in Consciousness: The Bible and the New Age Movement* (Liguori, MO: Triumph Books, 1994), p. 27.

80. Ibid., pp. 31ff.

81. Ibid., pp. 64–65.

82. Ibid., pp. 84–85. Cf. also Robert Quillo, *Catholic Answers to Questions About the New Age Movement* (Liguori, MO: Liguori Publications, 1995), p. 39.

83. *Companions in Consciousness*, p. 156.

84. *Catholic Answers to Questions About the New Age Movement*, p. 16.

85. Ibid., p. 30.

86. Ibid., p. 59.

87. *Mysticism and the New Age: Christic Consciousness in the New Creation* (New York: Alba House, 1991).

88. Ibid., p. 22.

89. Ibid., pp. 51ff.

90. *The Cosmic Christ: From Paul to Teilhard* (New York: Sheed and Ward, 1968), pp. 59–112.

91. *Mysticism and the New Age*, p. 124.

92. Ibid., p. 138.

93. 'New Age and Europe – a challenge for theology', *Mission Studies* 7.2 (1992): 190–220.

94. Ibid., pp. 198–206.

95. Ibid., pp. 211–12.

96. *Facing West from California's Shores: A Jesuit's Journey into New Age Consciousness* (New York: Crossroad, 1987).

97. In a similar approach, Bede Griffiths outlines some of the positive impact the New Age can have on both Christian theology and practice. See his *A New Vision of Reality: Western Science, Eastern Mysticism and Christian Faith* (Springfield, IL: Templegate Publishers, 1989).

98. 'Harmonic convergences and all that: New Age spirituality', *The Way* 32 (1992), p. 42.

99. Ibid., p. 35.

100. 'New Age spiritualities: how are we to talk of God?', *New Blackfriars* 74 (April, 1993): 178.

101. Ibid., p. 189.

102. Ibid., p. 188.

103. 'Spiritual wholeness: welcome to our New Age Catholic Web site', http://www.spiritual-wholeness.org/ [date modified: 11/11/97; date down-loaded: 12/12/97].

104. For a general description of this traditional Catholic position, see William D. Dinges, 'Roman Catholic Traditionalism in the United States' in *Fundamentalism Observed*, ed. Martin E. Marty and R. Scott Appleby (University of Chicago Press, 1991), especially pp. 86–87.

105. J. J. Wright, 'Patriotism' in *The New Catholic Encyclopedia* (New York: McGraw-Hill Book Co., 1967), vol. 10, p. 1102.

106. For a brief summary of what inculturation is, cf. Eugene Hillman, 'Inculturation' in *The New Dictionary of Theology*, ed. Joseph A. Komonchak, Mary Collins, and Dermot A. Lane (Wilmington, DE: Michael Glazier, 1987), pp. 510–13.

107. Mitch Pacwa, *Catholics and the New Age*, p. 68.

108. Towards the end of his book (*Catholics and the New Age*, p. 189), Mitch Pacwa counsels Catholics to 'look for good in their [i.e., New Agers'] ideas and relate it to the truth that God has already revealed'. He disappoints his readers, however, by not following his own advice.

109. For brief summaries see Zachary Hayes, 'Creation' in *The New Dictionary of Catholic Spirituality*, ed. Michael Downey (Collegeville, MN: Liturgical Press, 1993), pp. 238–42; and Denis Carroll, 'Creation' in *The New Dictionary of Theology*, pp. 246–58.

110. See, for example, John J. Heaney, *The Sacred and the Psychic: Parapsychology and Christian Theology* (Ramsey, NJ: Paulist Press, 1984).

111. Harold Sherman, 'Pastoral uses of ESP' in *Christianity and the Paranormal: A Collection of Writings from Periodicals of the Fellowship*, ed. Frank C. Tribbe (Independence, MO: Spiritual Frontiers Fellowship Press, 1986), pp. 58–64.

112. See, for example, Kelly Bulkley, 'Dreams, spirituality, and root metaphors', *Journal of Religion and Health* 31 (1992): 197–206.

113. *The New Age: A Christian Critique*, p. 273.

114. John A. Saliba, 'Dialogue with the new religious movements: issues and prospects', *Journal of Ecumenical Studies* 39 (1993): 51–80.

115. 'The hippo and the fox: a cautionary tale', *New Blackfriars* 73 (1992): 497. For another critical assessment of Fox's views, cf. Donna Runnalls, 'Matthew Fox and creation spirituality', *Touchstone* 10.2 (May 1982): 27–36.

116. *Companions in Consciousness*, pp. 155–56.

117. Ibid., p. 166.

118. 'Aquarian spirituality: the New Age Movement in America', p. 142.

5

TOWARD A CHRISTIAN EVALUATION
OF THE NEW AGE MOVEMENT

The presence and influence of the New Age Movement in the latter part of the twentieth century calls for a Christian response that is clear, reflective, and critical. But for any response to be effective it must avoid emotional outbursts, inaccurate representations, and wild accusations. What Christians who come in touch with the New Age Movement need is accurate information about its beliefs and practices and a solid background in Christian theology. They must also develop methods for evaluating the religious presuppositions and spiritual aspirations that underlie New Age theology and spirituality.

Unfortunately, Christian reactions to the New Age have been mixed and have ranged from complete rejection to unreflective acceptance. The result is that Christians are confused when they feel confronted or challenged by the New Age. Without the tools for discernment they can easily fall into the trap of identifying anything vaguely resembling the New Age with satanic interference or else of indiscriminately incorporating its teachings and practices into their own religious world view.

Whether the current apologetic attacks against the New Age are having a measurable impact on its popularity is debatable. The refutation of its philosophical and theological premises and the ridiculing of its magical beliefs (like those concerning the healing powers of crystals) and spiritual practices (like channeling) are probably having little effect on those already committed to them. Livid condemnation of New Age ideas, blanket accusations of satanic involvement, and emotional tirades against its ritual practices are more likely to reinforce New Agers' dislike of and attacks on Christianity.[1] The reasons why the popularity of the New Age has already peaked and might also be waning are due more to the problems endemic to the movement itself than to outside factors.[2] There is no doubt, however, that even if the New Age Movement will not survive, it has already left its mark on contemporary religion and culture. Thus, for example, Jungian psychology and holistic health, both of which are an integral part of New Age, have been incorporated in retreat programs and have influenced many Christians seeking growth in their spiritual lives. Christians are, therefore, justified in their concern for a growing religious or spiritual revival and in their efforts to draw up pastoral responses to its evangelical efforts.

Probably one of the major deficiencies in the Christian responses to the New Age Movement is that they do not outline from the very start the methodological and theological principles and/or assumptions that should guide Christians in both understanding the New Age and evaluating its teachings and practices. This chapter will attempt such a task and then reflect on a few select themes and issues to demonstrate how Christians could contribute to an assessment of the New Age and in the process broaden their knowledge and understanding of their own faith commitment.

PRINCIPLES FOR EVALUATING THE NEW AGE

A Christian evaluation of the New Age must be guided both by understanding and discernment. The following guidelines, some of which are applicable to New Agers, should contribute to a better Christian assessment of New Age ideas and practices and to a more productive relationship between Christians and New Agers:

(1) A response to the New Age must be conducted in the spirit of harmony and cooperation. While areas of disagreements need to be brought out, condemnations and accusations should be avoided.

(2) A response to the New Age must be based on a solid theology of religions which is aware of the pluralistic nature of the contemporary world that has been correctly described as a global village. People no longer live in relative isolation and modern conditions require that they learn how to relate to those of other faiths in a manner that will not only minimize rather than acerbate conflict, but also create harmony and cooperation.

(3) A response must start from a solid theology which is aware of theological developments throughout the centuries, of the variety of Christian belief, and of other religious traditions. Rejection of New Age ideas because they do not conform rigidly to the standards

of one particular Christian denomination is bound to increase misunderstanding and confrontation. Similarly, a refutation of the New Age that is based on a provincial theology that ignores other religions is bound to lead to theological bankruptcy and stagnation and to pastoral inadequacy.

(4) Criticism of the New Age Movement must rely on informed sources and must be conducted in an academic manner. The need to clarify, explain, and defend, when necessary, Christian doctrine must be attended to. But the Church's pastoral ministry must devise more positive ways of relating to and influencing those individuals attracted to the New Age.

(5) Refutation of New Agers' arguments that certain beliefs (such as reincarnation) are compatible with Christianity has its proper place. It is also important, however, to point out that many New Age ideas are hardly alien to Christian theology.[3]

(6) The good features of the New Age should be recognized. The tendency among many Christians to dwell on those New Age beliefs that are not compatible with the Christian faith ultimately serves no purpose. It will not convince those who are dedicated to the movement's ideals and goals that their involvement is evil. Neither will it lead to an effective ministry with traditional Christians and with those who have accepted some aspects of New Age ideology and incorporated them in their Christian world view.

(7) Stress must be placed on those elements of the New Age that can be harmonized with Christian doctrine and spirituality. For instance, in spite of the theological problems inherent in Matthew Fox's creation-centered spirituality, there are some elements in this spirituality that can be based on a Christian theology of creation.[4]

(8) Efforts must be made to reconcile some New Age ideology and practices with the Christian spirit. Thus, for example, the environmental movement to preserve the earth need not be based on a pantheistic viewpoint. It could easily be founded on traditional Christian theology.

(9) It should be recognized that the Church is in constant need of revitalization and that the New Age may be pointing to those areas where reform and renewal are most required. 'Spiritual innovation', writes William Dinges, 'is more often than not an indictment of organized religion and its failure to respond in creative and dynamic ways to new cultural trends.'[5] Some official Catholic reactions to the new religious movements have admitted that more can be done for the pastoral needs of the faithful.[6]

A question of method

The many Christian reactions to the New Age raise the question of what kind of response is appropriate to meet the challenge of a successful movement. Two major issues underlie the majority of these responses. The first is practical and pertains to the kind of influence New Age ideas and spirituality might have on Christians. More specifically, can any New Age practices be incorporated into Christianity? Or can they become so imbued with the Christian spirit that they can present Christians with viable options in their quest for God? The second is more theoretical and deals with orthodoxy. Are some New Age beliefs incompatible with basic Christian doctrines? And has the New Age anything positive to offer to Christian theological reflection? Granted that these are genuine concerns, how should a Christian go about evaluating what the New Age is teaching?

It is precisely how Christians have attempted to answer these questions that is at stake. The majority of Christian literature has been so negative and argumentative that the very issues have been clouded. In many instances the fundamental rules of interpersonal relationships have been disregarded. Dogmatic denunciations and emotional outbursts have stood in the way of real conversation between people who, even though they might adhere to different world views, might still find plenty of common ground and learn from each other's spiritual quest. The fundamentalist/evangelical response described in Chapter 2 shows that little communication has taken place between those Christians who wrote with such passion against New Age doctrines and practices and the New Agers who had committed themselves to a new spirituality and belief system.

The fault, however, does not lie exclusively with Christians. New Agers have often written about traditional Christianity as if it were bankrupt and had little to offer to the human spirit. And while many Christians have accused the New Agers of conspiratorial intentions, New Agers have, in their turn, also charged Christians with a conspiracy to suppress what Jesus actually taught. Joseph P. Macchio's work, *The Christian Conspiracy*,[7] represents a fairly common view in New Age circles. Macchio's main thesis is that authentic Christianity was suppressed by the early Church councils. The Church Fathers were responsible for destroying or repressing ancient texts that presented a different view of Jesus and

Christianity than the one depicted in the canonical Gospels. The original Christianity, according to this author, was diverse and gnostic in its beliefs, among which were included the doctrines of reincarnation, the preexistence of the soul, and the presence of a divine spark in all human beings. By the first century, Christian leaders felt it their duty to remold the doctrines of the oldest Christian sects and communities and to create a new belief system which included the resurrection of the body and the divinity of Jesus, which did not guarantee freedom of thought, and which denied the individual's freedom to pursue God according to one's conscience. And by the fourth century the so-called Orthodox Christianity was imposed by political and often destructive methods that enshrined distorted and narrow dogmas in the place of the much broader and diverse belief system preached by the first Christians. Macchio is aware of the inflammatory nature of his work and prefaces it with a kind of apology which confesses that his work is not intended to attack the present churches, nor to deny that these have upheld Christian virtues and nourished the spiritual lives of their adherents. None the less, his thesis is an indictment of Christianity particularly from the fourth century to the present day. Surely, labels like 'The bondage of orthodoxy' and 'The triumph of totalitarian Christianity' betray an attitude that is not conducive to any meaningful dialogue.

This kind of reciprocal bashing serves no purpose but that of increasing mutual antagonism which gives religion a bad name. People who participate in such charades are not listening to one another. In order for Christians and New Agers to carry on a conversation, such speculative accusations must cease. Exchanges on religious topics are better conducted in a spirit of calmness, cooperation, and learning. In such an atmosphere, people respect one another, avoid misunderstandings, and clarify their own positions without demeaning each other's sincerity and intellectual honesty. They can also learn that understanding does not imply agreeing or accepting another person's point of view and that faithful adherence to one's tradition does not require either the ridiculing or the condemnation of another's.

Equally irritating is the attitude of some Christians who appear willing to accept almost anything from the New Age and label it Christian. By neglecting to acknowledge that there are some real differences between Christianity and the New Age, they have rightly been accused of syncretism. Such indiscriminate lumping of incompatible beliefs does not do justice to either Christianity or the New Age, both of which are made up of coherent world views that present alternative spiritualities to their respective adherents.

ISSUES IN THE RELATIONSHIP BETWEEN CHRISTIANITY AND THE NEW AGE

The issues which have been debated in the manifold Christian responses to the New Age need to be examined in the light of the above principles. The following considerations on several major topics which repeatedly crop up in the Christian literature on the New Age are intended as examples of how Christians can engage in theological reflection with New Agers.

Towards a theology of religions

As was shown in the preceding chapters, three major theologies of non-Christian religions, namely, the exclusivistic, the inclusivistic, and the pluralistic, have influenced the responses to the New Age Movement. The issue of the theology of religions is a thorny one and cannot be resolved easily. One thing, however, seems certain: a contemporary theology of religion cannot be based solely on dogmatic grounds. In an age when people of different faiths go to school together, work together, and live together, a theology of religions must be constructed on a theology of communication and of interpersonal relationships. A religion that cannot or does not teach and encourage its members to live at peace with others and to respect other people's opinions is bankrupt. Probably one reason for the success of the New Age is its ability to incorporate elements from different traditions and to withhold making absolute, dogmatic statements of faith.

The exclusivist approach is the most popular. Its attractiveness lies in part in its ability to provide clear-cut answers to all the major theological points of contention and to create a sense of security by judging opposite religious beliefs heretical. Evangelizing and converting New Agers are its main concerns. Its major flaw, as seen in the negative responses to the New Age, is that it ends up creating or increasing conflicts between people who adhere to different religious commitments. From a Christian standpoint, this approach abandons charity for the sake of what is perceived to be true.

The inclusivist approach makes gallant efforts to acknowledge the good elements of the New Age. But it makes them subservient to Christianity. It frequently does not admit New Agers as equal partners in the religious quest. While it eschews confrontation and conflict and treats members of other faiths with some respect, it makes dialogue somewhat artificial and unproductive. It does, however, contain the necessary elements for a rapprochement between different religious traditions. For it admits that revelation can be extended to other faiths and that other religions are expressions of genuine religiousness and spirituality. It further does not equate the proclamation of faith and the task of mission with the practice of proselytization and the goal of conversion. It allows room for internal reform and is willing to learn from others. From a Christian standpoint, this position is also concerned with dogmatic truth, but it does pay attention to the importance of Christian love and is aware that there are some common elements shared by all religions.

The pluralistic approach is the most congenial to dialogue because it abandons the attitude of superiority and joins other religious seekers as equals in a common search. Its main flaw is that it ignores some of the main differences that exist between Christianity and the New Age. It could also easily fall into the error of relativism which has no criteria for evaluating truth claims and allows each individual to make up his or her belief system. Unlike the other two approaches, the pluralistic one puts less emphasis on absolute truths and deems charity to be the primary motivating force that should regulate the relationships between people of different faiths.

The New Age and christology

The debate about the nature of Christ and his mission has figured prominently in the Christian responses to the New Age. Christology is at the heart of Christianity and it is not surprising that it has often become a measure of orthodoxy even between the various branches of Christianity. There is little doubt that the New Age has developed its own view of Jesus. This development is hardly unexpected. In an age of cross-cultural and cross-religious contacts, each religion is bound to articulate its theological views about other religions. There are Jewish, Islamic, Hindu, and Buddhist views of Jesus. The New Age, because of its tendency to incorporate other belief systems, is bound to give Jesus a role in its theology. The concept of the New Age Jesus makes the transition easier for those Christians who have abandoned their traditional faith and become involved in the

New Age. It provides a link with their past. By incorporating Jesus in their belief system they feel that they are expanding on their theology, rather than abandoning it for an alternate one.

The exchanges between New Agers and Christians on the nature and role of Christ have been litigious and acrimonious not only because they bring into focus the question of orthodoxy, but also because of the New Age claim that its view of Christ is more attuned with early Christianity before the conciliar debates and dogmatic formulations. In order to prepare the ground for a fruitful dialogue between the New Age and Christianity on this touchy issue, it is necessary first to consider briefly what is the christology of the New Age and what are some of the theological issues it raises. Secondly, for a better understanding of the New Age view of Jesus, one must consider it not only in relation to the traditional christology of the early councils, but also in the context of current christological reflections. Only then can one attempt to point out which are those areas of christology where Christians and New Agers can engage in dialogue.

The New Age view of Jesus

In Christian theology the distinction between the Jesus of history and the Christ of faith has received a lot of attention and has been characterized by unending debates. Certainly, knowledge of the Jesus of history is, at best, very incomplete. Little is known of his early life. The so-called 'hidden years' of Jesus, roughly between the incident when he wandered off from his parents and was found in the temple (Luke 2:41–50) and the beginning of his public ministry, are open to all kinds of speculation.

The same issue is also part of New Age reflections on Jesus. New Age sources present a fuller account of his early history. It is a common view in New Age writings that during those years about which nothing is said in the New Testament, Jesus traveled far and wide throughout Asia. This historical reconstruction can be traced to Nicholas Notovitch[8] (b. 1858) in the nineteenth century, who claimed to have discovered documents that prove conclusively that Jesus traveled to the East and studied under several Hindu and Buddhist teachers. Notovitch, a Russian, describes his dangerous journey to Tibet where, in the library of an ancient lamasery, he discovered an old manuscript which contained reports of the travels and teachings of Jesus (known as 'Issa' or 'Isa' in Asia). Notovitch, through an interpreter, recorded various texts about Jesus which were found scattered in two large volumes, and grouped them together in a short book. Divided into fourteen chapters, this booklet first covers the human conditions that led to the incarnation of Jesus, his birth, and early life. Then it gives an account of the studies and teaching of Jesus in the East between the ages of 13 and 29. It finally covers his last few years when he was conducting his mission in Palestine. Besides some materials familiar to anyone acquainted with the New Testament, Notovitch's collection includes novel stories about Jesus. At the age of 13, Jesus is said to have secretly left his family and embarked on a trip to the East in order to perfect himself and to study the works of the great Buddha. He traveled in various Eastern countries where he became acquainted with Eastern religious and philosophical views. He ran into conflict with the Hindu upper castes when he tried to teach the scriptures to the lower ones. The section dealing with the last three years of Jesus, while including some of the data found in the canonical Gospels, adds some new materials. It is Pilate who finally condemns Jesus, while the Jewish priests and elders found no fault in him and implored Pilate to release him. Jesus was crucified between two thieves, but his body was removed by Pilate's order and buried elsewhere. The resurrection is omitted, if not completely denied. In general, Notovitch gives a picture of Jesus as a glorious, divine prophet chosen by God to fight idolatry, sun worship, and magic wherever they occur.

Notovitch's account of the hidden years of Jesus in Asia have been recently popularized by Elizabeth Clare Prophet[9] whose Church Universal and Triumphant is probably one of the most organized religious institutions based on New Age theology. Prophet reproduces Notovitch's work and other independent sources that claim to confirm his findings. She suggests that the evidence points to the sojourn of Jesus in the East and explains why his contemporaries in Palestine respected him as a great spiritual master. And she hints that the facts relating to his experiences among Asian peoples and gurus might have been intentionally suppressed.

Another account of the life of Jesus is provided by Levi H. Dowling (1844–1911).[10] Writing in the second half of the nineteenth century, Levi (as he is commonly known), unlike Notovitch, does not base his information on personal travels and the discovery of ancient literary sources. He rather claims to have unearthed the information through tapping into the Akashic Records, that is, chronicles that are believed by New Agers and Occultists to have been preserved in the astral plane, an alternate dimension of reality, 'which carries the imprint of everything that has ever happened'.[11] Levi, like many other psychics, believed he had the mental ability to read these records and thus succeeded in obtaining information that had not been recorded elsewhere. Unlike Notovitch's text, Levi's records provide a full-length book with a structure similar to that of those synoptic Gospels that include the infancy narratives, the ministry of Jesus, and his passion. Levi, however, provides numerous details that are missing in the Gospels. He adds, for example, an introductory chapter on the birth and early life of Mary. His description of how Jesus was lost and found in the temple is almost identical to that found in Luke's Gospel (3:41–50). Levi states that when Jesus returned home he took up carpentry with Joseph and provides a symbolic interpretation of the carpenter's tools. Unlike the records unearthed by Notovitch, Levi's transcriptions include a chapter on the resurrection in which he describes not just the empty tomb, but the way Jesus actually rose from death. The most conspicuous additions are six sections (35 short chapters) that relate the life and works of Jesus in different parts of the world, namely, India, Tibet, Persia, Assyria, Greece, and Egypt. The experiences of Jesus outside his homeland included studying under Hindu, Buddhist, and Persian masters, preaching in Athens, and joining an Egyptian brotherhood. Again, unlike the account of Notovitch, the records of Levi do not depict Jesus as secretly leaving for Eastern shores. Rather, Jesus was invited by an Indian prince visiting Palestine to continue his education in India and accepted the invitation with his parents' consent. For Levi, Jesus is a profound mystic, a great teacher who finally attains the great illumination and becomes the Christ.

Other accounts of the life of Jesus which include his travels in the East are available.[12] Among the most recent efforts to draw up a life of Christ which incorporates New Age materials is that of Richard Henry Drummond,[13] who departs from the customary exegetical method and accepts channeled materials (mainly those of Edgar Cayce) as authentic sources. Drummond seems to accept the view that Mary, Joseph, and Jesus were members of the Essenes, a Jewish religious community. Following New Age depictions of the life of Jesus, he treats at some length the education and preparation Jesus underwent for his missions in India, Persia, and Egypt.

There is no doubt that the Jesus of New Age literature is a great prophetic figure, a learned saint, who is to be numbered among the world's great religious leaders. He is revered by many New Agers as an enlightened cosmic master who, through his work and ministry, reached great holiness and who attained a high degree of unity with God. He became the 'Christ', a person with a high degree of personal development. He reached a close union with God or a state of perfection that is the goal of all human beings. Christ thus stands for the condition to which all human beings are evolving. While Jesus represents an individual person who existed in a specific historical period (or periods), Christ is a cosmic figure who transcends all cultural and historical boundaries. In fact his world-wide travels are symbolic of the universality of his message. Such a view raises questions about the divinity of Jesus and his uniqueness in the history of religion.

Christian reactions to the New Age Jesus

Several Christian responses to the New Age have concentrated on analyzing and refuting its portrait of Jesus. Arild Romerheim[14] provides a comprehensive treatment of the subject. He starts by giving a detailed description of the various New Age conceptions of Jesus Christ. He points out that in New Age christology Jesus is to be distinguished from Christ, the former referring to the historical figure who lived about 2,000 years ago, the latter to a state of consciousness which is achievable by all human beings. Various images of Jesus that consider him to have been an Essene who traveled in the East and to have been a master of meditation, a prophet, a healer and a magician are portrayed. Four ways by which New Agers legitimize their christologies are examined and criticized: (1) the existence of ancient, esoteric knowledge found in Rosicrucian and Masonic sources; (2) discoveries of ancient manuscripts that are accepted as authentic by various New Age writers; (3) reliance of Akashic records revealed by prominent New Agers; and (4) information received through spirits and channelers in the nineteenth and twentieth centuries. Finally, he summarizes what various religious movements teach about Jesus.

Romerheim's work is largely descriptive, though it is clear that he finds this view of Jesus unacceptable. Thus he rejects the historical data provided by New Agers because, among other objections, he finds disagreement among the various mediums and channelers who divulge information about the hidden years of Jesus. And he dismisses the literary evidence of Notovitch as a forgery.[15] In general, Romerheim makes no attempt at a theological evaluation of the New Age Jesus. He thinks that there is a great need by Eastern religions to claim Jesus as their own, just as there is a need for dissatisfied Christians in the West to acquire a new concept of wholeness. He alludes to some similarities between the views of Jesus propounded in New Age sources and in the New Testament. In both cases Jesus is regarded as Christ the glorious messiah, a prophet, a teacher, a healer, and a magician with great occult powers. The issue, for Romerheim, is whether Christ was unique, whether he was, in fact, the redeemer of the world; an issue he does not examine but simply links to the Christian world view which is basically different from that proposed by any other world religion.

More theological and apologetical in tone are the works of Ron Rhodes and Douglas Groothius that discuss specifically the New Age Jesus. Rhodes leaves no doubt as to what he thinks of the New Age Jesus by calling it from the very start a 'counterfeit'. He divides his analysis of the New Age Jesus into three parts. The first examines the Jesus of the New Age and refutes the various claims made by New Agers about the hidden years of Jesus. The second looks at the christology espoused by New Agers. And finally, the third part outlines the Jesus depicted in the New Testament. He points out that to understand New Age christology, one must begin with the New Age distinction between Jesus (a mere human vessel) and Christ (a divine, cosmic, impersonal entity). For him, the New Age view of Jesus is a revival of the old gnostic heresy. He finds nothing reliable and believable in the New Age reconstruction of the lost years of Jesus. And he argues at length that there is nothing to support the theories that Jesus went to Asia or that he was an Essene and that the New Age's historical reconstructions are littered with inaccuracies.

Rhodes also thinks that New Agers tend to read their own gnostic theology into the teachings of Jesus. While he admits that there is some disagreement among New Agers as to what Jesus taught, he maintains that there is a consensus on eight major points which he lists as follows:

1. Jesus taught that all is one, all is God, and man is god.

2. Jesus taught and believed in the unity of the world religions.

3. Jesus taught that he was not uniquely God, but was a human being who became enlightened.

4. Jesus taught that he was a way-shower for humanity, not a Savior.

5. Jesus taught that every human being has the potential and ability to save himself.

6. Jesus taught that esoteric knowledge (gnosis) is all-important to man's self-salvation.

7. Jesus taught that part of man's self-salvation involves a transformation of consciousness.

8. Jesus taught and believed in God the Father and God the Mother.[16]

Rhodes rejects all of these alleged teachings of Jesus as far-fetched reinterpretations of the Gospel sayings and as unsupportable by a correct reading of the canonical Gospels. New Agers are accused of making 'one of the most comprehensive attacks against the deity and uniqueness of Christ ever launched by the kingdom of darkness'. Rhodes, moreover, maintains that Christians should aggressively defend and proclaim the orthodox Christian position on the nature and role of Jesus. In fact he encourages Christians to 'mount an effective offense against a heretical view of Jesus' as propounded by the New Age.[17]

A similar refutation of the New Age view of Jesus is made by Douglas Groothius, who takes up many of the themes dealt with by Rhodes and reinforces many of the latter's objections to the historical reconstruction of the life of Jesus and to the understanding of his nature and mission. Like Rhodes he detects some basic unifying ideas in the New Age conception of the nature and mission of Christ. He writes that in New Age circles:

1. Jesus is revered or respected as a highly spiritually evolved being who serves as an example for further evolution.

2. The individual, personal, historical Jesus is separated from the universal, impersonal, eternal Christ or Christ Consciousness, which he embodied but did not monopolize.

3. The orthodox understanding of Jesus as the supreme and final revelation of God is dismissed as illegitimate.

4. Jesus' death on the cross (if recognized at all) is not accepted as having any ethical significance for salvation.

5. Jesus' resurrection from the dead is not viewed as a physical fact demonstrating his victory over sin, death, and Satan but is rather (if recognized at all) understood as a spiritual triumph not unique to Jesus.

6. Jesus' 'second coming' is not a literal, physical and visible return in the clouds at the end of the age but rather a stage in the evolutionary advancement of the race when the Christic energies escape the confinements of ignorance.

7. Exotic, extra-biblical documents are regarded as sources for authentic material about the life of Jesus not available from the canonical Scriptures.[18]

The works of Rhodes and Groothius are typical of the Christian response that is characterized by debate and refutation of New Age christology. In fairness to these writers, there is little doubt that the New Age Jesus differs substantially from traditional christology. But their approach constructs an impassable gulf between the two christologies. For these writers New Age and Christian theologies are mutually exclusive with no points of agreement among them. In which case neither the New Age nor traditional Christianity would have anything to say to, much less learn from, each other. They are doomed to live in mutual antagonism and confrontation.

However, it is possible that one can achieve a better understanding of the New Age Jesus by comparing it not only with the early conciliar statements but also with other contemporary christologies. It seems that both the New Age and its critics are conducting their theological inquiries within rather narrow and closed fields with the result that little communication is possible. The New Age view of the historical Jesus certainly relies (1) on questionable and insufficient historical materials that have not undergone the test of reliable historical criticism and/or (2) on channeling information that is very personal and eclectic and constantly growing and difficult to evaluate. There seems to be no limit and no parameters to what one can say about the life and role of Jesus gained through channeling. Unlike historical sources, channeling materials cannot be checked or subjected to independent scrutiny. The New Age will only neglect historical scholarship to its own detriment. It can never convince outsiders to even consider the authenticity of channeling information unless a method is developed for evaluating its contents and handling the disparate materials that channelers and those who accept their teachings accept as divine revelation.

On the other hand, Christians must remember that the canonical records on the life of Jesus are rather scanty and that the desire to learn more about him is a part of a Christian's genuine spiritual quest. Further, it must be conceded that, while the early conciliar pronouncements on the nature and role of Christ are definite and cannot be abandoned or drastically reinterpreted, our knowledge of Christ is not static. The definitions of the early councils were intended to solve the then current debates and not to close the doors on christological reflection.

Moreover, no matter how different and unreconcilable the Christian and New Age views of Jesus might be, the two can learn from one another. New Agers can learn a lot from the Christian debate about the Jesus of history and the Christ of faith and from exegetical methods that have been developed since the nineteenth century. Christians can learn from the New Age stress on the cosmic Christ, a concept found also in traditional theological reflection.

Contemporary Christian christologies

Over the last half century, christology has become one of the most fertile fields in current Christian theology with some remarkable contributions coming from various continents. Two factors have contributed to the growth of speculation on the nature and mission of Christ: (1) contact with the major world religions and (2) efforts to make the Christian faith relevant to converts from different cultural backgrounds. Besides the traditional christology,[19] which dwells on the person and nature of Jesus and maintains that Jesus is of one substance with, and the only Son of, God, there are at least the following seven types of christology:

Process christology. Christ, in this theology, is wherever the creative love of God is present and can be seen as the principle of creative transformation.[20] Anybody who is willing to be spiritually transformed is open to the presence of Christ in his or her life. Membership in any particular religion is not a requirement for an individual to become imbued with the spirit of Christ. While open to the presence of Christ in other religions, process christology considers Christ to be the norm of revelation and to be present wherever and whenever God is present in human life. This inclusivist theology is similar to the New Age because it is more inclined to stress the cosmic Christ; but it differs because it gives Christ a unique place in the history of religions and does not consider him to be simply one of the many cosmic masters.

Logos christology. This theology stresses that Jesus is the word of God made flesh. Basing its reflections on the biblical concepts of Wisdom (sophia) and Word (logos), it allows for the possibility that Jesus may not be the only incarnation.[21] Revelation and salvation are thus not restricted to the Christian faith, for Christ could have been incarnated in different historical periods and cultural settings. Yet the Christian logos remains the norm through which revelation and salvation in other religions are understood and achieved. Christ is unique and cannot be put on a par with other religious figures. This theology is inclusivistic, though it is more open to a pluralistic interpretation.

Theocentric christology. Those theologians who favor this theology argue that God, and not Christ, is the central figure in the New Testament. Jesus is the messenger of God, and not the message; the bringer of salvation, and not the savior as such. Consequently, he is not unique or normative, but only one manifestation of divine revelation and salvation.[22] Christ is the savior of all Christians, in the sense that God saves them through his mediation, but he is not the unique savior of all humankind. This christology is pluralistic and is in direct conflict with traditional christology.

Functional christology. Rather than attempting to define who Jesus is, this christology concentrates on what Jesus does. The function of Jesus is to lead people to God and salvation. As such, he is the savior in the sense that he hears and follows God's will to liberate the members of the community who follow him. Other prophets and religious leaders may fulfill similar functions in different religious settings. Like theocentric christology, functional christology is pluralistic. It is also in conflict with traditional christology because it ignores the nature of Christ and because it relativizes the mission of Christ, limiting it to those who are Christians.

Feminist christology. The main concern of women theologians has been that, in a tradition which has been patriarchal and androcentric, the maleness of Jesus becomes a prominent part of christology, thus making it difficult, if not impossible, for Jesus to become a model for women.[23] Hence it is argued that the humanity of Jesus, rather than his maleness, should receive attention and that his gender should be irrelevant to his mission of salvation. This theology concentrates on avoiding the patriarchal slant common in traditional theology, including christology. Though not directly concerned with the role of Christ in other religions, this theology is having some impact on Christians in Third World countries.

Liberation christology. This christology, while indirectly affirming the ontological christology of the traditional church, stresses the activities of Jesus on behalf of the poor and marginal people, of those who are social outcasts, enslaved, and/or neglected. Jesus is their liberator rather than their lord. For liberation theologians, salvation is achieved through social justice. Though originally initiated by Gustavo Gutiérrez in response to the conditions in Latin America and further developed by Leonardo Boff and Jon Sobrino, this theology has been applied to the Asian religious scene.[24] Liberation theology does not directly tackle the question of the theology of religions. It does present a view of Jesus which takes into account some of the cultural conditions of modern times and attempts to construct a christology that is relevant in third world countries.

Black christology. This Christology has much in common with liberation theology since it views Christ primarily as a liberator from oppression. Its focus, however, is on the plight of those who have been deprived not just economically and socially, but who play an inferior role in society primarily because of their race. Jesus is identified in black christology with black race and culture. Like liberation theology, black theology does not deal directly with Christ in the context of world religions. It favors a picture of Jesus that is more appealing to many who feel that they are treated as inferior human beings because of their ethnic origin.

African and Asian christology

Theologians in Asia and Africa have also been attempting to construct christologies that are more relevant to Third World countries. Besides accepting several of the above-mentioned christologies and adapting them to different cultural and social settings,[25] they have searched for new images to express the nature of Jesus and his mission. Christian theologians in Africa have observed that many of the traditional titles given to Jesus, such as Messiah, Son of Man, and Son of David, have no major significance in African religious thought. Africans find it hard to relate to Jesus since he did not belong to their clan, family, tribe, or nation.[26]

Efforts to build a christology that is congruent with African religious thought are common. Jesus has been seen as a master of initiation, a chief, ancestor or elder brother, and a healer.[27] Raymond Mooney, writing on African christologies, distinguishes between 'christologies of inculturation' and 'christologies of liberation'. African christologies of inculturation assume traditional themes and imbue them with christological meaning. They bestow on Jesus such titles as master of initiation, healer, and great ancestor. Mooney finds both strengths and weaknesses in these designations. Thus, referring to the christology which sees Jesus as master of initiation, the elder brother (Romans 8:29), who is rightly at home in his Father's house (Luke 2:4) for he is the son (John 8:35), he comments:

> The value of such a presentation lies in providing the preacher with some traditional concepts and terms in which to express the significance of Christ for us. It also helps to bring into a synthesis with our image of Christ some key Christian values, such as the role of the sacraments or the place of tradition. The weakness of the model lies in that, for many Africans today, initiation is no longer a living experience.[28]

African christologies of liberation have been inspired by the liberation theology of Latin America and have often been radical, aggressive, and revolutionary. Despite its tendency to be excessively political, if not racist, this theology offers a forceful image of the Jesus Christ, the black Messiah. Moreover, black christology incorporates the incarnation and the crucifixion into the daily lives of Africans.

Akintunde Akinade, an African theologian, has examined in some detail the various christologies in Africa. He points out that African Independent Churches often acknowledge Jesus as victorious over the spiritual realm and evil forces and proclaim that, together with God and the Holy Spirit, he can be called 'savior'. As a perfect human being, Jesus fulfilled all the rites of life. He is also called the mediator and intermediary between God and African Christians and the great ancestor. The latter title, according to Akinade, is very appropriate. He states:

> To use the title of ancestor for Jesus is very appropriate within the African context. Ancestors are very important in African world view; take away the ancestors from Africa and you destroy their roots in the past, their culture, their dignity and their understanding of *communio sanctorum*. Just as the ancestors watch and nourish their descendants, 'so does Christ continuously nourish the life of believers'.[29]

For Akinade, the most acceptable relevant title that Africans can give to Jesus is that of healer. He draws attention to the fact that the African world view is still dominated by belief in evil spirits, witches, and divinities. Christ as healer is the only antidote to the evil forces Africans believe still influence their lives. Finally, Akinade dwells on African liberation and feminist christologies which, he thinks, are founded on reactions to oppressive sociocultural conditions and structures.

Equally fertile have been reflections on christology by Asian Christians. There is some hesitation in using the word *avatāra*, which is the Indian concept that refers to the descent of God on earth or to the manifestation of the divine in human form, because it does not quite capture the theological conception of 'incarnation'. Richard De Smet compares Jesus, the incarnation of God, with Krishna, the avatāra of Vishnu, and discovers some major similarities and differences. For examples, he writes:

> Vishnu as Krishna many times assumes a creaturely body which does not seem to require a creaturely *ātman*. The Logos as Jesus takes a body animated by a human soul once and for all.
>
> In both, the motive is God's wise and potent compassion. The purpose is the salvation of man, either only through teaching, helpful grace, and love (Krishna), or through teaching, transforming grace and love, and suffering (Christ).
>
> In Krishna, the union of God and man is only manifestative and instrumental. In Christ, it is not only manifestative and instrumental, but also theandric and hypostatic.
>
> In both cases, God remains transcendent and 'unborn'; the human body or nature remains distinct from the divine as creaturely.[30]

Indian theologians have explored the use of several other titles to describe the nature and role of Jesus. Jesus can be said to be the true guru, the master who is teacher, guide, and exemplar. Jesus can also be referred to as 'mother', an appealing title in a society where Hindus worship several mother goddesses. In Hinduism the mother goddess is a symbol that refers to the origins and roots. It includes wisdom and wealth, victory over evil, healing, and grace and tenderness, all of which can be applied to Jesus.[31]

Like their counterparts in other Third World countries, Asian Christians contest that a relevant christology cannot ignore the cultural, religious and sociopolitical contexts of Asia. Poverty and oppression, the presence of communism, and the inherent religiousness of the populations of Asian countries all influence, if not determine, the method and the agenda of theology.[32]

Several attempts by Asian Christians to construct a Christology based on indigenous religious experiences are noteworthy. Aloysius Pieris,[33] for example, insisting on the need to take seriously into account Asian religions, argues that the only way by which Christian churches can become an effective force in Asia is by assuming the spirituality of non-Christian religions symbolized by the figure of the poor monk. Jesus is thus seen as a mendicant (Buddhist) monk, who is both a teacher and an exemplar. Others, like Jung Young

Lee,[34] use Taoist philosophy to explain who Jesus is. Basing his reflections on the classical Chinese Book of Changes (the *I Ching*), Lee maintains that Christianity requires both a theology of the absolute (being) and one of change (becoming) and suggests that Christ is the perfect realization of change. He utilizes the same Taoist philosophy to make theology more relevant to Asian immigrants in the United States. Reflecting on the state of these immigrants who, in his opinion, will always remain marginal no matter how much they adapt to their new sociocultural condition, Lee advances the view that Jesus can be seen as the marginal person *par excellence.* He rereads the story of Jesus' birth, life, death, and resurrection from the perspective of marginality. The self-emptying (*kenosis*) of Christ is a kind of divine marginality. Asian Christians in the United States (and in the West in general) can thus identify with Jesus and understand his mission because his life was characterized, like theirs, by being on the borderline of the dominant culture and/or religion.

Other theologians have applied the theology of liberation to more concrete situations in Asia. Thus Choan-Seng Song[35] bases his reflections on the stories of those who are poor, suffering, and powerless and who are oppressed by both church authorities and civil or military rulers. The suffering of Jesus, rather than his fulfillment of God's promise to Israel, becomes central in his christology. In an attempt to devise a christology from an Asian woman's perspective, Chung Hyun Kyung[36] starts, like Song, with stories, especially those of women. She sees Christ as a suffering servant to whom women can relate because they too have been suffering through oppression. Jesus is lord since he brings freedom from false authority. He is also 'emmanuel' (God with us) because he has experienced the poor and oppressed condition of women. Jesus is thus a liberator, a revolutionary, and a political martyr. He can also be described as a mother, a woman, and a shaman (healer).

Among the more original attempts to create an indigenous theology is the work of John F. Keenan who relies on theological and philosophical concepts from Mahayana Buddhism.[37] Applying his work to christology, Keenan[38] begins by pointing out that this particular branch of theology was developed by adopting Greek philosophical thought. The early Fathers and councils of the Church established a bond between Christian theology and Greek philosophy because of particular historical circumstances. They did not imply that the relationship between Greek philosophy and

Christian theology is necessarily applicable to all cultures and in all historical periods. On the contrary, Keenan thinks that the relationship is doctrinally fluid and historically contextual. He relies heavily, among other things, on a basic Mahayana Buddhist concept of 'emptiness' and applies it to Christ. This means that Jesus as a person is beyond definition. He is empty of essence, in the sense that one cannot understand him without reference to the relationships he formed in his life. The idea of self-emptying (*kenosis*) is also found in St. Paul (Philippians 2:6–11), where it is used to express what happened at the Incarnation. Paul explains that in his earthly existence Christ chose not to manifest the majesty of God that was his by nature and could thus become the servant of all.

Using other Mahayana Buddhist ideas, such as the concept and enunciation of truth as ultimate meaning, Keenan steers away from the understanding of the Incarnation as a synthesis of two natures. Though his analysis is difficult to follow unless one is steeped in the world of Mahayana philosophy, it is not hard to see what he is trying to achieve, namely, an understanding of who Jesus is in a philosophical language other than Greek. Though a christology in Mahayana terms is unlikely to be meaningful and appealing to Christians in Western culture, even though Keenan thinks it has some advantages over the essentialist christology of the West, it may be attractive to those who are immersed in Eastern thought and culture. It certainly offers a different kind of conception of who Jesus is and what role he fulfilled in the salvation of the human race.

Not all the christologies mentioned above are mutually compatible. Nor can they all be harmonized with traditional christology. They are a reminder that Jesus Christ is, in Christian theology, God incarnate, and as such a mystery. There is no one single christology which can provide a comprehensive, exhaustive, and completely satisfying explanation of the nature and role of Christ both within the Christian Church and in the context of the world's religions. At best, christologies can shed some light on who Jesus Christ is and the place he has in God's plan for revelation and salvation. Each individual christology might highlight one or more aspects of the Jesus mystery, but it does not provide one full and absolute answer to the exclusion of all others. And each christology has its particular weaknesses.

The New Age proposes another christology which places Jesus in a broader historical context than just first-century Palestine. It also ascribes to him a wider teaching role. In the light of the abounding christologies, the New Age Jesus enables us to see the universal character of God's salvific plan, but it does not do justice to the place of Jesus as depicted in the New Testament and proclaimed by the majority of Christians throughout the ages. Nor does it provide sufficient theological depth to enable us to express who Jesus is in terms of other philosophical and theological systems. Its attempts to reconstruct the life of Jesus are hampered by the lack of reliable historical records. Its view that there are Eastern influences on Jesus, however, may not be far-fetched. One writer[39] has remarked that Eastern religious concepts were not unknown in the time of Christ and that the lifestyle of Jesus may have fitted the model of an Eastern sannyasin (wandering ascetic or monk) more than that of a Jewish rabbi. Probably, one of the main contributions of the New Age to christology has been its endorsement of the idea of the 'cosmic Christ'. This view of Jesus has its basis in the New Testament and has also received plenty of attention by those scholars whose main interest is the theology of religions.[40] New Age reflections on Jesus may not coincide with the early conciliar statements, but they might still contribute to a broader understanding of the universal character of the Jesus mystery.

Reincarnation

One of the most common, if not universal, New Age beliefs is that of reincarnation (or metempsychosis, or the transmigration of souls),[41] which has become a topic of discussion in both academic journals and popular magazines[42] and which has further caused serious debates within Christian circles.[43] Reincarnation has become a recurrent theme also on the Internet, where one finds, for instance, a 'homepage' which gives world news pertinent to reincarnation.[44]

Reincarnation is a neglected theme in Christian thought. 'Christian theologians generally', writes Hans Küng, 'scarcely take the question seriously. To them the idea of living more than once, of reincarnation (reembodiment, rebirth) or migration of souls (metempsychosis, transmigration), seems most bizarre and ludicrous, superstitious purely and simply.'[45] To a large extent, it is equally ignored in Judaism and Islam.

Belief in reincarnation, however, is worldwide and not restricted to Eastern religions. Some ancient civilizations, like Greece and Egypt, and many nonliterate societies throughout the world have professed the belief that the souls of the departed returned to inhabit new bodies. Belief in reincarnation in the West never became extinct even after orthodox Christianity achieved dominance in the West. The early gnostics, the medieval Cathars, and the Jewish Cabalists were known to have included reincarnation in their belief system.[46] In modern times interest in reincarnation has been revived and strengthened by the presence, since the last century, of Eastern religions in the West. Spiritualism and Theosophy, in particular, have played a key role in the spread of the belief in reincarnation in Europe and North America where it is estimated that more than 20 per cent of the population of both continents believe in reincarnation.[47] For the vast majority of those involved in the New Age, reincarnation has become integral to their philosophy and theology. For them reincarnation and karma (the law of retribution) are alternatives to the Christian beliefs in the resurrection of the body and the final judgment which leads to a future eternal existence in heaven or in hell.

Just as there is a variety of beliefs regarding reincarnation among adherents to Eastern traditions,[48] so also there is diversity among New Agers. Some, for instance, believe that the soul comes into being at a certain moment in time and is then immortal, while others maintain that the soul has always existed. Some hold that reincarnation would one day end, others that it will go on eternally. Some believe that reincarnation takes place immediately when one dies, others that it occurs only after a lapsed period during which the soul is still on earth or in some other realm. And some think that reincarnation is governed by an automatic process of natural law, while others suggest that it is controlled by God or higher spiritual beings.[49] The belief that souls can be reincarnated as animals seems to have been universally rejected by New Agers.

The numerous writings on reincarnation cover three major related areas. The first deals with the attempts to provide empirical, philosophical, and theological arguments in support of the belief. These efforts have been rebutted by scholars who refute the scientific claims for reincarnation and by philosophers and Christian theologians who have respectively argued that neither rational thought nor faith can be adduced in support of the belief. The second covers arguments brought forward to show that reincarnation was originally an orthodox Christian belief and that the Bible actually teaches belief in reincarnation. The reaction of many Jews and Christians to this line of thought has been either to ignore it or else to mount a cogent refutation of the exegesis of those biblical passages that are interpreted as supportive of reincarnation. Finally, several writers have made a number of novel proposals which relate reincarnation to, or reconcile it with, traditional Christian theology.

Can reincarnation be proved?

Foremost among the proponents that empirical evidence might support belief in reincarnation is Ian Stevenson,[50] whose studies on children who remember past lives are routinely cited by New Agers as conclusive. His empirical research, however, is hotly debated and at times discredited,[51] though it has received endorsement not only by believers in reincarnation[52] but also by some scholars.[53] Equally debated are the philosophical arguments that have been adduced in favor of the belief. J. J. MacIntosh's[54] dismissal of reincarnation as a logical impossibility has been rebutted by other scholars.[55] Stevenson's approach raises other issues besides that of reincarnation. By proposing empirical support for what is clearly a matter of belief, Stevenson seems to be arguing that belief in reincarnation need not be based on scripture and/or revelation, but rather stands on rational and empirical grounds. In so doing, he has indirectly revived the debate regarding the relation between faith and reason.

Several philosophical and religious arguments have been advanced both in favor of and against reincarnation.[56] On the one hand, those who believe in reincarnation have strongly held that (1) the doctrine provides a plausible explanation to evil and human suffering; (2) it further gives a basis for hope to ignorant, imperfect human beings; (3) it lays the basis for respect to all life; (4) it puts one in the company of great sages; (5) it helps those who are dying; and (6) it removes the threat of eternal damnation. On the other hand, those who do not accept reincarnation maintain that (1) it does not guarantee a memory of a previous life; (2) it precludes responsibility and repentance; (3) it hinders the motive to relieve suffering; (4) it leads to extreme asceticism; (5) it justifies racism and sexism; (6) it was repudiated by both early Hinduism and Christianity; (7) it undercuts the philosophical foundations of morality; (8) it negates individual identity and significance; (9) it trivializes death; (10) it mocks our aspiration for immortality. Johannes Aagaard objects strongly against reincarnation because

> it contradicts the fundamental experience of gratitude. Because of this, the teaching of reincarnation is, in reality, highly unethical and destructive. It makes those who are fortunate and well-off to

be over-confident and self-satisfied; and it drives the unhappy and unfortunate out in even greater despair and passive acceptance of their misfortune.[57]

Arguments supporting reincarnation appear to be more logically convincing to those who have already committed themselves to the belief, while those that refute reincarnation are often based on a lack of understanding of its links with the doctrine of karma. Thus, for example, belief in reincarnation does not lead to or condone immorality since one's good or bad moral behavior in this life will guarantee a better existence in the next. And whether the belief in reincarnation actually militates against the very idea of charity is debatable, since, once again, charity has good karmic effects.[58] Neither does reincarnation necessarily imply fatalism or serve as an excuse for procrastination.[59]

Is reincarnation a Christian belief supported by the Bible?

Many proponents of the New Age have consistently argued that the belief in reincarnation is far from being incompatible with Christianity. They maintain, first, that the belief in reincarnation can be found in the Bible where many passages support or assume it. Second, they contend that reincarnation was the accepted doctrine in the early Church till it was opposed by some of the early Christian apologists and finally suppressed by various councils.

The Biblical quotations cited to confirm the belief in reincarnation by both the Israelites and the early Christians are relatively few.[60] Besides, in all of them, the reference to reincarnation is so obscure that they can just as easily be given different interpretations. The assertion that '[d]irect statements and inferences prove it [i.e. reincarnation] to be a definite teaching of the Bible'[61] is more likely to convince those who already accept reincarnation as a fact. Whether Jewish scriptures support the belief in reincarnation is a matter of debate. R. J. Zvi Werblowsky and Geoffrey Wigoder[62] have no doubt that the 'belief that after death the SOUL enters into a new body, though known in Eastern religions, is never encountered in biblical and talmudic Judaism'. Its appearance in Judaism dates from the twelfth-century Kabbalah. Others, like Joseph Head and S. L. Cranston, in their monumental compilation of religious and philosophical texts that allegedly endorse reincarnation, argue that the 'strictly orthodox [Jews] tend to reject it, and deny it a place in early Jewish philosophy. Others, including some orthodox rabbis,

accept rebirth as an integral part of Judaism.'[63] However, the handful of quotations from the Jewish scriptures quoted by Head and
Cranston in support of the idea of reincarnation appear rather far-
fetched and unconvincing.[64]

Attempts to pick out a number of texts from the New Testament
and to interpret them as either referring to reincarnation, or at least
not excluding it, are common.[65] Head and Cranston,[66] for instance,
quote or refer to about twenty New Testament texts that are said to
prove or at least suggest reincarnation. But different exegeses of the
same passages are possible and sometimes even more plausible.[67]
Ruth Montgomery, herself a New Age proponent of reincarnation,
after citing a few New Testament texts that are frequently adduced
to support belief in reincarnation, indirectly concedes that the evidence in the Bible is rather thin. She justifies this scarcity of
evidence by stating that, after the Second Council of
Constantinople (553), 'it is a logical assumption that most references to reincarnation were deleted from the Bible'.[68]

Some writers who look favorably on reincarnation still find the
biblical evidence unconvincing. Roger Anderson states that the
Christian who hopes to find a positive warrant for reincarnation in
the Bible is bound to be disappointed. He adds that though 'there
are a number of biblical pronouncements said to favor reincarnation, none can be said to unambiguously commend that
explanation above every other'.[69] The same hesitation is expressed
by Hans Tendam,[70] who concedes that in Judaic scriptures the few
passages that point to a belief in reincarnation are rather weak, even
though the suggestions that the soul preexists are more numerous
and stronger. While in the New Testament, he thinks, various passages do 'indicate pre-existence and some appear to indicate
reincarnation'. Geddes MacGregor,[71] who holds that the belief in
reincarnation is compatible with Christianity, states that the 'Bible
does not explicitly teach reincarnation'.

Other writers are careful in their efforts to interpret certain biblical passages as supportive of reincarnation. William L. De
Arteaga,[72] for example, explores two biblical themes or motifs: (1)
the relationship between biblical personalities across time or the
idea of the reappearance of the prophets of God, and (2) the existence and call of a person at the time of his or her birth. He
maintains that the Jewish Bible supports a belief in 'limited' reincarnation, where an individual has established a personal
relationship with God and hence would not be abandoned after

death in Sheol. He finds that the Elijah/John the Baptist relationship in the New Testament is a major theme that points to
reincarnation. Arteaga's work is certainly more scholarly than the
rumblings of Ruth Montgomery or the ordered, but brief and superficial, compilation of Head and Cranston. He argues that belief in
the imminent coming of Jesus and the fact that reincarnation was a
major gnostic belief led to its demise as the common Christian tenet
about what happens to the soul when a person dies. This explanation of why reincarnation ceased to be a major doctrine in the
mainline Christian Churches is more plausible than that provided
by Montgomery. It does not, however, resolve the major issue. Was
reincarnation foreign to and opposed to early Christian thought or
was it originally a common and orthodox belief which became suspect in the controversies over the influence of gnostic ideas?

Origen, one of the more influential writers among the early
Greek Fathers, is often mistakenly referred to as an early Christian
believer in reincarnation.[73] Actually Origen never expressed belief
in reincarnation in any form. On the contrary he categorically
denied that reincarnation is a Christian doctrine.[74] In fact, in his
commentary on Matthew's Gospel, he proposes several objections
against reincarnation. And he rejects the exegesis of the text from
Matthew's Gospel (11:14) that interprets the relationship between
John the Baptist and Elijah in terms that the former was the reincarnation of the latter. He writes: 'In this place it does not appear to
me that by Elijah the soul is spoken of, lest I should fall into the
dogma of transmigration, which is foreign to the church of God,
and not handed down by the Apostles, nor anywhere set forth in the
scriptures.'[75] In commentaries on both Matthew's and John's
Gospels he unambiguously states that one who belongs to the
Church repudiates the doctrine of transmigration as false and does
not admit that the soul of John was that of Elijah. For Origen, John
the Baptist had the spirit rather than the soul of Elijah.[76] In spite of
this patent and unquestionable rejection of the belief in reincarnation, MacGregor remains inexplicably convinced that Origen
taught reincarnation in some form. He does admit, however, that
there is no clear statement in support of the belief in any of
Origen's works and that Origen, while sympathetic to reincarnation,
believed that it did not fit into the Christian philosophy of history.[77]

Origen rather favored the theory of the preexistence of the soul
to counter some theological issues prominent at his time, such as
the controversies about the soul's origin and its relationship to the

body.[78] Though reincarnation was certainly a central belief among gnostic sects, it would be difficult, to say the least, to substantiate the claim that it was commonly held by early Christians or that many of the early Fathers of the Church believed in it. In fact one wonders whether reincarnation as such was ever a serious problem within the early Church, since it would be hard to find a direct condemnation of it. Norbert Brox, writing on the early debate on reincarnation, states:

> Early Christian interest in this theme was not intense. For the early Christians, reincarnation was an exotic and thus an alien idea. Origen already pointed out that it did not appear in the Bible and in the Christian tradition; neither of these knew the notion. Where it was mentioned among Christians, which seems to have been seldom enough, there was certainly an awareness that Greek philosophy was concerned with it. Primarily educated Christians will have come into contact with it.[79]

The Second Council of Constantinople did not condemn reincarnation directly, as it is often claimed, but rather the belief in the preexistence of the soul. And the councils of Lyons (1274) and Florence (1439) rejected reincarnation implicitly when they declared that, after death, the soul passes immediately to heaven, purgatory, or hell. Reincarnation was not the main issue discussed in these councils. In the words of one writer, 'the doctrine of reincarnation has hardly played a significant role in the historical development of Christianity'.[80]

It has been argued that many Church pronouncements contain indirect condemnations of the belief in reincarnation. The preexistence of the soul and the denial of final judgment after death are inextricably linked with the belief in reincarnation. Besides, for those who accept reincarnation, the link between the human soul and body is accidental and at death the individual transmigrates into another body. Given the Christian denial of the preexistence of the soul, the insistence on a final judgment, the belief that the body and soul are closely connected, and the conviction that the same body will rise again, it could easily be concluded that reincarnation has no place in Christian ideology.[81]

Probably the statement that comes closest to a condemnation of reincarnation is to be found in the 'Dogmatic Constitution on the Church' of Vatican Council II, where there is explicit reference to 'the one and only course of our earthly life', which is followed by judgment and the consequent reward or punishment.[82] This pronouncement, though not dogmatic, was explicitly intended to be an anti-reincarnation declaration.[83]

In the debate about the presence of the belief in reincarnation in the Bible and in early Christian history, one of the most troublesome findings is that there is little communication between Christian historians and biblical scholars on the one hand and the New Age advocates of reincarnation on the other. It would be next to impossible, for instance, to find a Church historian who would agree with the statement that reincarnation was the common and orthodox Christian belief in the first few centuries. It would be just as difficult to trace exegetical works which interpret certain biblical sayings as supportive of reincarnation. In fact, in mainline exegesis of the texts that refer to the relationship between John the Baptist and Elijah, the question of reincarnation is not even brought up. Rather, contemporary exegetes are likely to find the interpretation of certain passages in the Bible as evidence of the belief in reincarnation farfetched if not naïve. Since both Jesus and John the Baptist are associated with Elijah, the assertion that Luke is stating that John the Baptist is a reincarnation of Elijah is fraught with difficulties.[84] The issue is not merely one of the presuppositions that both Christian exegetes and New Agers bring to their respective reading of biblical texts. It is also one of hermeneutics, the methodology used to interpret the text. While Christian biblical scholars have developed a well-tested method for understanding scripture, New Agers have not. Consequently biblical scholars and New Agers are talking only to their respective audiences. One can only propose that the initiation of a dialogue between the two might be the first step to mutual understanding and resolution of some of the issues of method and interpretation.

Similar disagreements about early Christianity can, likewise, only be resolved by dialogue. Thus, the debate regarding early Gnosticism and its influence on the Church has been the subject of many books and articles since the discovery of the Gnostic Gospels.[85] Was there a pre-Christian Gnosticism that influenced some early Christians and was eventually declared unorthodox? Or was there a genuinely Christian form of Gnosticism which lost out against a more dominant belief system? Does the Gnosticism of the non-canonical Gospels represent the more authentic understanding of the Good News of Jesus Christ than the established canon of scripture, the writings of the majority of the Christian Fathers, and declarations of the council? Such questions must be answered by tested exegetical and historical methods of research and not by reliance on channeled materials, however sincere the channelers might be.

Can reincarnation be reconciled with Christian theology?

Several Christian theologians have held that belief in reincarnation cannot be reconciled with Christianity. F. L. Cross, for instance, has stated categorically that the belief in 'metempsychosis is fundamentally at variance with the Christian doctrine of the resurrection of the body'.[86] Even those who favor reincarnation sometimes see it as opposed to this central Christian belief.[87] Patrick R. Keifert thinks that, for the Christian, 'reincarnation seems to exchange the love of God for the cosmic justice of karma'.[88] It is also possible that the belief in reincarnation pinpoints some of the fundamental differences between Eastern and Western religions, differences that cannot be easily harmonized.[89] The majority of Christian responses to the New Age agree with such judgments and have dismissed and rejected reincarnation as an unorthodox belief that has no place in Christian theological reflection.

More recently, however, the debate about the compatibility or incompatibility of reincarnation with Christian belief has resurfaced. John Hick has pointed out some of the similarities between the Christian doctrine of the resurrection of the body and the belief in reincarnation. 'Resurrection and reincarnation', he states, 'both constitute reembodiment; heavenly resurrection is a kind of reincarnation in another world, whilst reincarnation is a kind of resurrection in this world.'[90] The two concepts may thus overlap, leaving room for some reconciliation.

In a more detailed study of the matter, Hick has distinguished three theories of reincarnation in Indian thought: (1) the empirical hypothesis about the rebirth of the conscious, memory-bearing self; (2) the metaphysical assumption that there exists a higher, spiritual self of which the normal conscious self is not aware; and (3) the ethical doctrine which links reincarnation to karma. He contrasts this with two strains of thought about the afterlife found in Christianity: (1) the view, central to Augustinian theology, that the soul, when it dies, is judged and then goes to heaven, hell, or purgatory; and (2) the belief, found in the theology of Irenaeus, that the soul, at death, goes through other spheres of existence beyond this earth on its way to its final destination in heaven. Hick thinks that Irenaean eschatology is not incompatible with the third interpretation of the idea of reincarnation and is readily capable of constructive debate with the first interpretation. For there is a basic agreement between them about the principle of continued responsible life, in which the individual may learn and grow by interacting with human beings in a common environment or series of environments. They differ only as to *where* this continued life is to take place.

I see no reason why a Christian should not come to believe in reincarnation instead of in continued life in other spheres, or why a Hindu should not come to believe in continued life in other spheres instead of in reincarnation.[91]

Another way of harmonizing the two concepts is to state that reincarnation fills in the gap between death and the Last Day (which includes resurrection and final judgment).[92] More precisely, reincarnation has been seen as functioning as a kind of purgatory where the soul undergoes a painful and purifying process. MacGregor[93] is among those who have strongly advocated this view. For him, purgatory, like reincarnation, is a waiting stage, a kind of spiritual reformatory, and a time for growth during which the soul is slowly transformed into a higher spiritual state, able to enjoy the vision of God. MacGregor, by seeing purgatory as a series of re-embodiments, attempts to fit reincarnation into Christian thought,[94] but at the same time he makes some adaptation of Hindu thought when, for instance, he suggests that karma and samsara conceptualize the journey of the soul towards the beatific vision in heaven.[95] Moreover, he is more careful to maintain the place of God's grace and of Christ's salvific work, to view matter much more positively, and to insist that working for salvation has to be founded in grace.

A similar idea is expressed by several Christian writers. Karl Rahner, for instance, after describing purgatory as a process of maturation that takes place after death, adds:

Let me just call attention to the question whether in the Catholic notion of an 'interval', which seems so obsolete at first, there could not be a starting point for coming to terms in a better and more positive way with the doctrine of the 'transmutation of souls' or of 'reincarnation', which is so widespread in Eastern cultures and is regarded there as something to be taken for granted. This is a possibility, at least on the presupposition that this incarnation is not understood as a fate for man which will never end and will continue on forever in time.[96]

Bede Griffiths agrees that purgatory is a kind of intermediate state during which the person is purified and rendered able to enter into the fullness of God. 'The question', he asks, 'is whether instead of that purgatory taking place in another world, it could take place in a physical world as well.'[97] And Charles DeCelles thinks that the doctrine of reincarnation is not embraced by Catholicism because, in its totality, it is neither correct nor precisely true. Souls do not preexist and men are not responsible for their condition at birth. But he does describe purgatory as a 'maturation process' analogous to psychotherapy and finds that, in this respect, reincarnation and purgatory are similar. And he goes on to ask the following questions to which he gives affirmative answers:

> is it possible that the Catholic notion of 'purgatory', while developed from an entirely different perspective, points essentially to the same truth as the Hindu idea of reincarnation – when both concepts are 'demythologized' or stripped of their anthropomorphisms and poetic imagery? Do both doctrines agree on the same basic religious point, namely, that before entering the presence of the All Holy, a person must undergo a painful and in-depth process of growth, out of which emerges a transformed individual, hardly recognizable as the original earthbound self, a person of perfection and maturity?[98]

The view that reincarnation and purgatory overlap, in that both are maturation processes that take place beyond this life, seems to be gaining a wider acceptance. Michael Stroeber,[99] like many other Christian writers, starts his reflectings by observing that there are some difficulties with reconciling the common Hindu view of reincarnation with Christianity, because belief in reincarnation fails to satisfy moral justice and is ambiguous about personal identity. However, he points out that there is a soul-making version of reincarnation, found in some Hindu philosophical systems, that is compatible with Christian theology. In this way he conceives of reincarnation as 'a teleological vehicle of moral and spiritual development of the soul' and as a means for moral, emotional, and spiritual development leading to union with God. In like manner Martin Israel[100] relates reincarnation to purgatory and sees it as a process of spiritual growth leading to the final consummation in God.

Other writers who have attempted to incorporate reincarnation in Christian theology have been less successful in upholding some of the fundamentals of orthodox Christianity. Karel Douven,[101] for instance, leans towards the Eastern view that there is an element of divinity in human beings and that the law of karma is the deter-mining factor in reincarnation. And he abandons the idea that Jesus is the savior who suffered and died vicariously for human beings, thus leading to the forgiveness of sins. But he still holds that rein-carnation is an evolutionary process which shows God's power in this world as well as a process of love in which God suffers with humankind on its way to salvation or liberation. He further incor-porates the linear into the cyclical conception of history and concludes that reincarnation can be harmonized with Christian eschatology.

Whether reincarnation can be incorporated into the Christian belief system is not an easy question to answer. Reincarnation does not exist in a vacuum. It is part of a system of thought and makes sense only in relation to several other beliefs. It cannot easily be extracted from its religious matrix and inserted into another. Reender Kranenborg expressed this difficulty when he wrote:

> A belief like reincarnation always stands within a religious context and cannot be easily extracted from it. When the notion of rein-carnation is introduced into a religion which is unacquainted with it, this means that other elements are also introduced. The system of this religion, therefore, is changed, for a religion is not a com-posite of loose beliefs, but includes relations and elements which are indissolubly connected with each other.[102]

He goes on to say that reincarnation is incompatible with the major creeds which the early Christian councils drew up.

More specifically, it can be argued that reincarnation fits into a cyclical world view but not in a linear one. Peter Lee, for instance, maintains that 'those faiths which emphasize linear views of time and history, with a revelatory value attaching to historical events in a single decisive time of choice in belief and morals, are less inclined to believe in reincarnation than those faiths (and branches of faiths) which place a greater emphasis on cyclical view of time and see personal religious experience as the ground of revela-tion'.[103] Both in Jewish thought and in the preaching of Jesus the stress is on a linear view of time and history, on historical revelation, and on personal judgment immediately the individual dies, all of which are incompatible with reincarnation.

Other theological problems abound when attempts are made to harmonize reincarnation with Christian theology. One obvious dif-ficulty is that Christianity presents a different view of the person than that found in Eastern religions. The concept of salvation in

Christianity depends on an anthropology which sees matter and spirit as united in one person and which considers matter good, even though in need of redemption. John R. Sachs goes to the heart of the matter when he writes:

> Salvation is for the whole person. Purgatory is not a purification from matter. Resurrection does not mean a departure or liberation of the soul from the body, but the liberation of the whole being, everything which one has done and become as a unique person, from sin and death. This is why the New Testament and the ancient creeds speak rather pointedly of the resurrection of the *flesh* or of the *body*.[104]

One thing seems certain: reincarnation cannot be harmonized with Christianity without some adaptation. Roger Anderson points out that, even though the doctrine of reincarnation and karma seems to be in conflict with the Christian view of salvation, there is still a possibility that the Christian can accept reincarnation. This could happen (1) if the idea of reincarnation was modified to exclude the natural retributive action of karma and the system of salvation by personal merit, or if (2) some traditional Christian doctrines were reinterpreted. He suggests that 'resurrection as the reunion of body and consciousness after separation by death rests upon basically the same understanding of man presumed by reincarnation, though resurrection conceived as a once-for-all rejoining of the present body and soul may require amendment'.[105]

The issue of whether Christianity can incorporate the belief in reincarnation is bound to be the subject of discussion for a long time. What is important in the dialogue between Christians and New Agers is not whether a solution can be found, but whether the beliefs in reincarnation and the resurrection of the body contain shared spiritual values which can contribute to mutual understanding.

NEW AGE PRACTICES: CRYSTALS AND CHANNELING

The New Age has become popular because it provides individuals with the option of choosing not only from a variety of beliefs, but also from diverse practices. It contains both a belief structure and a ritual system that deals with human problems and concerns. These rituals address themselves to human needs and experiences and are often the doors leading to involvement in the New Age and acceptance of its ideology. Two common practices are the use of crystals and channeling, both of which are still popular, even though the sale of books on both topics was, by the late 1980s, on the decline.[106] The use of crystals and channeling may not be immune to faddishness, but they still attract many New Agers in search of self-fulfillment.[107]

The healing power of crystals

One of the most popular New Age practices has been the use of quartz crystals for healing purposes. In the United States, interest in the healing power of crystals peaked in the mid-1980s, when many Americans followed the Hollywood star, Shirley MacLaine, and began carrying colored crystals to protect themselves against ailments.[108] The enduring popularity of crystals is manifested in their prominent display in New Age fairs and stores. This use of crystals is to be distinguished from crystal gazing (crystallomancy) which is an ancient form of divination through the aid of a crystal globe.[109]

Crystals are known to have certain physical properties that make them suitable for modern technological applications (such as watches and microcomputers). New Agers ascribe to them many other qualities and functions. Lawrence E. Jerome[110] has distinguished the claims for crystal power into five major categories: physical, medical, parapsychological, spiritual, and legendary. The belief that crystals have occult properties that can benefit the human body has recently become more common in Western cultures. According to Shepard, 'many people believe that the physical properties of the crystal in relation to electrical currents are parallelled by an ability to focus and modify cosmic energy or the life force and to harmonize the vital energies of the human body'.[111] Catherine Bowman, in a book which purports 'to provide the reader with the basic ground rules for working with quartz crystals', states:

> Crystals are here to teach and serve us. To the awakened mind, they are capable of performing a multitude of functions such as dream guidance and direction, cleansing the body of negative energies, focusing the mind, mental and physical healing, telepathy, linkages to special places, and other potentially limitless tasks.[112]

The tendency to ascribe magical and occult properties to crystals has a long history and has been found in many ancient civilizations. So also has the connection between crystals and astrological signs.

In the Western world the belief that crystals have healing powers dates at least since the Middle Ages.[113] In recent times much additional lore has been added to crystals by Edgar Cayce, a seer, and Frank Alper, a medium/channeler, both of whom linked them with the legend of Atlantis.[114] Work with crystals has also been tied with other New Age beliefs and practices, including the chakras (centers of energies within the human body), meditation and visualization.[115]

The use of crystals for healing purposes has not escaped criticism by the many writers who have questioned the scientific claims made by New Agers. Jerome, who conducted experiments on the power of crystals, concluded that crystal power and crystal energies simply do not exist. They are rather manifestations of the placebo effect (for medical claims) and/or the Hawthorne effect (for psychological claims).[116] J. Gordon Melton states that 'New Agers have attempted to build a base from science for their claims concerning the effects of crystals' without much success. 'There is', he asserts, 'no scientific evidence that crystals store or contain energy that can be transferred to humans.' New Agers, therefore, tend to talk about crystals in terms of paranormal energies. He further explains:

> Basically, believers view crystals as transmitters of the Universal Light. Clear quartz has taken on a special significance as the purest transmitter of that Light, but each crystalline structure qualifies (changes) the energy for a specific purpose. Each crystalline accumulates, stores, and, at the user's request or need, releases its inherent powers. Crystals can be recharged through specified processes after their use has drained them of power.[117]

The lack of scientific evidence for the claim that crystals have healing potentials is sometimes reflected in the way New Agers themselves promote their use. Loretta Elaine, for example, maintains that crystals have the power to heal all kinds of psychological and physical illnesses and provides one of the more comprehensive Internet sites on the healing power of crystals. She describes in some detail the therapeutic properties and cleansing powers of many gemstones, advises those who want to buy them, and gives references to various therapists. But she starts with the following disclaimer: 'This information is not meant to replace any medical treatment. It is offered here as a service. Use this information at your own risk. No guarantee is made towards validity. This is my personal belief on how high quality gemstones work for me.'[118] Other promoters of crystal therapy are even more cautious. J. S. Stuart, who believes strongly in the healing power of crystals, states, in his guidelines to the use of crystals, that 'crystals, minerals and precious stones should *not* be used on their own to treat serious conditions, but must be used in conjunction with other medical practices'.[119]

Other commentators have been more critical and have relegated the use of crystals to a superstitious and fraudulent custom. George Erickson,[120] for example, ridicules and dismisses as nonsensical the belief that crystals have inherent powers which can be applied to human needs and aspirations. According to him, people who have recourse to healing by crystals are gullible and easily deprived of their money. Jerome's view that the application of crystals for healing purposes functions more as a placebo effect is commonly held by scientists and sceptics alike. Seen from this angle, the use of crystals can be relegated to a magical ritual which is divorced not only from empirical reality but also from a spirituality that relies on God.

It must be admitted that many New Agers who rely on crystals for healing purposes are open to the accusation that they are practicing magic, which is based on the belief that there is some unseen (supernatural or psychic) power in nature that can be manipulated by human beings in a ritual context. However, the use of crystals might be better understood in relation to the rise of holistic medicine. In which case, the belief in the healing power of crystals is symbolical of both the limitations of, and the modern dissatisfaction with, medical care and treatment. Further, the mythology and ritual surrounding the power of crystals have religious aspects found also in other religious settings. Thus, for instance, crystals could function as sacraments and/or sacramentals and can be compared to the use of salt, oil, and holy water in some Christian churches. While crystals could be employed to the detriment of one's health and may provide false hopes to those whose physical, mental, or psychological illnesses might be more profitably addressed by traditional methods, they might promote the necessary mental attitude and courage that are needed in the healing process. Dissociated from its strictly magical mode, crystal healing may not be incompatible with Christianity.

Channeling

One of the characteristics that marks the New Age is the stress on personal development. Unlike traditional religions, where spiritual and moral guidance is based on sacred texts, traditional rules and doctrines, and well-established teachers or gurus, the New Age allows the individual more latitude in determining the path one follows in one's religious growth. Rather than consulting outside sources, the individual relies on inner sources of knowledge and advice, namely, his or her ability to make contact either with spirits of past human beings (known as spirit guides) or with the divine element which is present in everyone. When not able to do so, the individual can rely on the advice of noted channelers with whom they sometimes establish a patient/doctor or client/counselor relationship.

Channeling is hardly a new phenomenon. Claims of divine revelation and disclosures from the gods or the spirits of the dead have been common throughout human history.[121] The oracle, the seer, the shaman, the mystic, and the prophet have all functioned as intermediaries between humans and divine beings. The methods through which the information has been disclosed vary. Mediums[122] may deliver the messages from beyond while in various levels of trance, or while fully conscious, or through telepathy. In the Christian tradition visions and apparitions (like those of angels and the Virgin Mary) can be seen as a type of channeling. So also is speaking in tongues (glossolalia) which is held by Pentecostals and Charismatics to be a unique language through which God communicates messages to believers.[123]

There is little doubt that the knowledge or information provided by channelers is taken seriously. Marina Michaels McInnis, writing on mediumship in the modern age, states:

> Essentially, most people who approach a channeler for answers or who are first learning to channel hold some or all of the following beliefs: The channeler is a conduit through which the information comes. As such, he or she brings nothing to the party, so to speak, but instead can be thought of as a glorified spiritual radio tuning into the information being broadcast by the entities being channeled.
>
> The entities being channeled, by virtue of their being dead (deceased, departed from physical life) or by virtue of never having been in a physical body, are perfected beings who have only the highest thoughts and intentions towards we lowly and inadequate human beings.
>
> The information coming through is, therefore, always 100% accurate and always comes from a high and loving source.
>
> Anything that comes through a channeler, therefore, is never to be questioned, but instead should be accepted and followed verbatim.[124]

Channeling remains an essential part of the New Age, in spite of an apparent decline of interest. The Internet is bustling with information on the subject. One of the more comprehensive Web pages on channeling is offered by 'spiritweb.org',[125] where one finds references to channelers, various types of channeling, several essays on the subject, and plenty of references to books and other Internet resources.

The importance of channeling in New Age practice is stressed by several scholars. Melton, for example, thinks that

> channeling is possibly the single most important and definitive aspect of the New Age. It is certainly the activity which has had the greatest success in mobilizing support for the movement as a whole. It also provides an excellent illustration of the manner in which the movement has interaction with the older esoteric groups already established in the culture.[126]

The contents of channeling are fairly consistent with New Age themes described in Chapter 1. Suzanne Riordan, surveying channeled materials, states:

> Taken as a whole, this body of literature offers an analysis of the human condition and a set of prescriptions designed to assist humanity in discovering its true identity. The argument is based on certain assumptions about the nature of reality which the authors present from their presumably enhanced perspective. In essence they seek to convince us that we are not whom we think we are and that much of our suffering can be traced to our mistaken identity. Their tone is passionate and imploring, sometimes angry, ironic, or admonishing, but more often … tender and reassuring. In most cases it is respectful, but as a parent would comfort or admonish a well-meaning but misguided child.[127]

Among the themes which appear repeatedly in channeled materials is a criticism of organized religion, which is taken to task for denying that the human person is essentially good and for stressing the need for external sources of authority. The primacy of consciousness is assumed and various theories are proposed to explain why human beings have become materialistic and oblivious that the divine is immanent in their nature. Although a concept of original sin as found in traditional Christianity is not expressed in channeled materials, channelers reveal that human beings have become alienated from nature. Fear and guilt are serious obstacles to true spiritual progress. Various ways are suggested for improving the human condition and for helping individuals reach a true knowledge of themselves. According to Riordan,

> New Agers are crafting a polyphonic revelation proclaiming that the time has come for humanity to be delivered from its self-imposed prison. . . . The channeled sources offer a detailed diagnosis of the ailment which afflicts the modern psyche. It is guilt (self-loathing) and fear. Its etiology is the repudiation by an adolescent consciousness of its cosmic parent, the ego's denial of its divine source. The oracles' prescription is a reconciliation with Self and Spirit, a 'reawakening' from the illusion of separation – a 'remembering' of one's own divinity, of one's participation in Its wondrous creativity.[128]

A careful analysis of channeling shows that it is based on several religious beliefs or assumptions that are certainly not foreign to Christianity. Both channelers and those who consult them have a deep yearning for contact with the divine or for establishing a personal relationship with God. Both are convinced that there is an afterlife and that a relationship between the living and the dead is possible. And again, both acknowledge the need for spiritual direction. Channeling can be seen as a kind of private revelation, similar to that received by many Christian saints. When channeling is conceived as contact with some inner source, it can be compared to the inner voice of conscience which directs human beings in difficult choices.

Yet channeling is also beset by many problems. Probably the major one is that it leaves unanswered the question of who evaluates the channeler and the content. Since any person can become a channeler, and since the advice given is often addressed to the individual client who consults the channeler in the first place, it is difficult to see how a system of evaluation can be put into operation. While there is a consistent repetition of New Age themes in all channeled materials, differences abound. The beliefs, morals, and practices that flow from channeling support a kind of individualistic religion whose ultimate authority is not based on a community of faith. There is a clear anti-establishment element in channeling, just as there is in the New Age Movement as a whole. And this might be one of the major obstacles to a Christian understanding of, and coming to terms with, the phenomenon of channeling.

CONCLUSION

Christians have debated whether the New Age is compatible with their faith or whether there are any elements in this new religious movement that can be harmonized with Christian theology or practice. Their responses, irrespective of their theological stance, have indicated that the presence of the New Age might be an important event in the spirituality of the late twentieth century and that its influence on Christianity might be far from negligible.

Rather than bemoan its presence and decry its impact on culture, it might be more profitable to reflect on the positive contributions the New Age is making to religion and spirituality. One Christian commentator, Vivienne Hull, lists four of its major strengths that Christians should benefit from:[129] (1) the stress on the renewal of one's spiritual life; (2) the affirmation of the sacramentality of the natural world; (3) the profession of the value, uniqueness, and integrity of the individual person; and (4) its understanding of the power of a positive vision, of hope, and love to motivate human beings to be of service to the world. A Christian response to the New Age that does not take into consideration the above qualities is bound to be both ineffectual and short-sighted.

In conclusion, the advent of the New Age can be seen as a mixed blessing for Christians who are called upon to respond in faith to the presence of new religions towards the end of the twentieth century. While the New Age may be drawing away from traditional faith many dissatisfied individuals who have embarked on a personal religious quest, it might also be doing a service to Christianity by encouraging Christians to delve deeper in their religious tradition and rediscover its treasures.

Instead of being an indication of satanic conniving or an omen of impending apocalyptic doom, the New Age, like all new religious movements,[130] is 'a sign of the times' calling Christians to self-examination and reform in the light of the Gospel.[131] The New Age religion presents an excellent opportunity for the Christian Church to better understand and execute its mission, to adapt and react more meaningfully to the changing needs and cultural conditions of the modern age, to express its teachings clearly to an ecumenical and interreligious audience, and to reform and renew itself in the spirit of the Gospel.

NOTES

1. Paul McGuire, *Evangelizing the New Age* (Ann Arbor, MI: Servant Publications, 1989), p. 66.

2. J. Gordon Melton, 'Introductory essay: an overview of the New Age Movement', in J. Gordon Melton et al., *New Age Encyclopedia* (Detroit: Gale Research, 1991), pp. xxx–xxxi.

3. Consult, for example, Paul Collins, 'What's new about the New Age?', *St. Mark's Review* 144 (Summer 1991): 14.

4. See, for example, the whole issue of *The Way* 29.1 (1989), which is dedicated to 'creation-centred spirituality'.

5. 'Aquarian spirituality: the New Age movement in America', *The Catholic World* (May/June 1989): 141.

6. Cf. John A. Saliba, 'Vatican response to the new religious movements', *Theological Studies* 53 (1992): 3–39.

7. Subtitled 'The orthodox suppression of Original Christianity', several chapters of this book can be found on the Internet, http://www.newhopeent.com/ [date modified: 05/26/97; date downloaded: 01/05/97].

8. *The Unknown Life of Jesus Christ* (Joshua Tree, CA: Tree of Life Publications, 1996; first published 1894).

9. *The Lost Years of Jesus: Documentary Evidence of Jesus's 17-Year Journey to the East* (Livingston, MT: Summit University Press, 1987).

10. *The Aquarian Gospel of Jesus the Christ* (Marina del Rey, CA: De Vross & Co., 1972).

11. Eileen Campbell and J. H. Brennan, *The Aquarian Guide to the New Age* (Wellingborough, UK: The Aquarian Press, 1990), p. 16.

12. See, for examples, S. G. Ouseley, *The Gospel of the Holy Twelve: Known also as the Gospel of the Perfect Life* (Mokelumne Hill, CA: Health Research, 1974; first published c. 1900); Jane A. Welch, *The Known and Unknown Life of Jesus the Christ* (Geneva, IL: Yoga Publications Society, 1924); Janet Bock, *The Jesus Mystery: Of Lost Years and Unknown Travels* (Los Angeles: Aura Books, 1980); Jeffrey Furst, *Edgar Cayce's Story of Jesus* (New York: Berkley Publishing Group, 1991; first published 1968); Charles F. Potter, *The Lost Years of Jesus Revealed* (Greenwich, CT: Fawcett Books, 1990; first published 1958); Holger Kersten, *Jesus Lived in India* (Shaftesbury, UK: Element, 1995); and James W. Deardorff, *Jesus in India: A Reexamination of Jesus' Asian Tradition in the Light of Evidence Supporting Reincarnation* (San Francisco: International Scholars Press, 1994).

13. *A Life of Jesus the Christ: From Cosmic Origins to the Second Coming* (New York: St. Martin's Press, 1989).

14. *The Aquarian Christ: Jesus Christ as Portrayed by the New Age Movement* (Hong Kong: Good Tidings, Ltd., 1992).

15. Ibid., p. 29.

16. *The Counterfeit Christ of the New Age Movement* (Grand Rapids, MI: Baker Book House, 1990), pp. 91–92.

17. Ibid., p. 24.

18. *Revealing the New Age Jesus: Challenges to Orthodox Views of Christ* (Downers Grove, IL: InterVarsity Press, 1990), pp. 17–18.

19. This christology has been adopted in, for instance, *The Catechism of the Catholic Church* (Mahwah, NJ: Paulist Press, 1994). For a summary of the Catechism's christology see Sara Butler, 'Contemporary christology: getting one's bearings', *Chicago Studies* 36 (1997): 159–71.

20. *Christ in a Pluralistic Age* (Philadelphia: Westminster Press, 1976).

21. See, for instance, Leo D. Lefebure, *Toward Contemporary Wisdom Christology: A Study of Karl Rahner and Norman Pittenger* (Maryknoll, NY: Orbis, 1990).

22. Paul F. Knitter, *No Other Name?: A Critical Survey of Christian Attitudes Toward the World Religions* (Maryknoll, NY: Orbis, 1985), pp. 171ff.

23. Rebecca Pent, 'Can Jesus save women?' in *Encountering Jesus: A Debate on Christology*, ed. Stephen T. Davis (Atlanta: John Knox Press, 1988).

24. See, for instance, Aloysius Pieris, *An Asian Theology of Liberation* (Maryknoll, NY: Orbis, 1998).

25. R. S. Sugirtharajah, 'Third world christologies', *Theology Digest* 44 (1997): 213–23; and John R. Levison and Priscilla Pope-Levison, 'Emergent christologies in Latin America, Asia, and Africa', *Covenant Quarterly* 52.2 (1994): 29–47.

26. John Parratt, *Reinventing Christianity: African Theology Today* (Grand Rapids, MI: Eerdmans, 1995), pp. 80–81.

27. For various essays on African christology, see *Faces of Jesus in Africa*, ed. Robert J. Schreiter (Maryknoll, NY: Orbis Books, 1991); and *Exploring Afro-Christology*, ed. John Samuel Pobee (New York: Peter Lang, 1992). For an overview of African theology, cf. Raymond Justin S. Upkong, 'The emergence of African theologies', *Theological Studies* 45 (1984): 501–36.

28. 'African christology', *Theological Studies* 48 (1987): 507–08.

29. '"Who do you say that I am?": an assessment of some christological constructs in Africa', *Asia Journal of Theology* 9 (1995): 187.

30. 'Jesus and the avatāra' in *Dialogue and Syncretism: An Interdisciplinary Approach*, ed. Jerald Gort, Henrik Vroom, Reim Fernhout, and Anton Wessel (Grand Rapids, MI: Eerdmans, 1989), pp. 161–62. Cf. George John Hoynacki, '"And the Word was made flesh" – Incarnations in religious traditions', *Asia Journal of Theology* 7 (1993): 20–26.

31. Michael Amaladoss, 'Images of Jesus in India', *SEDOS Bulletin* 28 (February 1996): 48–53.

32. These contexts are discussed by Peter C. Phan, 'Experience and theology: an Asian liberation perspective', *Zeitschrift für Missionswissenschaft und Religionswissenschaft* 44 (1993): 101–11. Cf. also his essay 'Cultural diversity: a blessing or a curse for theology and spirituality?', *Louvain Studies* 19 (1994): 195–211, where he examines the impact of the context on the construction of theology.

33. *An Asian Theology of Liberation* (Maryknoll, NY: Orbis Books, 1988).

34. *The Theology of Change: A Christian Concept of God from an Eastern Perspective* (Maryknoll, NY: Orbis Books, 1979) and *Marginality: The Key to Multicultural Theology* (Minneapolis, MN: Fortress Press, 1995).

35. *Tell Us Our Names: Story Theology from an Asian Perspective* (Maryknoll, NY: Orbis Books, 1984).

36. *Struggle to be the Sun Again: Introducing Asian Women's Theology* (Maryknoll, NY: Orbis Books, 1990).

37. 'Mahayana theology: how to reclaim an ancient Christian tradition', *Anglican Theological Review* 51 (1989): 377–95.

38. 'The emptiness of Christ: a Mahayana christology', *Anglican Theological Review* 75 (1993): 48–62.

39. R. Sugirtharajah, 'Jesus in saffron robes?: the "other" Jesus whom recent biographers forgot', *Studies in World Christianity* 2.3 (1995): 103–10.

40. Cf., for example, Mariasusai Dhavamony, 'The cosmic Christ and the world religions', *Studia Missionalia* 42 (1993): 179–225.

41. Often metempsychosis is distinguished from reincarnation in that the former connotes the transmigration of the soul into either human, animal, or vegetable form, while the latter indicates the return of the human soul in another

human body. Such distinctions are sometimes found in standard English dictionaries. Cf. also Editorial, 'Che cosa pensare della reincarnazione?', *Civiltà Cattolica* 136 (June 15, 1985): 521.

42. Two recent bibliographies testify to the large amount of literature on reincarnation: Joel Bjorling, *Reincarnation: A Bibliography* (New York: Garland, 1996); and Lynn Kear, *Reincarnation: A Selected Annotated Bibliography* (Westport, CT: Greenwood Press, 1996).

43. See, for example, a report of the debate within the Danish Lutheran Church over whether two members on the parish council of a local church could maintain their position while professing belief in reincarnation: *Christianity Today* 111 (March 2, 1994): 222.

44. 'Reincarnation International' lists the past lives of various individuals. See http://www.dircon.co.uk/reincar/ [date modified: 07/14/98; date downloaded: 08/03/98].

45. *Eternal Life?: Life After Death as a Medical, Philosophical, and Theological Problem* (Garden City, NY: Doubleday and Co., 1984), p. 99.

46. For brief overviews of the presence of the belief in reincarnation in different societies and historical eras, see Ninian Smart, 'Reincarnation' in *Encyclopedia of Philosophy*, ed. Paul Edwards (New York: Macmillan/London: Collier Macmillan, 1967), vol. 7, pp. 122–24; J. Bruce Long, 'Reincarnation' in *Encyclopedia of Religion*, ed. Mircea Eliade (New York: Macmillan Publishing Co., 1987), vol. 12, pp. 265–69; *Reincarnation: The Phoenix Fire Mystery*, ed. Joseph Head and S. L. Cranston (New York: Julian Press, 1977); and Hans Tendam, *Exploring Reincarnation* (London: Arkana, 1987), pp. 29ff..

47. One of the earliest surveys, covering North America and Western Europe, was conducted by George Gallup, *The Gallup Poll: Public Opinion 1969* (Wilmington, DE: Scholarly Research Inc., 1967). For more recent data see George Gallup and Frank Newport, 'Belief in paranormal phenomena among adult Americans', *Skeptical Inquirer* 15 (1991): 138; and Eileen Barker, 'Whatever next? The future of New Religious Movements', *Religions sans Frontières: Present and Future Trends of Migration, Culture, and Communications*, ed. Roberto Cipriani (Rome: Presidenza del Consiglio dei Ministeri, 1994), p. 371. For the latest survey see George Gallup, *The Gallup Poll: Public Opinion 1996* (Wilmington, DE: Scholarly Research Inc., 1997), p. 205, where 22 per cent of the population in the United States of America are said to believe in reincarnation. This is a drop from 27 per cent recorded in the previous year. Cf. George Gallup, *The Gallup Poll: Public Opinion 1995* (Wilmington, DE: Scholarly Research Inc., 1996), p. 9.

48. See Geoffrey Parrinder, 'Varieties of belief in reincarnation', *Hibbert Journal* 55 (1956): 260–67.

49. Aidan A. Kelly, 'Reincarnation' in J. Gordon Melton et al., *New Age Encyclopedia*, p. 387.

50. *Cases of the Reincarnation Type* (Charlottesville: University Press of Virginia, 4 vols, 1975–77); *Children Who Remember Previous Lives: A Question of Reincarnation* (Charlottesville: University Press of Virginia, 1987); and 'Empirical evidence for reincarnation', *Skeptical Inquirer* 19 (May/June 1995): 50–51. See also Carol Bowman, *Children's Past Lives: How Past Life Memories Affect Your Child* (New York: Bantam Books, 1997).

51. See, for instance, Terrence Hines, *Pseudoscience and the Paranormal: A Critical Examination of the Evidence* (Buffalo, NY: Prometheus Press, 1988), pp. 72–76; and Paul Edwards and Antony Flew, 'Examining Stevenson's reincarnation cases', *Skeptical Inquirer* 19 (March/April 1995): 56.

52. Cf. also Robert Almeder, 'On reincarnation' in *What Survives?: Contemporary Explorations of Life after Death*, ed. Gary Moore (Los Angeles: Jeremy Tarcher, 1990), pp. 34–60; Joe Fisher, *The Case for Reincarnation* (Garden City, NY: Doubleday and Co., 1984); Sylvia Cranston and Carey Williams, *Reincarnation: A New Horizon in Science, Religion, and Society* (Pasadena, CA: Theosophical University Press, 1993), especially pp. 49–68; and Carol Bowman, *Children's Past Lives*, pp. 92–112.

53. See, for instance, Raymond Martin, 'Survival of bodily death: a question of values', *Religious Studies* 28 (1992): 165–84.

54. 'Reincarnation and relativized identity', *Religious Studies* 25 (1989): 153–65.

55. See Harold W. Noonan, 'The possibility of reincarnation', *Religious Studies* 26 (1990): 483–91; and Charles B. Daniels, 'In defense of reincarnation', *Religious Studies* 26 (1990): 501–04.

56. For a summary view of these arguments see, for example, Vishal Mangalwadi, 'The reincarnation of the soul', *Evangelical Review of Theology* 13 (1991): 135–47; Robert A. Morey, *Reincarnation and Christianity* (Minneapolis, MN: Bethany Fellowship, 1980), pp. 37ff.; and Quincy Howe, *Reincarnation for the Christian* (Philadelphia: Westminster Press, 1974), pp. 51ff. For several philosophical discussions see Ronald Bonan, 'On metempsychosis', *Diogenes: International Council for Philosophy and Humanistic Studies*, no. 142 (Summer 1988): 92–111; and Hywel D. Lewis, *The Self and Immortality* (New York: Seabury Press, 1973), pp. 93ff. For a radical refutation of the belief in reincarnation and its rejection as irrational and absurd, cf. Paul Edwards, *Reincarnation: A Critical Examination* (Amherst, NY: Prometheus Books, 1996).

57. 'Reincarnation or resurrection?', *Areopagus: A Living Encounter with Today's World Religions* 2 (Easter 1989): 23.

58. Ronald Bonan seems to lean towards this anti-reincarnation argument and

maintains that Gandhi 'condemned the foundation of refuges and hospitals'. But he fails to add that Gandhi worked tirelessly for independence and for the improvement of the lot of the 'harijans', the 'children of God', as he called the untouchables of India. See 'On metempsychosis', p. 99.

59. David S. Toolan, 'Reincarnation and modern gnosis' in *Reincarnation or Resurrection?*, ed. Herman Häring and Johann-Baptist Metz (London: SCM Press/Maryknoll, NY: Orbis Books, 1993), p. 33. This is, of course, a much debated issue. It can be argued that many Hindus have, under the influence of Christianity, reinterpreted their belief in reincarnation to include more explicit concern for social welfare and to exclude the fatalistic notions so often seen as the consequence of the doctrine of karma. See Harold Coward, 'Hindu–Christian dialogue as "mutual conversation"', *Studia Missionalia* 43 (1994): 177–92.

60. Cf. Joseph Head and S. L. Cranston, *Reincarnation: The Phoenix Fire Mystery*, pp. 127–28 and 135–40, where the relevant scriptural texts are explained.

61. Marilyn McDirmit, *Reincarnation: A Biblical Doctrine? Whose Time Has Come for the Evangelical Christian* (Maggie Valley, NC: Eagle Publication Co., 1990), p. 8.

62. *The Encyclopedia of the Jewish Religion* (New York: Holt, Rinehart and Winston, 1965), p. 389.

63. *Reincarnation: The Phoenix Fire Mystery*, p. 124. See also Sylvia Cranston and Carey Williams, *Reincarnation: A New Horizon in Science, Religion, and Society*, pp. 181–82, where the authors assert that reincarnation has never been denied in Jewish sources and that the Book of Job (14:14) may implicitly be referring to such a belief.

64. Joseph Head and J. L. Cranston, *Reincarnation: The Phoenix Fire Mystery*, pp. 126–28.

65. Ibid., pp. 135–40; see Sylvia Cranston and Carey Williams, *Reincarnation: A New Horizon in Science, Religion, and Society*, pp. 206–13.

66. Joseph Head and S. L. Cranston, *Reincarnation: The Phoenix Fire Mystery*, pp. 135–30; cf. Sylvia Cranston and Carey Williams, *Reincarnation: A New Horizon in Science, Religion, and Society*, pp. 206–13.

67. See, for example, David Jeremiah with C. C. Carlson, *Invasion of Other Gods: The Seduction of New Age Spirituality* (Dallas, TX: Word Publishing, 1996), pp. 47–48.

68. *Companions Along the Way* (New York: McCann and Geoghegan, 1974), p. 18.

69. 'Reincarnation: can Christianity accommodate it?', *Journal of Religion and Psychical Research* 9 (1986): 190.

70. *Exploring Reincarnation*, pp. 43–44.

71. *Reincarnation in Christianity: A New Vision of the Role of Rebirth in Christian Thought* (Wheaton, IL: Theosophical Publishing House, 1978), p. 16.

72. *Past Life Visions: Christian Exploration* (New York: Seabury Press, 1983), pp. 121ff.

73. Ruth Montgomery, *Companions Along the Way*, p. 17; and Quincy Howe, *Reincarnation for the Christian*, p. 62. The view that Origen believed in reincarnation appears to have been held also by some Christian theologians. See, for instance, Michael Maher, 'Metempsychosis' in *The Catholic Encyclopedia*, ed. Charles G. Herbermann et al. (New York: Robert Appleton and Co., 1911), vol. 10, p. 236. Joseph Head and S. L. Cranston state that Origen believed in the preexistence of the soul and in reincarnation, but none of the texts they reproduce supports the latter. See their *Reincarnation: The Phoenix Fire Mystery*, 144ff.

74. See Giuseppe Casale, *Nuova religiosità e nuova evangelizzazione* (Edizioni Piemme, 1993), p. 69. Cf. Joseph Wilson Trigg, *Origen: The Bible and Philosophy in the Third-Century Church* (Atlanta, GA: John Knox Press, 1983), p. 213.

75. 'Origen's Commentary on Matthew' in *The Ante-Nicene Fathers*, vol. X, ed. Allan Menzies (Grand Rapids, MI: Eerdmans, 1951), Book XIII, p. 474. Cf. Reender Kranenborg, 'Christianity and reincarnation' in *Dialogue and Syncretism: An Interdisciplinary Approach*, ed. Jerald Gort, Hendrik Vroom, Rein Fernhout, and Anton Wessel, pp. 18–81.

76. 'Origen's Commentary on Matthew', pp. 476 ff., and *Commentary on the Gospel According to John*, translated by Ronald E. Heine (Washington: Catholic University of America Press, 1989), Book VI, p. 186. Cf. Jean Daniélou, *Origen*, translated by Walter Mitchell (New York: Sheed and Ward, 1955), pp. 249–50.

77. *Reincarnation in Christianity*, pp. 51–58.

78. Henri Couzel, *The Life and Thought of the First Great Theologian*, trans. A. S. Worrall (San Francisco: Harper and Row, 1989), pp. 205ff.

79. 'The early Christian debate on the migration of souls' in *Reincarnation or Resurrection?*, ed. Herman Häring and Johann-Baptist Metz, p. 75.

80. Hans Tendam, *Exploring Reincarnation*, p. 45.

81. See Pietro Cantoni, *Cristianismo e Reincarnazione* (Torino: Editrice Elle Di Ci, 1997), pp. 57–58.

82. *The Documents of Vatican II*, ed. Walter M. Abbott (London: Geoffrey Chapman, 1966), p. 80.

83. Pietro Cantoni, *Cristianismo e Reincarnazione*, p. 57.

84. Robert J. Miller, 'Elijah, John, and Jesus in the Gospel of Luke', *New Testament Studies* 34 (1988): 611–22.

85. Cf. for example, Edwin M. Yamauchi, *Pre-Christian Gnosticism: A Survey of the Proposed Evidences* (London: Tyndale Press, 1973); and Elaine Pagels, *The Gnostic Gospels* (New York: Vantage Books, 1989).

86. *The Oxford Dictionary of the Christian Church* (London: Oxford University Press, 1974), p. 908. See also Johannes Aagaard, 'Reincarnation or Resurrection?', pp. 20ff.

87. A. T. Man, *The Elements of Reincarnation* (Shaftesbury, UK: Element, 1995), p. 46.

88. 'Resurrection and the New Age', *Word and World* 11 (Winter 1991): 46.

89. A. T. Mann, *The Elements of Reincarnation*, p. 47.

90. 'Reincarnation' in *The Westminster Dictionary of Christian Theology*, ed. Alan Richardson and John Bowden (Philadelphia: Westminster Press, 1983), p. 491.

91. *Truth and Dialogue in World Religions: Conflicting Truth-Claims* (Philadelphia: Westminster Press, 1974), pp. 153–54.

92. Rudolph Frieling, *Christianity and Reincarnation* (Edinburgh: Floris Books, 1977), pp. 43–57.

93. *Reincarnation as a Christian Hope* (Totowa, NJ: Barnes and Noble, 1982), pp. 69–79.

94. *Images of Afterlife: Beliefs from Antiquity to Modern Times* (New York: Paragon House, 1992), pp. 146–49.

95. *Reincarnation in Christianity*, pp. 18–19.

96. *Foundations of Christian Faith: An Introduction to the Idea of Christianity* (New York: Seabury Press, 1978), p. 442.

97. Wayne Teasdale, 'Reincarnation: a Christian view' [interview with Bede Griffiths], *Living Prayer* 21.5 (September/October 1988): 24.

98. 'Reincarnation: a maturation process like purgatory', *Sisters Today* 53 (1981): 163.

99. 'Pastoral identity and rebirth', *Religious Studies* 26 (1990): 496.

100. 'The nature of eternal life: a mystical consideration' in *Life After Death*, ed.

Arnold Toynbee and Arthur Koestler (New York: McGraw-Hill Book Co., 1976), pp. 159–61.

101. Cf. Reender Kranenborg, 'Christianity and reincarnation', pp. 184–85.

102. 'Christianity and reincarnation' in *Dialogue and Syncretism: An Interdisciplinary Approach*, ed. Jerald Gort, Hendrik Vroom, Rein Fernhout, and Anton Wessel, p. 179.

103. 'Reincarnation and the Christian tradition', *The Modern Churchman* 23 (1980): 106.

104. 'Resurrection or reincarnation?: the Christian doctrine of purgatory' in *Reincarnation or Resurrection?*, ed. Herman Häring and Johannes-Baptist Metz, p. 84.

105. 'Reincarnation: can Christianity accommodate it', p. 195.

106. Margaret Jones, 'Sorting out the strata', *Publishers Weekly* 236 (November 3, 1989): 20ff. For some recent works on crystals and channeling, see Liz Simpson, *The Book of Crystal Healing* (New York: Sterling Publications, 1997); J. S. Stuart, *The Colour Guide to Crystal Healing* (London: Quantum, 1996); Irene Dalichow, *Aura-Soma: Healing through Color, Plants, and Crystal Energy* (Carlsbad, CA: Hay House, 1997); Michael F. Brown, *The Channeling Zone: American Spirituality in an Anxious Age* (Cambridge, MA: Harvard University Press, 1997); and Larry Dreller, *Beginner's Guide to Mediumship* (York Beach, ME: Samuel Weiser, 1997).

107. See Lys Ann Shore, 'New Age books by any other name . . .', *Skeptical Inquirer* 15 (Summer 1991): 339–42.

108. 'The rocks with good vibrations', *Newsweek* 110 (October 12, 1987): 78; Lee Aiken, 'You don't need a crystal ball to see that New Age rocks are clearly on a roll', *People Weekly* 27 (June 15, 1987): 67ff.; and Martha Smilgid, 'Rock power, for health and wealth', *Time* 129 (January 19, 1987): 66.

109. 'Crystal gazing (or crystalomancy)' in Leslie Shepard, *The Encyclopedia of Occultism and Parapsychology* (Detroit: Gale Research, 3rd ed., 1991), pp. 362–65.

110. *Crystal Power: The Ultimate Placebo Effect* (Buffalo, NY: Prometheus Books, 1989), pp. 21–25.

111. 'Crystal healing' in *The Encyclopedia of Occultism and Parapsychology*, p. 365.

112. *Crystal Awareness* (St. Paul, MN: Llewellyn, 1992), p. 6.

113. See 'Crystals' in J. Gordon Melton et al., *New Age Encyclopedia*, pp. 138–39.

114. Cf. Dan Campbell, *Edgar Cayce on the Power of Color, Stones and Crystals* (New York: Warner Books, 1989); and Frank Alper, *Exploring Atlantis* (New York: Coleman Publishing, 3 vols, 1982).

115. See, for example, Liz Simpson, *The Book of Crystal Healing*.

116. *Crystal Power: The Ultimate Placebo Effect*, pp. 149–50. The Hawthorne effect is based on the observation that those participating in an experiment are inclined to please the researchers, thus providing the answers the researchers are looking for.

117. 'Crystals' in J. Gordon Melton et al., *New Age Encyclopedia*, p. 141.

118. 'Healing power of gemstones and crystals', http://www.gems4friends.com/therapy.html [date modified: 12/04/97; date downloaded: 12/30/97].

119. *The Colour Guide to Crystal Healing*, p. 12.

120. 'Crystal lights', *The Humanist* 56 (March/April 1996): 35. See also Mick Winter, 'How to talk New Age', http://www.well.com/user/mick/newagept.html [date modified: unknown; date downloaded: 01/02/98].

121. Susan Riordan, 'Channeling' in J. Gordon Melton et al., *New Age Encyclopedia*, pp. 76ff.

122. For the precise difference between mediums, channelers, and psychics see Larry Dreller, *Beginner's Guide to Mediumship*, p. 38.

123. Cf. Morton Kelsey, 'The former age and the New Age' in *New Age Spirituality: An Assessment*, ed. Duncan Ferguson (Louisville, KY: Westminster/John Knox Press, 1993), p. 54.

124. 'What is channeling? Mediumship and the modern age', http://www.sonic.net/~marina/channel/whatchan.html [date modified: 09/11/97; date downloaded: 12/04/97].

125. http://www.spiritweb.org/spirit/channelings.html [date modified: 11/21/97; date downloaded: 12/04/97].

126. 'New thought and the New Age' in *Perspectives on the New Age*, ed. James R. Lewis and J. Gordon Melton (Albany, NY: SUNY Press, 1992), p. 21.

127. 'Channeling: a new revelation?' in *Perspectives on the New Age*, ed. James R. Lewis and J. Gordon Melton, pp. 110–11.

128. Ibid., p. 124.

129. 'The New Age: the movement toward the world' in *New Age Spirituality: An Assessment*, ed. Duncan Ferguson, pp. 132–39.

130. This view was expressed by Cardinal Ernesto Corripio Ahumada in his report to the 1991 Consistory of Cardinals. Cf. *Catholic International* 2, 13 (July 1–14, 1991), p. 618.

131. The phrase 'sign of the times' has been frequently used by Catholic theologians since the Second Vatican Council where it can be found near the beginning of its 'Pastoral Constitution on the Church in the Modern World'. See *The Documents of Vatican II*, ed. Walter M. Abbott, p. 201.

INDEX